Policing and the Legacy

Policing and the Legacy of Lawrence

Edited by

Nathan Hall, John Grieve and Stephen P. Savage

WILLAN
PUBLISHING

Published by

Willan Publishing
Culmcott House
Mill Street, Uffculme
Cullompton, Devon
EX15 3AT, UK
Tel: +44(0)1884 840337
Fax: +44(0)1884 840251
e-mail: info@willanpublishing.co.uk
website: www.willanpublishing.co.uk

Published simultaneously in the USA and Canada by

Willan Publishing
c/o ISBS, 920 NE 58th Ave, Suite 300
Portland, Oregon 97213-3786, USA
Tel: +001(0)503 287 3093
Fax: +001(0)503 280 8832
e-mail: info@isbs.com
website: www.isbs.com

First published 2009

ISBN   978-1-84392-505-7 paperback
       978-1-84392-506-4 hardback

British Library Cataloguing-in-Publication Data

A catalogue record for this book is available from the British Library.

Project managed by Deer Park Productions, Tavistock, Devon
Typeset by GCS, Leighton Buzzard, Bedfordshire
Printed and bound by T.J. International Ltd, Padstow, Cornwall

To Mrs Doreen Lawrence and Mr Neville Lawrence

Contents

Part Three: Lawrence – Widening the Agenda

List of abbreviations

ACPO	Association of Chief Police Officers
BCS	British Crime Survey
BME	Black and minority ethnic
BPA	Black Police Association
CALT	Centre for Applied Learning Technologies
Centrex	Central Police Training and Development Agency
CIA	Community Impact Assessments
CIM	Critical Incident Management
CJA	Criminal Justice Act
CPS	Crown Prosecution Service
CRE	Commission for Racial Equality
CRR	Community and Race Relations
CSU	Community Safety Units
DCLG	Department for Communities and Local Government
DCSF	Department for Children, Schools and Families
DfEE	Department for Education and Employment
DfES	Department for Education and Skills
EHRC	Equalities and Human Rights Commission
ELS	Emergency Life Support
ESRC	Economic and Social Research Council
FLO	Family Liaison Officer
HMIC	Her Majesty's Inspectorate of Constabulary
HOLMES	Home Office Large Major Enquiry System
IAG	Independent Advisory Group
IAN	Independent Advisory Network
ICAS	Intelligence Cell Analytic System

ICF	Integrated Competency Framework
IMC	Independent Monitoring Commission
IPCC	Independent Police Complaints Commission
IPLDP	Initial Police Learning and Development Programme
LGBT	Lesbian, gay, bisexual and transgender
METL	Minimum Effective Training Levels
MIRSAP	Major Incident Room Systems, Administration and Procedures
MPA	Metropolitan Police Authority
MPS	Metropolitan Police Service
NCIS	National Criminal Intelligence Service
NDM	Naturalistic Decision-Making
NIM	National Intelligence Model
NORIS	Newham Organised Racial Incident Squad
NOS	National Occupational Standards
NPIA	National Policing Improvement Agency
OBTJ	Offences brought to justice
PACE	Police and Criminal Evidence Act (1984)
PCA	Police Complaints Authority
PDTN	Police Diversity Trainers Network
PRDLDP	Police Race and Diversity Learning and Development Programme
PSI	Policy Studies Institute
RVCTF	Racial and Violent Crime Task Force
REC	Racial Equality Councils
RPD	Recognition Primed Decision-making
RR(A)A 2000	Race Relations (Amendment) Act 2000
SEU	Social Exclusion Unit
SID	Systems for Investigation and Detection
SIO	Senior Investigating Officer
SLI	Stephen Lawrence Inquiry
SMoCIT	Strategic Management of Critical Incidents

Figures and tables

Acknowledgements

The account offered in these pages contains a consilience of a vast number of disciplines, ideas, conversations and developments that were the buckled-together thoughts of many people. Amongst those individuals are: Carol Bewick, Joe Chowdry, Ron Cuthbertson, Dave Field, Michael Fuller, Howard Gosling, all the members of the first Independent Advisory Group, Ian Johnston, Mick Jones, Steve Kavanagh, Barry McDowell, Duncan McGarry, Pat McLoud, Denis O'Connor, Bob Quick, George Rhoden, Miriam Rich, Mark Simmonds, John Sutherland, Betsy Stanko and several PhD and other students, Sarah Thornton, Dave Thomas, Ron Woodland and many, many others to whom the editors express their thanks again.

Notes on contributors

John Azah OBE has been Director of the Kingston Racial Equality Council since 1990 and is Chair of the Independent Advisory Group for the Independent Police Complaints Commission, the latter a legacy of the Stephen Lawrence Public Inquiry. He has taken an active community role in many campaigns for justice and assisted police thinking in *causes célèbres*. He has been an advocate and participant in many efforts to promote the interests of and create job opportunities for BME young people in London over the past 25 years. John was a founder member of the Metropolitan Police Independent Advisory Group and was the second chair they appointed. He has taken part in many simulated and real critical incident resolution activities, not least as Gold and Diamond Group member. He was appointed OBE for his services to the communities of London and elsewhere in 2007.

Ben Bowling is Professor of Criminology and Criminal Justice at King's College, London and is the author of *Violent Racism*. He was a witness to the Stephen Lawrence Inquiry Part 1. He was a founder member of the Metropolitan Police Independent Advisory Group and has advised on many *causes célèbres*. He has worked as a researcher at the Home Office and has assisted senior police leaders' learning at the Police Staff College. His PhD was awarded for his study of violent racism and the police response to it. He has taught criminology and criminal justice issues at John Jay College of Criminal Justice in New York and at the University of Cambridge. He is Visiting Professor at the University of the West Indies.

Jeffrey Brathwaite QPM is an independent consultant, community engagement specialist and an authority on independent advisory groups and staff associations. He was the deputy director of the Racial and Violent Crime Task Force (RVCTF) at New Scotland Yard from 1998–2002. His doctoral research was on the role of internal and external pressure groups in police policy-making.

Phil Clements is a Principal Lecturer at the Institute of Criminal Justice at the University of Portsmouth where he is course leader for the Professional Doctorate in Criminal Justice. Prior to joining Portsmouth he served with the Metropolitan Police for 25 years. He has been involved in police equality issues for many years and has experience of equal opportunities, diversity, and police training. Whilst on secondment to the former National Police Training and Development Authority (Centrex) he worked on projects to implement the training recommendations of the Stephen Lawrence Inquiry. He has published several books on related topics, including the *Equal Opportunities Guide*, the *Diversity Training Handbook* and *Policing a Diverse Society*. For his doctoral thesis he researched the education and training implications for police officers' learning in the field of equal opportunities. He is currently researching in the field of police education and specialist policing.

Ben Crane is a Police Inspector in a medium-sized provincial force. He has worked in a wide variety of posts in two police forces including community policing, corporate development, public order and response policing. Ben currently works in the roads policing department with particular responsibility for Automatic Number Plate Recognition (ANPR) and motorcycle operational issues. In 2007 he completed a Masters Degree in International Criminal Justice at the University of Portsmouth and his interest in community policing led him to specialise in the area of hate crime.

Jonathan Crego MBE has worked for the Metropolitan Police and on national projects for nearly 20 years. He currently directs major elements of the Leadership Academy at Hendon Police College. He is the creator of Minerva, Hydra and 10 thousand volts IT solutions for assisting learning and simulating policing activities and debriefing operations and experiences. These projects are delivered at sites worldwide. With John Grieve and Bill Griffiths he created the Strategic Management of Critical Incidents training regime that delivered the opportunity to learn from many of the experiences of the Stephen Lawrence Public Inquiry. His debriefing tools have enabled him to facilitate learning from terrorism, public order, murder reviews, multi-agency perspectives and disasters. He holds a research chair and is the co-Director of the International Centre for the study of Critical Incident Decision Making at the University of Liverpool.

John Grieve CBE QPM joined the Metropolitan Police in 1966 at Clapham. He served as a detective throughout London and in every role from undercover officer to policy chair and as a Murder Squad senior investigator. He organised the 'Community, Fairness, Justice' Conference and was first Director of Intelligence for the Metropolitan Police. He led the Anti-Terrorist Squad as National Coordinator during the 1996–1998 bombing campaigns. He was the first Director of the Racial and Violent Crime Task Force, in which role he gave evidence to part two of the Stephen Lawrence Inquiry. Now he is a Senior Research Fellow at the University of Portsmouth and Professor Emeritus at London Metropolitan University, and a Commissioner of the Independent Monitoring Commission for the Peace Process in Northern Ireland; he was also appointed Independent Chair of the Home Office/Ministry of Justice Independent Advisory Group on Hate Crime in 2007. In 2008 he was awarded the ACPO Homicide Working Group Lifetime Achievement Award for contributions to murder investigation.

Bill Griffiths CBE BEM QPM served in the Metropolitan Police mostly as a detective for 38 years and on retiring became the Director of Leadership for them – a post he still holds. He created the Leadership Academy. With John Grieve and Jonathan Crego he was responsible for driving many of the changes required by the Stephen Lawrence Public Inquiry, not least in his case the creation of a Murder Command, which he directed as their first leader, professionalising detective skills and with critical incident learning. Together they created the Strategic Management of Critical Incidents Training regime that provided opportunities to learn from many of the experiences of the Stephen Lawrence Public Inquiry. He has been the Director of the critical incident management course which has developed many of the recommendations of the Stephen Lawrence Public Inquiry for the past decade. He was created CBE in 2007 in recognition of his contribution to twenty-first-century policing in London.

Nathan Hall is a Senior Lecturer in criminology and policing at the Institute of Criminal Justice Studies at the University of Portsmouth. His main research interest lies in hate crime, which he has extensively researched, particularly in relation to criminal justice responses in England and Wales and in the United States. His first book, *Hate Crime*, was published by Willan Publishing in 2005 and he is currently involved in comparative research on the policing of hate crime in London and New York. In addition to working with a number of police services across the country, Nathan has also acted in a consultative capacity to the Association of Chief Police Officers (ACPO) and Her Majesty's Inspectorate of Constabulary (HMIC) and the Home Office.

John Jones is a Senior Lecturer at the Institute of Criminal Justice at the University of Portsmouth where he is responsible for external development. John was a police officer for over 20 years and during this time had a period of responsibility for the Community and Race Relations Team at the former National Police Training and Development Authority (Centrex). Prior to joining the University of Portsmouth John was a senior consultant and worked with a number of government and other agencies in regard to the implementation of the Race Relations Amendment Act. He is currently working on a collaborative project with Surrey Police and is researching and working on joint projects relating to the management and training of critical incidents. John is co-author of the *Diversity Training Handbook*.

Sam Poyser is a Lecturer in Criminology and Criminal Justice at the Institute of Law and Criminal Justice Studies, Canterbury Christchurch University, Kent. She is currently engaged in doctoral research on miscarriages of justice and has researched and published in the areas of crime prevention and miscarriages of justice.

Nicola Rollock is a Research Associate for the Runnymede Trust where she has been researching progress within the criminal justice system in meeting the Stephen Lawrence Inquiry recommendations. She is the author of *Failure by any other name? – Educational Policy and the continuing struggle for Black academic success* published by the Runnymede Trust. Nicola is also a Visiting Research Associate at the Institute of Education, University of London.

Stephen P. Savage is Professor of Criminology and Director of the Institute of Criminal Justice Studies, University of Portsmouth, which he founded in 1992. He has published widely on policing and the politics of criminal justice policy, including his most recent book, *Police Reform: Forces for Change* (Oxford University Press 2007). He has recently researched and published on miscarriages and justice, and his current research is on the independent investigation of complaints against the police.

Foreword

Doreen Lawrence OBE

This book examines the ten years since the publication of the Stephen Lawrence Inquiry, seen as a watershed in the history of British policing, and the 70 Recommendations that were accepted by the Labour Government. The book also examines the shortfalls in policing intelligence in the investigation of the murder of Stephen Lawrence and considers what changes, if any, have taken place over the last ten years.

The Stephen Lawrence Inquiry came at a time when there was lack of confidence in the police service from the black community. The many murders that had taken place before Stephen Lawrence had not challenged the justice system in the way that Stephen's murder did. The racism and the incompetence of the police service in relation to Stephen's murder, which came to light during the Inquiry, were starkly evident.

The input of the many authors giving their views of what has happened in the last ten years is welcome because for the first time there is a concentration of individuals looking at how many of the recommendations have been implemented since the publication of the Inquiry. The Inquiry into Stephen's death had highlighted the many flaws in the Metropolitan Police Service and the wider criminal justice system, including the lack of respect that the Metropolitan Police Service showed towards the African-Caribbean community that it served.

In the early days after the publication of the Lawrence Inquiry some of the police officers tried to undermine the report. There were some police officers who viewed the recommendations from the

Inquiry as stopping them from carrying out their work of stopping individuals for fear that they would be labelled as racist. The fact is that some officers were missing the point for the need for change to take place in officers' behaviour towards the black community.

There have been many changes since the publication of the Stephen Lawrence Inquiry, the latest of which now sees the Government moving its focus from 'race' to 'diversity'. The question we should ask before we change to diversity is this: have we fully addressed the issues of race? Another question is this: do the police service think they have achieved their goals of addressing racism in the force? And if so, do they think they could be accused of institutional racism again? With the recent high profile cases that have taken place in the last month of 2008, racism, it seems, continues to plague the police.

Training in the police service is another area where change has taken place since the Lawrence Inquiry. Indeed it was one of the main recommendations. A lot of work has gone into police leadership and improving their skills. The question to ask is how much has trickled down to the officers on the beat who have regular contact with members of the public? Another change is in race relations with the improvements derived from the Race Relations (Amendment) Act 2000. There is also the introduction of the IAG - an independent body of professionals from the community. I believe this to be essential in today's policing.

Collectively all of the authors talk of the changes that have taken place since the Stephen Lawrence Inquiry and all are agreed that there is still some way to go. I would agree with this. Over the last ten years I have worked with the Metropolitan Police Service and Government departments as an independent supporting the work that came out of the Lawrence Inquiry. One of the changes I saw was when I recently visited the West Midlands Police with Richard Stone, who was one of the Advisors to the Lawrence Public Inquiry. Richard Stone and I were able to see at first hand how they had increased the confidence of the community by working closely together with them. Other changes that have taken place concern how the police investigation into crime and the use of family liaison officers have helped some families to receive justice for the loss of loved ones, although we as a family are still waiting for justice.

Overall this book gives the reader a record of achievement (or otherwise) of the implementation of the recommendations from the Stephen Lawrence Inquiry. It also shows the clear shift from the race agenda to the wider diversity agenda that the Government have now moved on to.

Introduction: the *legacies* of Lawrence

*Nathan Hall, John Grieve and
Stephen P. Savage*

Crimes motivated by racial prejudice have a long history in Britain (Hall 2005), yet official recognition of the problem can be traced back to as recently as the early 1980s. The re-emergence of victimology in the late 1970s, and in particular the subsequent development of victim surveys, began to reveal the extent, nature and impact of racist victimisation that had hitherto been largely unknown. The problem of racism was further thrust into the public consciousness in the early 1980s by widespread public disorder across the country, most notably in inner-city areas (Scarman 1981; Bowling 1999). Together, these issues ensured that racism could no longer be ignored as a contemporary social problem, particularly as earlier official denials of the problem were justified by an apparent lack of reliable information (Bowling and Phillips 2002).

In 1993, the same year that Stephen Lawrence was murdered, the first calls for racially motivated violence to be made a specific offence were made by the Commission for Racial Equality, but these calls were rejected by the then Conservative government, as were the Commission's calls for a strengthening of existing anti-discrimination legislation. Despite these rejections, John Major, the then Prime Minister, strongly condemned racism in a speech to the Board of Deputies of British Jews; and, perhaps somewhat ironically, tackling racist offending was also named as the top priority of the Metropolitan Police Service (Bowling and Phillips 2002). Nevertheless, Bowling and Phillips (2002) note that in reality very little practical action of note occurred for a number of years.

Arguably the most significant single event that was ultimately to propel the issue of violent racism to the top of the political and social agenda was the murder of black teenager Stephen Lawrence in April 1993. At approximately 22:30 on the evening of 22 April 1993, 18-year-old Stephen and his friend Duwayne Brooks were subjected to an unprovoked racist attack by white youths in Well Hall Road, Eltham, south-east London. Stephen Lawrence was stabbed during the attack and died shortly afterwards. His killers were never convicted and serious questions concerning the police investigation remained unanswered.

In the run-up to the 1997 general election the then shadow Home Secretary Jack Straw expressed hopes that, if New Labour were elected, a public inquiry into the death of Stephen Lawrence and the failure to bring his killers to justice, which had previously been rejected by the Conservative government, would be possible. Shortly after New Labour's landslide election victory, Jack Straw announced a full public inquiry into the matters arising from the death of Stephen Lawrence to be conducted by Sir William Macpherson of Cluny.

The Stephen Lawrence Inquiry was by no means the first report to critically examine the issues of race, policing and criminal justice. However, Sir William Macpherson's report into matters arising from the death of Stephen Lawrence has been described as 'the most radical official statement on race, policing and criminal justice ever produced in this country' (McLaughlin 1999: 13).

The Stephen Lawrence Inquiry was divided into two parts. Part one was concerned with the matters arising from the death of Stephen Lawrence and part two with the lessons to be learned for the investigation and prosecution of racially motivated crimes. The Inquiry concluded that the investigation was 'marred by a combination of professional incompetence, institutional racism and a failure of leadership by senior officers' (Macpherson 1999: 46.1). The Inquiry team made 70 recommendations, including a new Ministerial Priority for all police services 'to increase trust and confidence in policing amongst minority ethnic communities' (1999: rec. 1).

Crucially, however, the Inquiry went beyond just policing and made a number of recommendations for responding to racism and racist violence in much broader terms through, for example, the education system. Recommendations 67, 68 and 69 related directly to the role of education in *valuing cultural diversity and preventing racism*; and to reflect the particular attention paid to this area by the Inquiry, the issue of education is examined in Chapter 11 of this volume. This wider agenda meant that the focus on racism was not simply restricted to the police, but also to other organisations and institutions. The Inquiry, and the sharp public focus that it drew, therefore necessitated official action against racism as a matter of urgency.

A decade on from the publication of the final report, the purpose of this book is to examine the legacy of Lawrence. Each of the 11 chapters examines a particular area or theme that has been affected or shaped in some way by the Lawrence Inquiry and its aftermath. The book identifies a series of dimensions and processes associated with British policing in terms of the role that the Lawrence 'agenda' has played in forming and/or moulding policy and practice in that particular area, and in doing so assesses the extent to which the original recommendations and issues raised within the Lawrence Inquiry have been reflected in policy, practice and, importantly, policing outcomes in service delivery. The book offers both practitioner and academic reflection on the impact of Lawrence which includes contributions from some of the key policing figures, and others, who were involved in post-Lawrence implementation and development programmes; those who, in a very real sense, have 'lived' the Lawrence agenda in their professional capacities. In this sense, then, the reader should be clear from the outset that this is a very different kind of book. It goes beyond the traditional academic approach of simply critically discussing the issues in hand and includes chapters that are personal reflections. In so doing the book opens the door for readers to explore information, thoughts, feelings, stories and experiences that might not otherwise be known and which, in our view, serve to bring the academic contributions to life.

In this introductory chapter we offer an overview of the 'Lawrence legacy'. To do this we identify a number of overlapping dimensions of the legacy of Lawrence which, taken together, we contend, offer some measure of the massive impact of the Stephen Lawrence Inquiry on the landscape of British policing and beyond. We will present the legacy of Stephen Lawrence in six dimensions in all: the *cultural* legacy; the *governance* legacy; the *political* legacy; the *legal* legacy; the *intelligence* legacy; and the *international* legacy. Before addressing these themes we shall comment on where Lawrence sits in terms of policy change and reform.

Lawrence as police reform

One of our main concerns in this collection is to assess the impact of the Stephen Lawrence Inquiry (SLI) on police reform and change in policing. In order to do this we need to consider the nature of policy change in general and police reform in particular. The assessment of the 'impact' of Lawrence on policing needs to go beyond identifying particular recommendations of the SLI and tracing their realisation or non-realisation in specific policies, although that is a perfectly legitimate and indeed valuable process, as the work of the 'Lawrence Steering Group', set up by the Home Office in 1999 to monitor the implementation of the recommendations of the SLI (Home Office 2005d), exhibits. There are two reasons why we need to move beyond the linear tracking of recommendation–policy outcome.

Firstly, many of the 'legacies' of Lawrence involve changes which were already in motion, as will be made clear at various points in this book, and the impact of Lawrence in these cases has been to *accelerate* and *shape* change rather than just to initiate change as such. One example of this, considered later in this discussion and elsewhere in this book (see also Savage 2007: 36–7), is the role of the Family Liaison Officer (FLO). The SLI was to have much to say about the way in which the Lawrence family was treated by the police after Stephen's murder, and much to propose in terms of the role of the FLO in the process of investigation. However, FLOs were already a part of the policing landscape when the SLI reported, albeit in a fragmented and inconsistent form. What Lawrence served to achieve was to provide a powerful 'push' to enhance the function, status and professional development of FLOs within the policing and investigative process. This is not at all to downgrade the significance of Lawrence in these areas of police reform, rather to acknowledge that the landscape of British policing confronting the SLI was an uneven and complex one, and the key role of Lawrence has been in these respects to drive change faster and further than would otherwise have been the case. In addition to a range of new policing reforms one can attach to Lawrence, the agenda associated with Lawrence has also been effective as a 'midwife' of reforms already lying somewhere within the policing body.

Secondly, we need to view reform and change as multi-tiered and, as a consequence, the assessment of the impact and legacy of Lawrence should address the different levels at which the Lawrence agenda has and still does shape policing policy practice. In this regard Hall's differentiation between 'orders of change' in public policy – in his case applied to economic policy (Hall 1993) – is helpful. Hall talks of three orders of change, reflecting degrees of continuity and discontinuity with previous or past policies. 'First-order change' is change which is essentially in continuity with the past and which might be quantitative rather than qualitative and tend to occur frequently or even as a matter of course. For example, in the policing context this might involve an increase in police numbers but without change to policing structures of styles of policing. 'Second-order change' is less common but still 'normal' and may involve changes in the techniques or instruments of policy, or qualitative changes to the way things are done or delivered. For example, the creation of the National Policing Improvement Agency in Britain through the Police and Justice Act 2006 reflected a structural change in the management and delivery of services such as police training and police research (Savage 2007: 118–119). 'Third-order change' is an altogether much rarer occurrence and concerns changing *goals* in the form of what Hall, following Kuhn (1962), refers to as 'paradigm shifts'. Hall differentiates the orders of change as follows:

> First and second order change can be seen as cases of 'normal policymaking', namely of a process that adjusts policy without challenging the overall terms of a given policy paradigm … Third order change, by contrast, is likely to reflect a very different process, marked by the radical changes in the overarching terms of policy discourse associated with a 'paradigm shift'. (Hall 1993: 279)

We suggest this framework helps capture the legacy of Lawrence. As we shall see, the SLI has been instrumental in generating or accelerating a range of second order changes, such as the formalisation of murder investigation reviews (see Chapter 5), the establishment of the Independent Police Complaints Commission (see below) and the framework for the police response to hate crime (see Chapter 10). However, and in relation to such changes, we would argue that the Lawrence agenda for policing also constitutes a *paradigm shift*, or third order change, in policing. This paradigm shift relates to fundamental, if uneven, changes in the police 'mind-set' and in external expectations of what policing is there to deliver. Paradigm shifts may not be sudden, and may take the form of 'slow fuse' change and reform which takes considerable time to unfold – and may still be at work at present. As will be made clear at other points in this book, this paradigm shift relates to such things as the rethinking of racist crimes (Chapter 10), the (further) relocation of the community within the policing and investigative process (Chapters 2 and 3), the importance of independent sources of oversight and insight for policing and investigation (Chapter 8), and the rethinking of the role of families in serious crime investigations (Chapter 4). In our outline of the various dimensions of the 'legacy of Lawrence' below, and in the chapters that follow, we aim to demonstrate that the Lawrence agenda is indeed about a paradigm shift in policing, one which makes the publication of the Stephen Lawrence Inquiry Report a watershed in the history of British policing.

The legacy of Lawrence

In the remaining sections of this Introduction we attempt to identify the range of police reforms and policy changes which owe a debt to the legacy of Lawrence by grouping changes in policing under various overlapping dimensions of 'legacy'.

The cultural legacy

By the cultural legacy of Lawrence we mean the impact of the Lawrence agenda on the police 'mind-set'; ways of thinking about policing and the police role which have direct or indirect consequences for policing practices. Obviously one area where new ways of thinking about policing can be developed and transmitted is the police training process, which is discussed in depth in Chapter 9. Here we reflect on other areas of mind-set change which relate to the cultural impact of Lawrence.

One key change to emerge in the wake of the SLI was the adoption of a new definition of a racially motivated incident, which shifted the emphasis from the perception of the police to the views of the victim. Between 1986 and 1999, police services in England and Wales used the Association of Chief Police Officers' definition, which defined a racist incident as:

> Any incident *in which it appears to the reporting or investigating officer* that the complaint involves an element of racial motivation; or any incident which includes an allegation of racial motivation made by any person. (ACPO 1985, emphasis added)

Evidence presented at part two of the Stephen Lawrence Inquiry left Macpherson and his advisors to conclude that this definition, with its emphasis upon motivation, was potentially confusing, poorly understood by police officers, and that the apparent priority of the views of investigating or reporting officers was unhelpful. Indeed

Macpherson (1999: para. 45.36) concluded that the failure of the police to recognise Stephen's murder as racially motivated had contributed to the failure of the investigation. A change of definition to one that was significantly more victim oriented was one outcome of these conclusions. Therefore, following the Stephen Lawrence Inquiry, police services adopted the definition recommended by Sir William Macpherson (1999, rec. 12, emphasis added) and as such:

A racist incident is any incident which is perceived to be racist *by the victim or any other person.*

This revised definition, although clearer and simpler than the original (Home Office 2002), is in essence the same as the previous ACPO definition in that an incident has a racial element if anyone perceives that it has. The important difference here is that the apparent priority given to the views of the police officer, and thus the element of discretion afforded to the police in the recording of such incidents by the old definition, is now removed. This new definition is plainly more victim oriented, and crimes and non-crimes reported as racially motivated must now be recorded as such and investigated with equal commitment regardless of the perception of the reporting or investigating officer in line with recommendation 13. Theoretically, at least, it is now impossible for a police officer to refuse to accept that a reported incident is racially motivated if that is the view held by the complainant or anyone else.

Part of the underlying rationale for the change in definition was to encourage reporting of racist incidents to the police. The views aired at the public hearings held during part two of the inquiry illustrated significant distrust and dissatisfaction with the police, which in turn had led to a disinclination amongst black and minority ethnic (BME) people to report racist and other incidents. To help address the dual issues of underreporting and public distrust, Macpherson highlighted the importance of third-party reporting, identifying the need for people to be able to report at locations other than police stations, and the ability to report 24 hours a day (recommendation 16). One such legacy to emerge from this is today known as 'True Vision'.

Although third-party reporting had already been established in a number of police forces, 'True Vision' was launched in May 2004 and is aimed at improving the service the police provide to a range of diverse communities. In short, more than 20 different police forces have joined together to produce a single self-reporting and information pack together with an online facility (www.report-it.org.

uk) that allows anyone to report hate crime directly to the police. The packs are also available in all police stations signed up to 'True Vision', and in line with Macpherson's recommendations, have also been distributed to a range of different locations including, for example, pubs, clubs, libraries and health groups.

A further legacy in this category has been the shift towards recognising the needs of victims in relation to service provision. As Rowe (2004: 141) suggests, prior to the Lawrence Inquiry the predominant policing approach was based around the provision of a similar level and style of policing to all members of society. This 'colour-blind' approach to policing was, however, identified as problematic by the Lawrence Inquiry. Macpherson (1999: para. 45.24) concluded that:

> The provision of policing services to a diverse public must be appropriate and professional in every case. Every individual must be treated with respect. 'Colour-blind' policing must be outlawed. The police must deliver a service which recognises the different experiences, perceptions and needs of a diverse society.

This legacy of recognising the different needs of a diverse community, and the acknowledgement that service provision cannot be uniform but instead must be appropriate to those needs, leads to a further legacy of the Lawrence Inquiry, namely that of a fundamental shift of focus towards diversity issues. Whilst the main focus in Britain remains largely on issues of race, Rowe (2004) suggests that the Lawrence Inquiry provided additional impetus to the development of policing policies designed to meet the needs of an increasingly multifaceted society and may similarly have created a political climate in which interest groups other than those concerned with race have been able to advance their agenda.

Evidence of this widening of the 'diversity net' can be seen in the relatively recent shift from a narrow focus on racist crime to a broader concern with issues relating to 'hate crime' motivated by a range of prejudices other than just racism (Hall 2005), and in various legal developments (discussed below). This legacy is reflected in the police response to recommendation 18 of the Lawrence Inquiry, which suggested that:

> ACPO, in consultation with local Government and other relevant agencies, should review its *Good Practice Guide for*

Police Response to Racial Incidents in the light of this Report and our Recommendations. Consideration should be given to the production by ACPO of a manual or model for such investigation, to complement their current *Manual of Murder Investigation*. (Macpherson 1999: rec. 18)

The police response, in the shape of the publication of the Association of Chief Police Officers' *Guide to Identifying and Combating Hate Crime* (2000), and latterly the revised *Hate Crime: Delivering a Quality Service* (2005), emphasised this broadening agenda – a process that will continue with the proposed publication of a third ACPO guide in 2009. In identifying the post-Lawrence era as a window of opportunity for change, and with a desire to improve standards of service delivery to minority groups other than just those identifiable by race, the ACPO guides incorporated other strands of diversity, including for example sexuality, religion and faith, disability, and gender. This shift in focus has led to the wider definitions of 'hate crime' now in use, which are, in their victim-oriented approach, clearly inspired by Macpherson's definition of a racist incident:

any incident, which may or may not constitute a criminal offence, which is perceived by the victim or any other person, as being motivated by prejudice or hate. (ACPO 2005: 9)

In addition, the ACPO guides also document the outcomes of shifts in thinking in terms of the way in which investigations are conducted and in which the needs of diverse communities might be better met. A significant legacy of the Lawrence Inquiry can be found in developments in policing relating to critical incidents, family liaison, community engagement and independent advice, and changes in the way that murder investigations are conducted, each of which are discussed in chapters of this book.

Whether the outcomes of the legacies touched upon here have been substantive or merely predominantly symbolic has, perhaps unsurprisingly, been a matter of some debate, as has the question of whether the widening focus on diversity has served to 'water down' the original focus on the issue of race (Rowe 2004; Azah, this volume). The chapters contained within this book will, we hope, serve to address some of these controversies. Whilst at least in theory these legacies, on balance, represent change for the good, it is nevertheless important to note the existence of some less positive outcomes to emerge from the Lawrence Inquiry.

An unintended consequence of the current definition of a racist incident, for example, relates to the type of incident that is being reported, and by whom. In unquestioningly accepting the perception of victims (or any other person) of a racist incident, there is evidence that the situation is being abused in order to further personal or group interests, and to secure the services available to victims of hate crime. For example, McLaughlin states that:

> There is evidence that police officers and white residents in certain neighbourhoods, as part of a backlash, are interpreting virtually any conflictual encounter with non-whites as a 'race-hate' act and reporting it as such. Hence, we are witnessing, through the mobilisation of white resentments, a determined effort to subvert the meaning and purpose of the new policy on racial incidents. (2002: 495)

These concerns are (arguably) reflected in British Crime Survey findings that suggest that approximately two-thirds of the victims of racially motivated incidents are white (see, for example, Clancy, Hough, Aust and Kershaw 2001, cited by Rowe 2004). This is not to suggest that white people cannot be victims of racist incidents, but rather to illustrate that the change in definition has also produced outcomes that, it might be argued, are unintended and perhaps in some instances undesirable, not least in terms of the consumption of finite investigative resources by 'dubious' reporting (see Hall 2005 for a further discussion of these issues).

Questions can also be raised concerning the impact of the Lawrence Inquiry on the morale of police officers; a potential problem not lost on Macpherson (1999: para. 6.46), who in the Inquiry report warned of the dangers of misunderstanding the term 'institutional racism':

> We hope and believe that the average police officer and average member of the public will accept that we do not suggest that all police officers are racist and will both understand and accept the distinction we draw between overt individual racism and the pernicious and persistent institutional racism which we have described.

This 'understanding', however, appears not to have been universally forthcoming, particularly amongst police officers. A number of research studies (Hall 2002; Foster, Newburn and Souhami 2005; Souhami 2007) have highlighted the extent and depth of anger and resentment amongst police officers caused largely by a misunderstanding of the term 'institutional racism', in which many officers felt that they were being individually accused of being racist. Souhami (2007: 77) also points to the importance of the media in this misreading of the Inquiry's intent. The negative impact on the morale of the police service, and indeed the duration of this impact, represents both an unintended and undesirable legacy, and one that has had, at least to some degree, negative consequences for service delivery, driven by fears of misinterpretation, accusation and sanction (Hall 2002; Bowling and Phillips 2002). This important issue is touched upon in a number of the chapters in this book.

A final area of concern here, alluded to above, relates to whether the post-Lawrence changes in policing are predominantly symbolic or substantive; or, in layperson's terms, to what extent has the Lawrence Inquiry resulted in a 'tick-box exercise' by those impacted upon by the recommendations? This is of course a difficult question to answer, largely because the myriad of areas touched by the Inquiry ensure that a 'blanket answer' on the extent to which the Lawrence Inquiry has been a success or a failure is both impossible and inappropriate. Nevertheless, it is an issue that is important to address, not least because of the very public exposure of the racist attitudes and behaviours of the police in 2003 by the BBC's undercover investigation of police training shown in the *Secret Policeman* documentary, which inevitably raised the question of whether anything had really changed as a result of the inquiry. Such issues are discussed in the chapters contained within this book.

The governance legacy

In terms of the legacy of Lawrence in the sphere of police governance, the SLI can be associated with a range of 'second order' changes which, taken together, form elements of deeper 'third order changes' in British policing, particularly in terms of the role of independent, lay and community representatives in overseeing and informing policing and police decision-making. In most cases they fit the profile of influences referred to earlier, as changes that were in motion at the time of the SLI but which Lawrence helped to accelerate and shape. When it comes to governance it is possible to detect the hand of Lawrence on virtually every corner of British police governance: in complaints processes; in the constitutional arrangements for local governance; and in the machineries of inspection and performance management.

In terms of complaints processes, recommendation 58 of the SLI, which reflected concerns over the way complaints against the police made by the Lawrence family were dealt with, asked that the Home Secretary 'consider what steps can and should be taken to ensure that serious complaints against police officers are independently investigated'. The case for the independent investigation of complaints against the police had been suggested as long ago as 1981 with the Scarman Report (Scarman 1981: 118), but had not been embraced by policy-makers, who had opted for the staged enhancement of independent *oversight* of investigations undertaken by the police themselves (Smith 2004). In one of the most evident expressions of translating Lawrence into policy, the Labour Government, through the Police Reform Act 2002, established the Independent Police Complaints Commission (IPCC), which went live in April 2004. The IPCC went short of its sister body and precursor in Northern Ireland, the Office of the Police Ombudsman, by restricting the fully independent investigation of complaints to more serious complaint cases – the Police Ombudsman investigates *all* complaints against the police (see Savage 2007: 71–2) – but nevertheless went as far as the SLI had itself proposed. Furthermore, the IPCC stands out as one further institutional embodiment of the principle of independent, non-police, involvement in the policing process.

As regards the constitutional arrangements for local governance, the SLI had in recommendation 6 stated:

> that proposals as to the formation of the Metropolitan Police Authority be reconsidered, with a view to bringing its functions and powers fully into line with those which apply to other Police Services, including the power to appoint all Chief Officers of the Metropolitan Police Service. (Macpherson 1999: rec 6)

The thrust of this recommendation was to strengthen the local governance of the MPS as a means of generating more openness and accountability and to help restore confidence in policing. The MPS had long had special status in comparison with other police services – the Home Secretary was still technically at that point the 'police authority' for the MPS, although a Metropolitan Police Authority (MPA) existed at the time of the SLI as a nascent body-in-waiting. The legislation which brought the MPA into full existence, the Greater London Authority Act 1999, did in section 311 formally bring the MPA into line with the other local police authorities in terms of general functions as the SLI had proposed, and partially at least reflected the recommendation for the MPA to appoint chief officers. Section 315 (3) of the Act left the power to appoint the Commissioner of the MPS with the Home Secretary, but did require the latter to 'have regard to any recommendations made by the Metropolitan Police Authority and any representations by the Mayor of London'. This partial homage to the SLI, however, had left a degree of confusion which was later to be exposed by the resignation of Sir Ian Blair as Commissioner in October 2008, which Sir Ian had blamed on a 'lack of support' by the Mayor of London, Boris Johnson, who had also adopted the position of Chair of the MPA. This might not have been the type of 'local accountability' of the MPA which the SLI was concerned to pursue. However, what the Inquiry had to say about the MPA served more generally, one could argue, to help shape the MPA as a body highly engaged with and very much a beacon of the pursuit of the Lawrence agenda for diversity in policing and the policing of diversity in London.

One of the functions of the MPA as with other police authorities is to set targets for police performance and monitor performance against those targets as part of the framework of police performance management (see Golding and Savage 2008). Recommendation 2 of the SLI was concerned with a variety of ways in which police performance might be measured by performance indicators which focus on such issues as: measures to encourage reporting of racist incidents; the extent and achievement of racism awareness training; directives governing stop and search; levels of complaint against racist behaviour; and levels of recruitment, retention and progression of minority ethnic groups (Macpherson 1999: rec 2). The SLI coincided with a period of rapid expansion of performance measurement and management regimes for policing (see Savage 2007: 102–4); the proposal to develop a suite of indicators around the behaviours and actions which were of concern to Lawrence could therefore land on fertile soil. Since Lawrence the inclusion of measures and monitoring along the lines proposed is clearly evident in subsequent performance measurement frameworks for local governance. For example, the 2005 Police Authorities (Best Value) Performance Indicators included such indicators as 'satisfaction of victims of racist incidents', 'ratio of minority ethnic groups resigning to white officer resignations' and 'percentage of PACE [Police and Criminal Evidence Act 1984] searches which lead to arrest by ethnicity of the person searched' (OPSI 2005). These are all performance indicators directed at concerns raised in the SLI but which have become routinised in that arm of police governance which draws upon performance management.

Linked to this, in recommendation 3 the SLI also proposed that Her Majesty's Inspectorate of Constabulary (HMIC) 'be granted unfettered powers and duties to inspect all parts of Police Services including the Metropolitan Police Service' (Macpherson 1999: rec 3). At that time HMIC, as the primary body for audit and inspection of police organisations and central to police performance management (Savage 2007: 95–7), did not have full powers to inspect the MPS, although engagement with the MPS had certainly increased in the years just prior to the SLI. The Inquiry gave a final push to the extension of the reach of HMIC into the depths of the MPS, significant not least because one of the roles of HMIC became very quickly one of overseer of the implementation of the SLI recommendations across the police service (see HMIC 2002).

The political legacy

The political legacy of the SLI overlaps to some extent with the governance legacy but also embraces some quite different issues. There are two main areas of the political legacy. The first relates to the lessons offered by justice campaigns and in particular how seemingly powerless individuals and groups can be successful in achieving quite major outcomes through the political process, something this book itself stands testimony to. The second relates to the 'space' which the SLI gave to minority police associations and the impact this has since had on the work and activities of such associations.

One of the many lessons of the SLI is what we might call the 'power of the seemingly powerless'. It is difficult to ignore the fact that SLI did not begin its deliberations until 1998, some five years after the murder of Stephen. As the Chronology (see Appendix 1) makes clear, the public inquiry only took place after a series of prior events and processes relating to the case, including an inquest, a private prosecution and various reinvestigations of the murder. The Inquiry itself and much of that which preceded it was the result of a variety of factors (some of which are examined in more depth in Chapter 1), but central amongst them was the resilience of the Lawrence family. One of the most striking features of the whole Lawrence case has been the huge role played by Stephen Lawrence's parents, Doreen and Neville Lawrence, in campaigning for justice in Stephen's name. In the words of Cathcart (1999: 418), Mr and Mrs Lawrence 'never took no for an answer'. Despite being new to the 'art' of campaigning at the time of the murder – of fighting for a cause, of mobilising others in support of that cause, and so on – the Lawrence family nevertheless showed enormous determination, courage, energy and integrity in fighting for what they saw as justice in Stephen's case. This included demanding a thorough investigation of the murder, honesty and contrition from those who had failed in Stephen's case, the prosecution of those responsible for the murder, and, of course and in relation to these, a full public inquiry into the circumstances surrounding the response to the murder of their son – which the SLI would eventually become. That alone stands as a measure of the critical and powerful role that victims and families play in securing justice when faced with what are in effect miscarriages of justice (Savage, Poyser and Grieve 2007; see also the following chapter).

The Lawrence campaign of course was not by any means an easy one, faced as the campaigners were by the predictable reluctance of those in power and authority to accept fault and respond to pressure from those 'outside' the political process. Indeed, during the early years of the campaign the Lawrence family had to confront denial, dismissal, refusal and even suspicion of their motives (Cathcart 1999) from those at the heart of the case. That they could succeed and achieve the public inquiry they sought – and also leave the wider and longer-term legacy with which this book is concerned – was a reflection of their own refusal to give up and, we might say, of the potential power of the seemingly powerless. In policy analysis terms, the Lawrence family succeeded, largely through their own endeavours and using their own particular qualities, in moving from 'outsiders' to (at least to an extent) 'insiders' (Grant 1989) in the political process. The Lawrence campaign demonstrated that quiet voices can sometimes be heard, whatever the odds against them.

The political legacy of Lawrence also encompasses another set of voices: those of minority groups *within* the police service. It is significant that, in trying to arrive at an appropriate conception of the nature of 'racism', institutional and otherwise, in the police service, the SLI took and clearly valued submissions from the MPS Black Police Association (BPA) (SLI: paras 6.27–6.29). The Inquiry reported that the evidence presented by representatives of the BPA on police culture in general and institutional racism within the police in particular was 'illuminating' (para. 6.27) and that the views of the BPA representatives 'should be closely heeded and respected' (para. 6.28). This was with reference to such statements made by BPA representatives as:

... we should not underestimate the occupational culture within the police service as being a primary source of institutional racism in the way we differentially treat black people. (para 6.28)

Not only were academic specialists influential in shaping the SLI in terms of its working definition of 'institutional racism', but here were officers themselves, with their own particular opinions and concerns, doing so. This form of 'giving space' to those minority voices in the police service acted as a clear acknowledgement that the opinions and concerns of the BPA, as a minority grouping within the police service, were being granted legitimacy in this the most fundamental review of the issue of police racism in Britain since Scarman (Scarman 1981), and possibly of all time. The SLI gave a voice to the BPA and in doing so helped empower that Association to spawn a national framework of BPAs (Holdaway and O'Neill 2007). Furthermore, by serving to further the legitimation of this particular minority police association, the SLI may have indirectly aided the legitimacy and standing of other minority police associations such as the Lesbian and Gay Police Association and perhaps even the more long-standing British Association of Women Officers.

What underpins the key role of the Lawrence family in both the establishment of the SLI and the recognition of the legitimacy of the voice of the BPA is the process of empowerment. The political legacy of Lawrence includes the space given to the formerly relatively powerless in helping shape agendas which otherwise would be the exclusive province of those in power and authority. The empowering effect of Lawrence, both in the run-up to the Inquiry itself and through the Inquiry process, has been to give voice to those otherwise on the margins of influence and decision-making.

The legal legacy

A fourth legacy to emerge is the legal legacy. In addition to announcing the inquiry into Stephen Lawrence's death, the Labour government further maintained its focus on racist crime by acting where the previous government had failed to, by implementing its pledge to make racially motivated and aggravated crimes specific offences with the introduction of the Crime and Disorder Act in 1998. Although this legislation clearly predates the Lawrence Inquiry, Rowe (2004: 99) rightly points out that it was implemented against the context of the debate surrounding racist violence, of which Stephen's murder was clearly a significant part. Iganski (1999) further suggests that, in addition to responding to concerns about a perceived increase in racist offending, the Crime and Disorder Act also served to provide something of an impetus for the police and the wider criminal justice system to take these crimes seriously, to respond appropriately, and to be accountable for those actions.

The widening focus on diversity issues, discussed above as part of the cultural legacy of the Lawrence Inquiry, is similarly reflected in post-Lawrence legal developments. The Criminal Justice Act (CJA) 2003 is particularly significant for a number of reasons. First, section 146 of the Act allows for homophobia and disability (mental and physical) bias to be taken into account as aggravating factors in an offence at sentencing and allows for increased penalties, but stops short of making them specific offences in the same way that the Crime and Disorder Act does for offences relating to race and, by amendment in 2001, religion.

Second, section 145 of the Criminal Justice Act 2003, which also allows for the imposition of increased penalties, applies where a court is considering the seriousness of an offence other than one under sections 29 to 32 of the Crime and Disorder Act 1998 (c. 37) (in other words, for offences other than racially or religiously aggravated assaults, criminal damage, public order offences and harassment).

Third, in relation to recommendation 38 of the Lawrence Inquiry, namely that consideration should be given to the Court of Appeal being given power to permit prosecution after acquittal where fresh and viable evidence is presented, the CJA 2003 allows for the retrial of people who have been acquitted of an offence where there is 'new and compelling evidence against the acquitted person in relation to the qualifying offence'. In short, this effectively abolished the 'double jeopardy' rule that had prohibited a person from being tried twice for the same offence.

A further legal legacy, brought to fruition by the Race Relations (Amendment) Act 2000, relates to recommendation 11 of the Inquiry. This recommended that the full force of the Race Relations legislation should apply to all police officers, and that Chief Officers of Police should be made vicariously liable for the acts and omissions of their officers relevant to that legislation. Bowling and Phillips (2002: 257) identify this as the most important post-Lawrence development in anti-discrimination law because it makes it unlawful for police and other authorities to provide demonstrably inferior treatment to people on the basis of their ethnic origin in terms of both service provision and the use of coercive powers.

Finally, recommendations 32–44 relating to the prosecution of racist crimes have also left a legacy, evidenced both in the policy documentation produced by the Crown Prosecution Service (CPS) with its clear victim focus, and of course by the increase in prosecutions for these types of offences since the publication of the Lawrence Inquiry. The latter is perhaps evidence of recommendation 33, which stated that once the CPS evidential test is satisfied there should be a rebuttable presumption that the public interest test should be in favour of prosecution.

Despite this, however, two particular areas of concern stand out, both of which relate to recommendation 34 in particular. This recommendation stated that police services and the CPS should ensure that particular care is taken at all stages of prosecution to recognise and to include reference to any evidence of racist motivation. In particular it should be the duty of the CPS to ensure that such evidence is referred to both at trial and in the sentencing process. Recommendation 34 also recommended that the CPS and counsel ensure that no 'plea bargaining' should ever be allowed to exclude such evidence. There is, however, evidence that racist motivation is still not consistently identified, particularly by the police (John 2003; Rowe 2004), and that plea bargaining regularly occurs, often because the racist element is difficult to prove evidentially (Burney and Rose 2002).

The intelligence legacy

We can treat the 'intelligence legacy' of Lawrence very briefly because Chapter 6 deals specifically with the issue. The intelligence legacy, however, warrants mention here because it illustrates very powerfully the extent both of the reach of Lawrence and of the capacity of the Lawrence agenda to transmute evident failure into more positive change. As Chapter 6 makes clear, the findings in the SLI of wholesale failures in the collection and handling of intelligence in the Lawrence case were to act as stimulators of an already shifting mind-set on the role of intelligence in criminal investigation. With the encouragement of the Audit Commission (see Savage 2007: 100–101), in the early to mid 1990s the police service had begun, with tentative steps, to engage with the principles of 'intelligence-led policing' (ILP), with an emphasis on an appreciation of the role of front-line uniformed officers as sources of local intelligence, the use of civilian staff as crime analysts, the use of information technology in crime mapping, and so on. What the SLI served to achieve was to offer an important boost to this movement by drawing attention to the vagaries of intelligence failures and the value of information gathering (recommendation 21) and the sharing of information between the police and other agencies (recommendation 17), both of which can be included under the 'intelligence' umbrella. ILP was to acquire formal government approval with the arrival of the National Intelligence Model (NIM) soon after the publication of the SLI, and legal standing with the Police Reform Act 2002 (Savage 2007: 116–7). ILP was on the move before the SLI but it seems difficult to deny that Lawrence was to concentrate the minds of those responsible for policing policy, particularly criminal investigation policy, and add momentum for the push towards thinking in terms of the role of the 'intelligence cycle' as at the core of investigative strategy. In this sense the 'reach' of Lawrence was to extend into national policy on the investigation of serious crimes.

The international legacy

Although the Stephen Lawrence Inquiry focused solely on issues relating to the UK, there is no doubt that it has also left an international legacy. The impact of the Lawrence Inquiry on the international stage takes a number of forms.

Perhaps the most obvious relates to the number of incidents now coming to the attention of the police in this country compared with other jurisdictions. Under the cultural legacy we discussed the significance of the change in definition of a racist incident to acknowledge the impact of non-crime incidents, the widening of the net to incorporate other strands of diversity, and the possibilities for third-party reporting. Whilst it was noted that the changes were not always positive in their outcome, the net effect has nevertheless been, at least to some degree, to uncover more of the 'dark figure' of unreported crimes of this nature.

This is illustrated by Hall (2005) in the following comparison between England and Wales and the United States. In 2001 the population of the United States officially stood at 284,796,887. In that year 11,987 law enforcement agencies recorded 9,726 hate crimes, of which 4,366 were racially motivated (FBI 2002). In the same year the population of England and Wales stood at 52,041,915 and the 43 police forces of England and Wales recorded 54,351 racially motivated incidents alone (Home Office 2002). Statistically, then, in 2001 England and Wales suffered almost twelve and a half times as many racially motivated incidents as the US, despite the population of the US being almost five and a half times greater than England and Wales. Indeed, West Midlands police recorded similar figures for racially motivated incidents to the whole of the US (4,058 incidents), and the

Metropolitan Police recorded just under four times as many racially motivated incidents as the whole of the US (16,711 incidents).

Some commentators have argued that such statistics simply present an inaccurately negative picture of the state of intergroup relations in a country (Jacobs and Potter 1998: 64), and also between countries. Nevertheless, as far as shedding a little more light on the 'dark figure' is concerned, and not withstanding the issues discussed above concerning the cultural legacy, the situation remains that efforts to encourage greater reporting and recording of racist incidents seem to have had some impact, particularly when viewed in a comparative context, and despite the fact that racist victimisation remains significantly under-reported (Home Office 2006). In other words, in comparison with other countries (in this example the US), the figures recorded by the police here are closer (albeit still some way off) to those recorded by victim surveys.

A second area of the international legacy relates to family liaison. The shifting focus towards victims and families, and in particular the issue of police interaction with families, was noted above as part of the cultural legacy of the Lawrence Inquiry. The formalisation of the FLO role following the Lawrence Inquiry has resulted in the training of over 700 FLOs in England and Wales. Their work with families has, however, extended far beyond national boundaries on a number of occasions, and since the Lawrence Inquiry the expertise of FLOs has been sought by, and deployed in, a number of countries around the world, often to great acclaim.

Perhaps the best endorsement of the early work of FLOs in supporting families abroad can be found in the responses to the terrorist attacks in the US on 11 September 2001, in which former President George W. Bush, former UN Secretary General Kofi Annan and the then Prime Minister Tony Blair united in their praise of FLOs. Indeed Tony Blair (cited by Grieve 2002) said:

> I pay tribute to our own consular staff in New York and London and to the family counsellors and Metropolitan Police officers who have supported relatives of the British victims. A lot of people here, such as the Metropolitan Police, played an enormous part in helping to co-ordinate the efforts to sustain those involved, which was obviously difficult for reasons that we know.

More recent examples of the deployment of FLOs abroad can be found in the responses to the Bali bombings in 2002 and the Tsunami in South-east Asia in 2004.

A third area within the category of international legacy relates to critical incidents, and in particular critical incident management and training. In Chapter 7 in this volume, Jonathan Crego firmly attributes the significant developments in the field of critical incidents to the Stephen Lawrence Inquiry. The developments he discusses, particularly in terms of immersive training for police officers in responding to critical incidents, have been exported around the world to both police and non-police organisations, leaving a truly international legacy.

In this Introduction we have sought to demonstrate that the 'legacy of Lawrence' is far-reaching and complex. If one disaggregates what the SLI has achieved into discrete policing policies (or non-policies) it is possible to argue, at least in some respects, that Lawrence has had modest impact on contemporary policing. However, we would argue that, important as such disaggregation is for tracking particular policy developments and outcomes, we should also seek to consider the SLI in the round and assess the extent to which, as a package, the SLI leaves a substantial legacy. On the basis of what we have already argued in this Introduction, and of what will follow in this collection of essays as a whole, we would contend that the legacy of Lawrence is huge.

Part One:
Lawrence in Context

Chapter 1

Stephen Lawrence as a miscarriage of justice

Stephen P. Savage, John Grieve and Sam Poyser

In this chapter we will attempt to place the Stephen Lawrence Inquiry (SLI) into a broader context, in two closely related ways. Firstly, we shall consider the Lawrence case as a particular form of miscarriage of justice to enable us to understand how the case sits in the lexicon of British miscarriages of justice and how it exists as an example of system failure. Secondly, and one reason why we consider Lawrence as a miscarriage of justice, we shall build on existing work about the role of miscarriages of justice and more generally system failure in driving change and reform in policing (Punch 2003; Savage 2007: 11–45) and where Lawrence sits in that respect. In that regard, rather than examine *how* Lawrence has had an impact on policing, or in what ways Lawrence has left a legacy – these are the primary concerns of other parts of this book – we shall in this chapter attempt to explain *why*: why Lawrence was to become so powerful an influence on policing. If, as this collection of essays as a whole indicates, the Lawrence agenda has constituted a watershed in British policing, we need to ask what it was about the Lawrence case which made it so. The chapter will proceed firstly by reflecting on definitions of 'miscarriage of justice'; secondly by examining the relationship between system failures and police reform; thirdly by outlining how the Lawrence case constitutes a miscarriage of justice; before finally asking the question, 'Why Lawrence?'

Defining and categorising 'miscarriages of justice'

In a sense, one of the 'legacies of Lawrence' has been the role of the Lawrence case in stretching and deepening academic thinking on the nature of 'miscarriages of justice'. Traditionally, the term has been used to refer to wrongful convictions and catalogues of the *causes célèbres* of miscarriages of justice would tend to consist of notorious cases where wrongful convictions have come to light, such as the Guildford Four and Birmingham Six cases (Rozenberg 1994). However, increasingly, commentators and researchers in the field of miscarriages of justice have adopted more nuanced conceptions of what constitutes a 'miscarriage of justice'. Walker in particular has argued for a more inclusive and broader classificatory framework:

> A miscarriage occurs whenever suspects or defendants or convicts are treated by the State in breach of their rights, whether because of, first, deficient processes or, secondly, the laws which are applied to them or, thirdly, because there is no factual justification for the applied treatment or punishment, or fourthly, whenever suspects or defendants or convicts are treated adversely by the State to a disproportionate extent in comparison with the need to protect the rights of others, or, fifthly, *whenever the rights of others are not effectively or proportionately protected or vindicated by state action against wrongdoers* or, sixthly, by the state law itself (Walker 2002: 506 – emphasis added).

It is the fifth category in Walker's framework (in emphasis) which is of most significance in this context. It incorporates, amongst other things, what we have elsewhere referred to as miscarriages of justice based on *failures to act* (Savage, Poyser and Grieve 2007). Rather than wrongful conviction, such miscarriages of justice may involve the failure to convict, or to act in appropriate ways to make conviction possible. 'Miscarriages of justice' can also apply when there is *no action, inaction or questionable actions* in the sense that an act has taken place (an offence against a victim) but no action or insufficient action or intervention has followed. Indeed, each time a wrongful conviction is exposed, another 'miscarriage of justice' is exposed at one and the same time, in the sense that the revelation of a wrongful conviction leaves an offence for which no one stands convicted. Whilst much of the research on miscarriages of justice – and indeed most of the media attention – has focused on 'wrongful convictions', miscarriages based on what we have called failures to act also warrant attention.

Such 'failures to act' embrace as broad a range of system failures as wrongful convictions (on the latter see Walker 1999: 52–55). They include police poor practice, malpractice and incompetence (failure to identify an event as a potential crime; failure to identify an event as a certain type of crime; failure to investigate effectively; poor treatment of victims and their families), inadequate prosecution processes (poor communication with the police; 'risk avoidance') and problematic trial practices (hostile cross-examination of witnesses; weak presentation of the prosecution case). More specifically, failures to act embrace the failure of the police to identify suspects, the failure of the police to press charges, the failure of the prosecution to mount a case, the collapse of the prosecution case during the trial and, throughout all of these, the failure of the agencies involved to inform or support victims and their families. One can add to this category those miscarriages of justice which relate to the failure of the authorities to *protect* citizens from known danger. Examples of this would be the Mubarek case, where a young Asian offender in custody was murdered in a prison cell having been placed with another offender known by the prison authorities to be both racist and violent (Kennedy 2005), or the Zito case, where a man was killed on an Underground train platform by a man known by the police and health agencies to be mentally disordered and dangerous but who, for a variety of reasons, was not made safe by being kept in secure accommodation (Jones and Mason 2002). Later in this chapter we shall attempt to locate the Lawrence case within this lexicon of system failures as 'failures to act', but it is evident at this point that most at issue in this case were *police* failures at early and critical stages of the investigative process. Before elaborating on that, we can reflect on the role of system failures, including the range of types of miscarriages of justice, in stimulating or furthering change and reform in policing, and how in turn they can be identified with periodic watersheds in the development of policing.

System failure as a driver of change in policing: watersheds in police reform

In the public policy literature a distinct sphere of study relates to the relationship between what Dunleavy (1995) calls 'policy disasters', or what Boin and t'Hart (2000) refer to as 'crises and fiascos'. The case for focusing on this issue for public policy analysis is that 'policy disasters' can be an important stimulus for change and reform, or 'institutional renewal', in public sector institutions. In that sense system failures can offer what has been called 'windows of opportunity' for reform (Keeler 1993), creating conditions where change and reform become more possible and more likely than would otherwise have been the case. System failures and the crises they engender provide opportunities for policy-makers and those close to influencing policy to think the previously 'unthinkable' and enable change agendas to enter the scene. This capacity was expressed famously many years ago by Sherman (1978), in his case concerned with system failure in terms of 'scandals' and what they can lead to:

> Scandal is a mighty weapon. It can topple governments and destroy careers. It can tarnish the reputation of an entire profession. It can cause misery and suffering among the families of its subjects ... *But it can also be an agent of change.* (Sherman 1978: xv – emphasis added)

Boin and 't Hart (2000) suggest a staged process by which crises within the public sector can lead to 'institutional renewal'. Firstly, a stable and established policy sector is faced with problems, generated externally or internally, which seriously undermine the status quo in that sector. This is often a scenario of 'things going wrong'. Secondly, and as a result, the existing or traditional routines and procedures within that sector come under increasing scrutiny and criticism. Thirdly, the authority and legitimacy of policy-makers within the sector are subsequently challenged and an institutional crisis ensues. In turn, this provides a 'window of reform' where institutional change becomes possible, although not certain. If change is to take place then the response to that opportunity might be incremental change ('adaptation' to the problem or 'restoration') or more fundamental reform ('reconstruction'). This framework can be applied across the public sector. For example, tragic events such as the fire at King's Cross Underground station in 1987 (Fennell 1988) and the Paddington rail crash in 1999 (Crompton and Jupe 2002) both played a key part in driving fundamental reforms of the British public transport sector. In these cases 'system failure' was indeed a driver for fundamental change, or a *midwife of reform*. Exactly the same, perhaps even more so, can be said about the role of system failure in driving police reform.

What then are the system failures most frequently associated with policing, failures which are, in turn, most frequently associated with drivers for police reform? Each policy sector has its own particular configurations of 'stress points' which, for that sector, provide most opportunities and vulnerabilities for 'things going wrong'. For the health sector, that might include outbreaks of infection in hospitals (Martin and Evans 1984); for the education sector it might include breaches of security for children in the classroom, such as those identified in the Dunblane shootings (Cullen 1996). In terms of policy sectors closer to the police sector, it is evident that the prison sector, for example, is particularly vulnerable to failures surrounding prison disturbances or 'prison riots' (Carrabine 2005), escapes from prison (Barker 1998) and deaths in custody, such as the killing of Zahid Mubarek (Zahid Mubarek Inquiry 2005). In all of these cases, system failures are prone to the process of the delegitimation of the status quo, periods of review and criticism, followed by designs for institutional renewal as outlined earlier – and possibly actual reform itself. What, then, are the 'stress points' as far as the police sector is concerned?

There is a case for viewing the police sector as particularly prone to system failure. To begin with, police work can position the police in highly sensitive and potentially volatile situations where, either as a result of their own activities and behaviours, or as a result of wider social problems and divisions, police interventions may provoke or at least be the catalyst for outbreaks of social disorder – a relatively frequent form of system failure in the policing context. The potential for public order problems is never that far from certain types of police work (Baker 2002); when social disorder occurs the police may be blamed, rightly or wrongly, for some or all of the problems which become evident. In addition to this level of vulnerability, some police decisions, such as the use of firearms or the hot pursuit of vehicles, have to be taken at very short notice with little opportunity for detailed consideration, and yet they may result in death or serious injury to others or the officers themselves. In turn such decisions may become the focus of intense scrutiny, with the potential for exposing a range of system failures in such areas as police training, the supervision and management of officers, police communications, and so on. The involvement of the police in such critical incidents, a consequence of the police role, creates a unique propensity for the police sector to be vulnerable to 'things going wrong', or system failure. Furthermore, policing is often undertaken in situations where public safety is at issue, and when public safety is compromised police actions and decisions may be identified as causal factors. Perhaps the most notable example of this was the Hillsborough disaster in 1989, when 96 football fans were killed as a result of injuries sustained during crushing on the terraces, and after which the police were to take much of the blame for the ways in which crowd control was handled (Taylor 1989).

However, to return to the theme raised earlier, major system failures may be and have been critical drivers of reform and positive change in policing, in Britain and elsewhere. In his comparative study of police deviance Punch (2000) has developed the convincing thesis that whereas in some countries police corruption tends to be the main form of policing 'scandal', in the European/British context 'scandal' tends to be around other sorts of system failures:

> ... in Europe the concerns about corruption and deviance revolve around two matters. First, 'noble cause' or 'process' corruption, particularly in specialised units, which is oriented to achieving results. And – at the other end of the scale – non-performance, incompetence and failing to perform adequately. (Punch 2000: 308–9)

This captures conveniently the core areas of system failure which, it could be argued, have been driving forces for police reform in the British context. 'Noble cause' corruption is a label which has been given to the police role in miscarriages of justice based on wrongful conviction; performance-related 'scandals' concern the 'other' type of miscarriages of justice referred to earlier: failures to act. 'Performance'-related scandals could also embrace another key source of system failure in the British context – police failures concerning police–community relations and policing styles, as evidenced in the Scarman Inquiry into the Brixton disorders (Scarman 1981). If we take these together it is possible to draw up a threefold sequence of the role of system failures, through official inquiries (public or otherwise), in creating the conditions for 'paradigm shifts' or 'third- order' changes in policing in postwar Britain, watersheds or 'mind-set changes' in the history of police reform, including Lawrence. This framework summarises a wider study (Savage 2007) of the role of system failure in British police reform.

Watershed 1: Confait – Fisher Inquiry – Police and Criminal Evidence Act 1984

The Confait case involved the wrongful convictions in 1972 of two boys, Colin Lattimore and Ronald Leighton, both of whom suffered learning difficulties, for the murder of Maxwell Confait. They were convicted on the basis of confession evidence, subsequently denied, which was eventually shown at the Court of Appeal to have been seriously fallible, leading to the quashing of their convictions in 1973. Part of the fallout of this particular case of miscarriage of justice was the ordering of an official inquiry, to be known as the Fisher Inquiry, which reported in 1977 (Fisher 1977; Savage 2007: 23–26). The Fisher Inquiry was to raise a series of concerns about protections for persons under interview, rights to consult a solicitor, the recording of interviews with suspects and the treatment of vulnerable people in police custody. Given these concerns, Fisher was to call for a Royal Commission to review police powers and practices, to become known as the Royal Commission on Criminal Procedure (RCCP, or 'Phillips'). The RCCP in fact embraced a much wider remit than Fisher had adopted and undertook a root and branch review of the full panoply of police powers, from stop and search in the street right through to powers and practices when dealing with suspects in police custody. The RCCP was to offer much of the framework of what was eventually to become the Police and Criminal Evidence Act 1984 (PACE), by all standards the most comprehensive package of reforms of police powers ever to appear in the UK. This was not only a matter of legal provisions and codes of practice, critically important as they were; PACE involved fundamental shifts in the balance of police powers and the rights of suspects which, arguably, were in the longer term to have more subtle effects on the police mind-set concerning the police role. This particular 'paradigm shift' could be found in both provision for and attitudes to:

- the position of vulnerable people under police control;
- the value of record-keeping of policing processes and decisions and, through this, issues of transparency and accountability;
- the general question of the rights of those subject to police actions.

These fundamental issues of policing policy, practice, ethics and orientation formed the basis of the watershed in British policing which the miscarriage of justice associated with the Confait case helped bring forth.

Watershed 2: Brixton, Scarman and the rebirth of community-priented policing

The Brixton disorders of 1981, involving sustained and violent clashes between the police and large numbers of young, mainly black, people in London over one weekend in April 1981, have been widely acknowledged to have played a hugely formative role in guiding the direction of British policing during the 1980s and beyond (see Reiner 1992). Lord Scarman's inquiry into the disorders (Scarman 1981) was to stand not just as a powerful and forensic analysis of the system failures peculiar to the policing of London in that area at that time, but also as (on reflection) a timely judgement of the 'state of the police' in Britain in the early 1980s and where the police (service) might be going in the future. The shock waves created by the Brixton disorders, and the gravitas which Lord Scarman brought to the subsequent review of the forces and factors at issue in these disorders, combined to create a stage for fundamental change in policing to be placed on the agenda. Crisis had created opportunity; that opportunity would eventually be associated with both particular policy reforms and, perhaps more significantly (as a form of 'slow-fuse' reform), a paradigm shift in relation to the question of the *purpose* of policing. The paradigm shift in this case would involve (Savage 2007):

- a call for the reorientation of policing towards community-based policing;
- the growth of the 'service' ethos in policing at the expense of the 'law-enforcement' or 'crime-fighting' missions of policing;
- the enhancement of the independent element in the police complaints process;
- the value placed on social skills and human awareness (including race awareness) training for recruit police officers.

Although much of the critical response to the Scarman Inquiry related to the dismissal of any finding of 'institutional racism' as a factor in the events leading up to the Brixton disorders (largely because Scarman chose to define 'institutional racism' as the institution 'knowingly' discriminating against black people (Scarman 1981: 11)), the fact that Scarman recommended a panoply of *institutional* reforms of policing in response to any problem of 'racism' arguably means that if it had employed the definition employed by the SLI, Scarman would have reached the same conclusion as the SLI. More generally, the Scarman agenda helped inculcate within a generation of future leaders of the British police service (Reiner 1991) a 'vision' of the purpose of policing quite different from that which had prevailed amongst their predecessors. Scarman involved a classic form of paradigm shift.

Watershed 3: Stephen Lawrence – Macpherson Inquiry – the Lawrence legacy

In relation to the two 'watersheds' in policing which Confait and Scarman were part of, and which can be associated with a range of what are referred to in the Introduction to this volume as 'second-order' and 'third-order' changes in policing policy, Lawrence stands as the 'third pillar', the third phase of paradigm shift which postwar British policing has experienced in the formation of the contemporary police mind-set. We do not need here to track or identify the range of policy changes or deeper mind-set transformations which Lawrence has been about, because that is the subject of this volume as a whole. Suffice to state at this point that, in the inventory of radical changes in British policing in the postwar period, Lawrence stands with the other watersheds as responsible for a veritable paradigm shift. As other chapters in this volume make clear, this paradigm shift includes:

- the recentring of racism as a focal concern of policing;
- the repositioning of families and communities at the core of police investigative processes;
- the enhancement of the 'independent' element in police governance, police decision-making and police strategies;
- the renewal of diversity-based policing within and outside of the police service.

Confait was a system failure involving a miscarriage of justice based on wrongful conviction which was to have long-term consequences for the way we exercise – or, more importantly, think, about – police powers. Scarman pointed to a system failure based on shortfalls in the quality of policing and in police strategies and responses to what were seen as 'policing problems', which in turn helped shape how the 'police purpose' was articulated. Lawrence was a system failure involving a miscarriage of justice based on *failures to act*, which subsequently became an engine for change within the very processes of action which the police were to be identified with. If Lawrence was a miscarriage of justice which was to have such a consequential impact on the policing landscape, what type of miscarriage of justice was it?

Stephen Lawrence: a miscarriage of justice

We have outlined earlier how the notion of miscarriage of justice should be and has been extended to embrace miscarriages of justice based not just on wrongful convictions but also on failures to act. The Lawrence case stands out as the classic example of this dimension of miscarriage of justice, not least because the 'failures' in this case have been spelled out in the glare of a full public inquiry which the Lawrence family did so much to instigate. Rather than repeat the extensive catalogue of the failings documented in the SLI, we shall at this point attempt to render the failures of Lawrence down to those which form the elements of miscarriages of justice which constitute those failures to act. What *types* of failures to act were evident in the Lawrence case?

In order to answer this question we will utilise two sources of information: on the one hand Doreen Lawrence's own powerful statement on the response to the murder of her son Stephen (Lawrence 2006); on the other hand our own previous research on miscarriages of justice (Savage, Poyser and Grieve 2007) which involved interviews with a number of those (n=37) who had been engaged with miscarriages of justice as victims, families of victims or victim-families, and those involved in campaigns against miscarriages of justice, including those attached to the Lawrence case.

We propose that the miscarriage of justice in the Stephen Lawrence case can be broken down into a categorisation of a range of failures.

Failure to protect. Directly following the murder, and while Stephen was still alive, steps might have been taken by those officers first on the scene to provide first aid: '[there was] no attempt to apply First Aid ... nobody had put Stephen in the recovery position ... no police officers at the scene ... attended to Stephen's injuries ... the police did not even look to see if he was seriously hurt' (Lawrence 2006: 169).

Failure to treat the Lawrence family as victims. In the early responses to the death it was alleged that the police failed to offer the family support on the basis of them being victims; rather there appeared a degree of suspicion of Stephen himself, as one interviewee in the research by Savage, Poyser and Grieve stated: 'Some of the things they said ... like hearing about the gloves and hat [in Stephen's possession] it was said in a way as if [Stephen] was a cat burglar and was preparing to do a robbery that night.'

Failure to treat the Lawrence family appropriately as victims. While Mr and Mrs Lawrence visited the hospital, officers who were with Duwayne Brooks, who accompanied Stephen on the night of the murder, failed to respond to them in ways they might have expected: '... the police must have seen us coming in – especially when Neville recognised Duwayne and went up to him – and yet no police officer there said anything to us. No one offered to take us home after we were told Stephen was dead' (Lawrence 2006: 73). When the Lawrences returned home from the hospital, no police officer went with them and they had no idea at this time how their son had died. Doreen Lawrence explained that when she went to the mortuary to view the body, the police officers' attitude towards her wanting to go into the room and see Stephen's body was one of agitation: '... they did not give us space to mourn our child, but were standing over us, as if watching to see what we were going to do' (Lawrence 2006: 72). The failure to treat victims appropriately also applied to Duwayne Brooks: 'There was no sympathy for him whatsoever, no suggestion that he had been traumatised by what he had gone through ...' (Lawrence 2006: 128).

Failure to communicate and liaise appropriately. Many of the failings of Lawrence relate to poor or non-existent family liaison and communication between the police and the Lawrence family about the investigation into the murder of their son. Doreen Lawrence referred to the 'one-way' nature of communication and information giving: '... they constantly wanted information from us, but we were never given any by them' (2006: 81). An interviewee in the research by Savage, Poyser and Grieve (2007) put it that 'Members of the public were giving [the family] information about who had done it [the murder] ... which [was passed on to the police ... But [the family] never got any feedback on whether it was useful. The police would never tell [the family] how the investigation was progressing.' As Doreen Lawrence also expressed it, 'Each time I asked a question they could not answer it' (2006: 116).

Failure to investigate properly or thoroughly. Of course, much of the SLI pointed to ineffective or incompetent investigation on behalf of officers attached to the Lawrence case and we cannot capture the depth of the failings in this regard. Suffice to note that, in the words of Doreen Lawrence (2006: 87), 'They dragged their feet, mishandled witnesses and slowed things down'; in the immediate aftermath of the murder, '... it seemed strange to me that they had not searched more thoroughly in the area around the place where the killing happened ... it was obvious ... that there was nothing serious being done down there – no roadblocks or barriers or police cars ... Duwayne had pointed the police down Dickson Road ... but they hadn't bothered to search [it] ...' As one interviewee expressed it, 'just after Stephen was killed you assumed the whole force would just kick in and that they would be knocking on doors ... and have this sense of urgency to gather evidence ... We soon realised that this wasn't the case.'

Failures of police leadership. Linked to the points above, there were evident failings in the coordination, management and leadership on behalf of those involved at various levels of the Lawrence investigation and its aftermath. As one interviewee in the research by Savage, Poyser and Grieve expressed it, one problem with the immediate response was that '... [the family] did not know who was in charge that night'; and that '... The man who took charge of [Stephen's] murder case in the first instance wasn't going to be there for the whole period of time, only two or three days ... the case was doomed from the start ... a person who is not going to continue to the end of a case should never be in charge of a case, especially a murder investigation.'

Failures to admit fault and apologise. One of the possible failings of leadership is to fail to reveal fault and accept responsibility. Research has shown that what victims of miscarriage of justice often seek more than anything else is an understanding of what went wrong in their particular case – the 'truth' – and an acknowledgement by those responsible for failings that they 'did wrong' (Savage 2007a). In the Lawrence case it is clear that early failings in the investigation were compounded by later failings to remedy those failings or to accept responsibility that they had occurred. For example, one interviewee in the research by Savage, Poyser and Grieve claimed that 'people wanted to cover up their mistakes to protect their own backs'. Another commented that during the Inquiry itself, '... when he [a senior officer] sat in the witness box he said that the only thing that went wrong was the liaison with the family ... They [the police] are a closed shop.' Although the SLI did serve to uncover much of what went wrong in the Lawrence case and was instrumental in gaining the apology which the Lawrence family had sought for so long, the fact that it took a full public inquiry to achieve that was itself an indication of the nature of the failures in this regard.

It should of course be acknowledged that the miscarriage of justice in the Lawrence case did not only involve failures on behalf of the police. Doreen Lawrence also documented failures on behalf of the

Crown Prosecution Service to communicate with the Lawrence family over their decisions (and non-decisions) (2006: 153), and of the trial process in the failed private prosecution (2006: 157). After all, what was in question in the Lawrence case was indeed *system* failure. This only adds weight to the conclusion reached by Macpherson that the Lawrence case was about system failure on a grand scale; what we would classify here as a miscarriage of justice based on a catalogue of *failures to act*.

In relation to this, and given what has been argued here and throughout this volume concerning the depth and breadth of the legacy of Lawrence, we conclude this chapter by reflecting on the question of *why* the Lawrence case and the SLI were to have such far-reaching consequences and such an impact on the landscape of British policing.

Conclusion: why Lawrence?

It is never easy to determine why or how particular cases of system failure in policing come to have long-term consequences or play a key role in inaugurating a period of major change in policing. Why, for example, did the Brixton disorders of 1981, through Scarman, have such an impact on the police mind-set nationally, as discussed earlier, when other major outbreaks of disorder, such as the Handsworth riots of the mid 1980s (Gaffney 1987), whilst significant in a number of respects, did not have anything like the impact of Scarman on the police mind-set? Almost certainly, it is not solely as a result of a specific system failure that fundamental change is set under way, however dramatic that failure might be. More likely, particular cases of system failure come to act as signifiers of deeper problems which may already have been evident, or they may be only one dimension, even if the key dimension, of a complex set of factors coming into play, even coincidentally, at one and the same time. In this sense *timing* might be a critical issue determining whether this or that system failure is to have major and longer-term consequences.

For these reasons we need to have some sense of why this particular miscarriage of justice, and its aftermath, holds the fundamental position it does as one of the great drivers of change and reform in British policing, and beyond. Answering this question is a project in its own right so we can only here offer a speculative inventory of the factors which, taken together, served to make Lawrence 'special', in addition of course to the sheer weight of the evidence of policing

37

failures which the SLI presented. In this respect it is clear that the 'Lawrence agenda' would not have been set without the Stephen Lawrence Inquiry itself. In that sense the question 'why Lawrence?' is to an extent the question 'why the Lawrence Inquiry?' – what were the factors critical to the establishment of the public inquiry into the circumstances surrounding the investigation of the murder of Stephen Lawrence?

We would argue, as others have done (Cathcart 1999) that top of the list in the answers to the questions 'why Lawrence?' and 'why the Inquiry' has to be the Lawrence family. As has already been noted in the Introduction to this book, the holding of the SLI owes much to the endeavours and determination of Doreen and Neville Lawrence in campaigning for justice in their case. This point was made clear in the Inquiry Report itself (Macpherson 1999: para. 4.1):

> Neville and Doreen Lawrence have together been the mainspring of this Inquiry. Their persistence and courage in the face of tragedy and bitter disillusionment and disappointment have been outstanding ... Their dignity and courtesy have been an example to all throughout.

The character and dignity exhibited by Doreen and Neville Lawrence throughout their campaign to have a public inquiry and since the Inquiry itself have been widely acknowledged as the major driving force behind the Lawrence campaign for justice. This stands as classic testimony to what we have referred to as the critical role of families in campaigns against miscarriages of justice (Savage, Poyser and Grieve 2007). Families can provide the resilience which is crucial to justice campaigns. As one campaigning lawyer in our research expressed it:

> ... families ... are the best people to take any [miscarriage of justice] case forward because nobody can impeach their motives ... they are essentially the best protagonists of change ... I am a firm believer in families being the hero of any campaign because without them there is nothing. All those other organisations exist only because of them ... ultimately it's the families which drive you and which lead the change.

Without the commitment and character of Mr and Mrs Lawrence it is difficult to doubt that the Inquiry would not have taken place; without the Inquiry there would have been no 'Lawrence agenda'. In this respect the family were well supported by their legal advisors and legal team (Cathcart 1999: 418), a second factor in answer to the 'why Lawrence?' question. Imran Khan, who was to emerge during the 1990s as a major player in campaigns for justice, worked closely with the Lawrence family throughout their campaign, advising them on campaigning networks and the mobilisation of support for their quest for a public inquiry.

A third factor in answer to the 'why Lawrence?' question appears to be the media (Cathcart 1999: 418) and an alliance which was formed between Mr and Mrs Lawrence and sections of the media, including, perhaps surprisingly, the *Daily Mail*. Exposure of the Lawrence case was partly due to space given to it by the *Daily Mail*, often as front page coverage. This appeared to be the result of a chance encounter between Neville Lawrence and Sir David English, editor of the *Mail*, when Neville worked on Sir David's house as a craftsman. With the strange bedfellow of the *Mail* on their side, the Lawrence family could look to the media, at least in the later stages of their campaign, for critical support.

A fourth factor, and a major one, behind the Lawrence agenda was the political will to support the Lawrence case which was exhibited by the Labour Party. This was crucial not only to establishment of the SLI but also to the official response to Lawrence and the recommendations of the SLI. In this respect Jack Straw MP was to play a key role. In the mid 1990s Jack Straw was Shadow Home Secretary and had made a personal commitment to the Lawrence family that Labour, once in office, would follow through the family's demands for a public inquiry into Stephen's case. As one interviewee in the research by Savage, Poyser and Grieve (2007) expressed it:

> Jack Straw had some empathy with the Lawrences ... a certain respect for what the family had suffered and [he] was keen to ensure they had some access to justice which thus far they had had denied to them by the Conservative Government.

It is fair to say that this personal commitment on behalf of Jack Straw to the Lawrence family was maintained throughout Straw's terms of office, both as the Home Secretary and as Lord Chancellor at the Ministry of Justice. Having secured the SLI itself, it was inevitable with that level of political support that the findings of the Lawrence Inquiry would also find their way into government-led actions. Political support for the Lawrence agenda may, however, have stemmed from more than the personal commitment of Straw to the Lawrence cause.

It is clear now that New Labour was eventually to become heavily engaged with the police reform agenda. In the early years of the new millennium, Labour was to launch the most comprehensive and radical package of reforms ever witnessed on the policing front (Savage 2007), a package which stretched from the creation of new national policing institutions through to 'workforce modernisation'. The thrust for this agenda was the case that the police sector remained the 'last great unreformed' part of the public sector (Savage 2007: 187–9). It was not until Labour entered its second term of office that this case and the reforms attached to it were openly presented. However, it is highly unlikely that such an agenda for police reform was not already being mapped out in Labour's first term, or even before. The relevance of this for our discussion is that it could help to account, in part at least, both for Labour's commitment to hold a full public inquiry into the Lawrence case and its subsequent determination to ensure that the Inquiry recommendations would find their way into police reforms. We might speculate that one answer to the 'why Lawrence?' question is this: that Lawrence offered the prospect of providing a critical review of policing and in turn a menu of police reforms which Labour was already thinking were necessary. Politically, the holding of the Lawrence Inquiry may have been particularly timely.

Chapter 2

Violent racism, policing, safety and justice 10 years after Lawrence

Ben Bowling in conversation with John Grieve

JG: Ben, one of your earliest works is your book *Violent Racism*.[1] Can you run through for me how you became involved with research and policy in the area of violent racism and hate crime, and then how you came to give evidence to the public inquiry into the death of Stephen Lawrence?

BB: Well, I started my doctorate in 1986 on the police use of stop and search powers, particularly its targeting of the UK's black population. And then, in 1988, I shifted my PhD topic to the study of what became *Violent Racism*, when I got a job on a Home Office-funded action research project under the supervision of Bill Saulsbury. Bill had just come over from Washington DC to do work around multi-agency policing. This role gave me access to interview police officers, to carry out observation of policing and to observe in detail the functioning of a multi-agency project attempting to combat racist violence in the London Borough of Newham. That was a project which involved the police, the local authority, their housing department, education department, social services, the local victim support scheme and so on. I worked on that between 1988 and 1991 and published the report, *The Multi-Agency Approach in Practice* in 1991.[2]

The idea was to use the material generated from doing this narrow evaluation of a multi-agency project for my doctoral research. I had a survey of victims of racist violence, interviews with police officers, group interviews with all the various agencies involved, a certain amount of observational work, such as observing police officers carrying out targeted patrol and so on. The evidence collection was substantially complete in 1991 and I finished the PhD in the spring of 1993. It then took about five years to get the book published.

My conclusion was that there was a mismatch between the victims' experiences and the response of the statutory organisations, specifically the police. Based on interviews and all the case material that I had, it seemed clear that violent racism was experienced as a process, but the police responded to 'incidents' and therein lay the roots of the failure of the statutory response. The study showed that racist violence often involved a sequence of events and could only be understood in the context of narratives of racism, 'race' and nation within particular localities. It concerned ideas about who is supposed to belong, and who does not belong, which inflected the racist content of the incidents themselves, such as the use of racist language and symbolism and exclusionary rhetoric. There was, in other words, a connection between the extremely violent incidents, such as physical assault, and mundane, 'everyday' racist harassment, abuse and exclusion.

In fairness, I should say that by this time, the police had already made some quite significant strides in that part of London. They had created the Newham Organised Racial Incident Squad – nicknamed NORIS – which had some quite interesting characters involved. One was a career detective of Asian descent and there were a couple of other people who had detective experience, who actually began to document some of the pattern of violent racism within a locality. At one point they produced a list of incidents around two or three streets in the borough and they charted the various incidents that had occurred, from egg throwing, graffiti, broken windows, verbal abuse, common assault, culminating in an incident where a group of men pushed their way into the home of an Asian family and attacked them with snooker cues. But the value of the work that this specialised squad undertook was that they had put this very violent incident in the context of a whole sequence of events, and to me it made the final, most serious incident intelligible. It also provided a kind of context and a way of understanding what the experience of racist violence was within the locality.

So, that was very good police work which led to the prosecution of the offenders. However, this systematic and nuanced understanding of the experience of racist violence that was produced by this kind of analytical work really didn't match the usual incident based 'fire-brigade-policing' type response which was prevalent in the late 1980s. Most of the police officers who responded to these incidents couldn't understand, they really couldn't understand, why somebody who'd been shouted at in the street or spat at, or had kids banging on their door, was calling the police. The police line was, 'When a serious incident occurs, of course we'll respond to it; of course, if it's a real crime then we'll investigate it, we'll take it to court and we'll prosecute these people; we know who the offenders are and their families and so on ... but why is somebody calling us because someone's thrown an egg at their house?' The front-line police constables couldn't see the relevance of these incidents because they couldn't see the bigger picture.

I would go further than that. Not only could many police officers not see the bigger picture from the victims' perspective, but much of their sympathy expressed in the group interviews lay with what Rae Sibbitt refers to as to the *offender community*.[3] As far as they were concerned, the white population of Newham had had their tolerance tested by the arrival of black and Asian communities who they thought were loud, noisy and often smelly. They empathised with the man whose living environment, in their view, had been undermined and disrupted by the arrival of ethnic minority communities in the previous couple of decades. They empathised strongly with the sense of resentment and anger among East End white communities. They obviously didn't support their violent actions, but in terms of the idea that these black people had come into a white neighbourhood, perhaps shouldn't even be there, they could understand why 'indigenous' people felt resentful about them. They couldn't see the world from the victims' perspective, the way that an accumulation of minor incidents and sometimes more serious incidents needed to be seen alongside the everyday abuse and exclusionary language that was still, I think, very prevalent in the politics of the late 1980s and early 1990s, and which was how the victims experienced it. The victims – and ethnic minority communities more generally – experienced the political rhetoric of the time, both nationally and locally, as a kind of language that said, 'You shouldn't be here.' The minor incidents were an expression of that and when very serious violent incidents occurred it was in that context.

So, the conclusion was that violent racism was experienced as a process, the police responded to incidents, and as a consequence the police routinely failed to satisfy the victims when they called for help.

JG: That timescale of course overlapped with Stephen's murder in April 1993 – you were just completing your research that spring – and then your five years of getting the book into print overlapped with the years leading up to the Inquiry. When did you first become aware of Stephen, and did you map your thinking on to Stephen prior to the publication of your book or prior to your appearance at the public inquiry?

BB: Well, I was certainly aware of the murder of Stephen Lawrence because at this point I was still working in the Home Office, but now as a research officer working on *Young People and Crime*.[4] Although I was working on something completely different in my day job, I was writing up the PhD of an evening. However, the Home Office subscribed to a press cuttings service and I saw the cuttings every day and I was particularly interested in those relating to 'race relations' and policing, which was how they were categorised. I recall hearing of Stephen Lawrence's murder on the news and I saw all the press cuttings.

I remember it vividly because I was a boy scout and 23 April, St George's Day, is an important day in the scouting calendar. I'd carried the flag and done the whole thing. I wondered immediately whether at least part of the motivation for the attack was the idea of an English nationalist newspaper headline for St George's Day. I was looking at the press cuttings and thinking, for an extremist English nationalist, this is a 'good headline' for the day.[5]

I'd been monitoring the media. Racist murders were periodically news stories throughout that time. My research had gone back to the murder of Kelso Cochrane in 1959 and I tried to keep a record, as full a record as I could, of all the reported racist murders in the UK. So, even though I was on the very last leg of the PhD, I still kept the press cuttings in a file. So I was looking at it and I was looking at the ways in which the response to the murder of Stephen Lawrence looked similar to or different from all the previous ones, and I think I probably at first thought that it was unlikely that the trajectory of this case would be substantially different to the other cases that had been reported in the previous few years. For example, Rolan Adams and Rohit Dougal were murdered nearby in the years prior to the murder of Stephen Lawrence and I wasn't sure at that time that the future of the case – in terms of the quality of the investigation or the public response to it – would actually be any different from what had occurred in the previous cases. What was really very clear from my research was that, whether it was more serious or more minor incidences of racist violence, for reasons that we were discussing earlier, ultimately the state response was likely to be inadequate.

Relatively soon after that, from the support that the family campaign had in the years after 1993, it began to become clear that Stephen Lawrence was going to be *the* case that would run and run; the one that would make the difference in terms of the politics of racist violence and the politics of the police response to racist violence. And clearly the interventions of people like Nelson Mandela affected Jack Straw's decision to order the public inquiry and to take the issues of racist violence, racism and racial justice, social justice generally, more seriously. Even though the New Labour manifesto in 1997 talked about being 'tough on crime, tough on the causes of crime', except for a pledge to introduce an offence of racially aggravated violence, there wasn't really a major equalities agenda in there; the Stephen Lawrence Inquiry in a way stood in for it.

JG: So, how did you come to be involved in the Inquiry?

BB: My involvement came about by chance. I left England in January 1995 to work at John Jay College of Criminal Justice in New York for 18 months and returned in the summer of 1996, still working on the book. I didn't incorporate any commentary or analysis of the murder of Stephen Lawrence into the book, partly because it was substantially written and partly because, in 1995–6, I'm not sure that there would have been a case for saying that here was a case which was so dramatically different from the other tragic and disturbing murders that had occurred previously and indeed subsequently. With hindsight, I could have said more in the first edition of *Violent Racism* and when the revised edition came out in 1999, I included a new preface in which I discussed the Lawrence case and set it in the context of what I had written in the book.

Anyway, I had lunch with a colleague and the topic of conversation came round to the forthcoming Lawrence Inquiry and this professor said, 'Presumably you'll be putting evidence in.' I have to say, it literally had not occurred to me that would be something that I would do. At that point, I'd never made anything that could be described as a public intervention in any major policy debate. I'd certainly never given any evidence to a public inquiry previously, I was just pleased to have a contract with Oxford University Press and I was looking forward to getting the book out. And this professor's reply to this was, 'Well, if not you, then who? Who else has done thoroughgoing theoretically informed empirical research in this field with such obvious policy implications?' And I said, 'Well, there's *Beneath the Surface*[6] by Barnor Hesse and others, published a few years ago, and plenty of other studies.' And he said, 'Well, your book is about to be published with Oxford University Press; you should submit the book as evidence at the very least. There's probably a word limit on what you can put in so why not write a synopsis of the book, draw out your main themes and what your policy recommendations would be and submit it.' So that was what I did.

JG: And how much of your thinking or how many of those recommendations do you think were reflected in the Lawrence Inquiry recommendations? Let's split it up, in the final report and then in the recommendations, because I want to ask you something about the recommendations in a minute.

BB: Well, among the many curious things about the Inquiry, the most obviously curious thing was the invisibility of part two of the Inquiry. In terms of the content of the Report, the bulk of it is the chronology of events – the murder, the investigation, the reinvestigation and the aftermath. From memory, part two of the Inquiry in terms of the write-up was despatched in just a few pages and then from there it more or less moved straight into the recommendations. And given the extent of the evidence that was submitted to the Inquiry, and I remember you remarking on this yourself, this was a travesty really, that so much material had been submitted and then there was no significant analysis of part two of the Inquiry on the matters surrounding the murder, the context. I have, I think, three box files of all the submissions. The evidence was extensive as well as, of course, all the oral evidence.

JG: You just used the word curious, about invisibility and absence. Can I ask you about something very specific? The finding of institutional racism came as a shock – to put it mildly – to the police, yet for lots of reasons that I could go into, I can see now why it shouldn't have come as a shock; there was plenty of evidence that it was coming.

But despite its presence in the Inquiry Report, and the great deal of time spent explaining the finding in the Report and in the background material in Chapter 6 of the Report, at no point in the recommendations and nowhere in the Home Secretary's first action plan do the words 'institutional racism' appear; in fairness I should say of course that the word 'racism' appears a lot. I was wondering how you interpret that and how significant you think that is for what occurs later.

And yet there is a great deal about the organisation as an institution. So perhaps this is splitting hairs, but on the other hand, if you want to make a very strong point, you could write a recommendation that says the Metropolitan Police must address the issue of institutional racism, and the Home Secretary could then have identified a number of tasks that came under that heading, or the Inquiry could have done. It doesn't appear in that form and I'm not even sure that we ever get to it; we have all the practical things that we're going to do.

BB: Well, in my submission, I tried to articulate the ways in which my research showed that racism – as an ideology and as a practice – was apparent in the Metropolitan Police Service and could be understood at individual, cultural and institutional levels.

I argued that some individual police officers are unashamedly and explicitly racist in their ideas and in their practice. This, we can call individual racism. Then there is cultural racism, which is like individual racism, but shared collectively. I was able to point to examples from my interviews where groups of police constables shared ideas about who 'belonged' and who 'did not belong' in the London Borough of Newham. Officers described how offensive they found ethnic minorities' customs, language and appearance and I was able to show how these shared understandings influenced the way in which the police behaved towards victims of crime.

I think that by 1998 most senior police officers were able to admit that individual and cultural racism were problems in

47

the police service. At the very least, they were happy to admit that – back in the 'bad old days' – quite extreme racism was widespread across the police service. You only have to look back at the Policy Studies Institute (PSI) study of *Police and People in London*.[7] Rereading Smith and Gray's work on race and class makes your jaw drop when you realise what police officers were willing to say to, or at least in the presence of, researchers in the early 1980s. The extreme racist views and the extraordinarily offensive language are quite staggering.

JG: I know, I've just been rereading it. And that they should be so relaxed about it. Also, there is the conclusion that 'They talk like this but they don't behave like this.'

BB: The point is that during the time of my fieldwork – 1988, 1989, 1990 – you still had very clear shared and unashamedly racist ideas about how the world worked, with individuals who were really quite extreme in their views.

But it was obviously my conclusions about institutional racism that were the most controversial and uncomfortable for the police service. What I argued was that although individual and cultural racism were significant – not least because they were so very clearly articulated – what was more important was the connection between individual and cultural racism and the way in which the police service functioned *institutionally*. I felt that this was more important because although some of the experiences of the victims of racist violence or people assaulted by the police or abused by the police could be clearly attributed to individual and cultural racism, some of the organisation's failure was a result of routine practices. In other words, the racist impact on victims was very difficult to pin down to an explicit racist antagonism.

I think that stop and search was one example of that. In the PSI study when Smith and Gray conclude – quite wrongly in my view – that they had no evidence that the well-documented racist talk was ever manifest in racist behaviour towards ethnic minorities, their only caveat was to say, except where police officers make an unthinking assumption that there's a link between colour and crime in their selection of who it is they're going to stop and search. One reason I felt that this was something that went beyond individual and cultural racism was that officers, for example those interviewed by Roger Graef in

Talking Blues,[8] would say things like, 'I don't think of myself as racist but we're expected to do certain things because that's how we work. How we work is to stop the people who look suspicious and black people naturally fall into that category.' And whilst you could argue that this sits in the cultural racism bit of the analysis, it came back to this idea that racist outcomes could be the product of unthinking, or at least unreflective, forms of behaviour.

If someone challenged a police officer – 'Why exactly did you decide that you were going to stop and search that person?', or 'Why exactly did you decide that this wasn't an incident worth investigating?' – they might gradually come to a realisation that racism had affected their judgement but it wasn't explicit, it was automatic and unthinking. I felt that an important component of the analysis was the way in which routine organisational practices have racist outcomes. For example, *Violent Racism* showed that in the police response to isolated 'racial incidents' rather than to racist violence in its context, routine police actions led to outcomes which systematically disadvantaged communities of colour. I thought, and still think, that is an important way of understanding the problem.

JG: Did you actually go to the public inquiry and speak about your paper or did you just submit the paper?

BB: I submitted the paper cold and I attended the oral hearings as an observer. Then, some time later, I got a call from Bishop John Sentamu, now Archbishop of York. He said something along the lines of 'Of the submissions, this one strikes us as a scholarly analysis of the evidence of how the murder of Stephen Lawrence fits into the broader picture. Obviously the fact that you're at the University of Cambridge and you're publishing with Oxford University Press lends credibility to it, would you come to speak to us in London?' So I did.

Sentamu quizzed me on various aspects of my submission. I think one of the key things was the question of institutional racism because the argument that the failure to investigate properly and get a result from the Stephen Lawrence investigation was explained by institutional racism had been made in various other submissions, but perhaps hadn't quite been pinned down.

I can't really say how influential my intervention was. Obviously, I was cited in Macpherson's report along with others like Robin Oakley and Simon Holdaway, and this confirmed what others were saying – the Black Police Association, the Commission for Racial Equality, the 1990 Trust and so on. But I do remember seeing the Bishop a couple of years later when I was with my mother and some friends – I just happened to see him out shopping in Solihull and he said in his jovial way something like, 'This man is responsible for institutional racism.'

How I read it was that the Inquiry team had bashed this idea backwards and forwards trying to agree whether or not there was an analytical or evidence-based case for it. During the writing of the Report I got a second call from Sentamu saying, 'Could we run through this again, could you say a bit more about the provenance of the idea of institutional racism, could you get the Carmichael and Hamilton (a book on Black Power written in the 1960s) reference for us?' I got the sense that it was contested within the Inquiry team and that Sentamu was sticking his neck out to make sure that it was in the Report. I think that's right but I'm speculating really.

JG: OK, so while that's going on, which is from October through to well into mid February, say, because the leak occurs, I think, around about 14 or 15 February and the report is published on 24 February, Assistant Commissioner Denis O'Connor gets in touch with you; can you remember how that came about?

BB: Yes, I was approached by Sara Thornton and Mark Simmons.

JG: Had we been to the United States and looked at institutional racism? This is where I think we get knocked off track. Officers go to the United States and come back and say, it's not a concept that is sound academically, even amongst the black academics out there. It was a classic example of us making up our mind what the evidence was going to be and then sticking with the evidence that supported this. So you get a phone call?

BB: Sara and Mark contacted me and reminded me that somewhere in the book I'd said that police officers need to be 'anti-racist' in order to provide a fair response to violent racism and to ethnic minority communities more generally.[9] So they asked, 'What do you mean by anti-racist policing?'

In the book I had argued that – at best – the police saw themselves as neutral on the subject of racism: they were neither for it nor against it. If a victim of crime had evidently been targeted because of their race or ethnicity and the offender had used explicit racist language, the police orientation was to say, 'People say things like that in this area, that's just East End banter.' I would go further than that to say that when I was doing the fieldwork in 1988, 1989, 1990, there was quite a lot of support for racist and exclusionary politics. So, my argument was: if you're serious about protecting ethnic minority communities then you need to be able to express an explicitly anti-racist position.

JG: Had you included anti-racism in your submission?

BB: Not in the synopsis but in the book. But in the brief submission I recommended that individual, cultural and institutional racism within the police service had to be tackled in order to prevent police practice from disadvantaging people from ethnic minorities, which is the essence of the idea of anti-racist policing.

JG: Then you could reply to Archbishop John's remark, 'Yes, but I was also responsible for anti-racist policing.' I think that's something to be very proud of, because it doesn't appear in the Lawrence Inquiry recommendations, it doesn't appear in the Report, but it does appear in our response. So, how effective do you think you were at getting the anti-racist policing concept into policing and how did that lead in to your further involvement?

BB: Mark and Sara were perhaps both Denis O'Connor's staff officers?

JG: Yes, they were the specific staff officers to deal with the Stephen Lawrence and diversity agenda. The way it was packaged up was, Bob Quick was responsible for the submissions for part two and ran a team for part two, but Sara and Mark were responsible for the day-to-day monitoring and for thinking up how the responses would work. And then, when I was brought in, I was given the operational side of it but they would be doing the staff officers' side, so I spent a lot of time with them.

BB: The sense that I got was that the police service recognised they were going to take a big hit.

JG: Do you think they recognised they were going to take the hit and that they would actually have to accept the finding of institutional racism?

BB: I don't know about that. I certainly had the sense that it was looking bad and that whatever the response was going to be, it could not be more of the same. It was going to have to be something quite radical. And if the claim in my book was accepted that the police organisation contained individuals who fully expressed racist views, that there was a culture of racism within the organisation and that routine institutional practices created racist outcomes, my challenge was that the organisation needed to have a thoroughgoing response to this. In which case, an explicitly anti-racist response was at least part of the answer. So that the organisation could say, we can now move on from this because we are going to be explicitly anti-racist in what we do.

I felt that there were some very important things that were achieved. I think that what was needed was a recognition that racist violence was a reality and that it was a reality that affected the lives of a large number of black, Asian and other visible minorities in Britain, not just in London, but in Manchester, Birmingham, Bristol and so on. Much of the response to racist violence from the most senior politicians – and perhaps a little bit earlier in policing – was to simply deny that racism was a problem; to deny that racist violence existed. While this view from the leadership of the Metropolitan Police had begun to change in the preceding years it was still there among the rank and file. Basically, the Lawrence Inquiry drew a line under denial.

JG: Do you think that's still true then, from your outside observer status?

BB:	I think it is true – because of the recommendation that a racist incident is any incident where the victim says it is. You know, prior to that recommendation it was only a racist incident if the police said it was. And even though things had begun to change, this was still the case. After the Inquiry I think that at least the most explicit denial went away. Police officers might mutter under their breath, 'Well, I think it is just plain thuggery actually', but it was no longer part of the official discourse. It was almost as if, to put it cynically, the denial of the racial motive was now banned by the organisation. We no longer do that; we accept the reports as they are and we investigate from there. Of course there is a downside to that, which is that the police have to deal with vexatious and entirely spurious allegations and counter-allegations, but nonetheless I think for the black community, for the Asian community, for Britain's ethnic minority communities, the sense of recognition was enormously powerful and enormously valuable. It was a vindication not just of the experiences of the Lawrence family, but a vindication of all of those community organisations and individuals who had been saying 'This is something which we are experiencing, please recognise it and do something about it.'

Finally, and in the most explicit and public way possible, this was accepted. I think all the broadsheets had a special pullout supplement and all of them, without exception, reported the Inquiry's findings about racist violence: that the murder of Stephen Lawrence was an unprovoked racist attack and this was an indication of a broader problem of racist violence in British society which needed to be dealt with by the police and by others. I think that was very, very important. I think Jack Straw's presentation to Parliament on the day the Inquiry Report was published, when he said that the Commissioner of the Police accepts that the Metropolitan Police is institutionally racist, and beyond that, institutional racism is a problem for the Home Office where I sit as Home Secretary, and indeed for other institutions in society, including education, was also very important. It gave a voice to, or validated, the experiences of people in a variety of different spheres. I think that was important and continues to be important.

So are things like recommendations to improve the response to victims of racist violence, improvements in the response to ethnic minority victims in general; obviously the creation of the Racial and Violent Crime Task Force, the response to critical incidents, the development of Family Liaison Officers. These things are not just the recommendations from the Inquiry, but the policy initiatives that followed – the creation of the Community Safety Units, Independent Advisory Groups, and of course this is all prior to the creation of the Metropolitan Police Authority and the Independent Police Complaints Commission. You have got all the issues around accountability and governance; all of those things I think have been important developments. So have acknowledgement, taking those issues seriously, developing a robust response, creating new mechanisms, structures, processes of accountability. And even though all of those things were in play already, obviously the Inquiry Report and the subsequent policy development acted as a sort of lightning rod or some way of linking all of these issues together in ways which I think have been progressive.

JG: Would you pick out, say, two or three issues and maybe talk them through? It would be interesting for you to talk through why you left the Independent Advisory Group (IAG), for example, because I think that is very important, but maybe you could also talk about the IAG, gold groups and critical incidents as a bit of learning and then say why you came to the conclusions that you did.

BB: The experience of the Independent Advisory Group speaks to both the promise and the limitations of the initiatives coming out of the Lawrence Inquiry. Because I had already given evidence to the Inquiry and offered my advice in the lead-up to the publication of the Report, when Jeff Braithwaite invited me to be involved in some sort of process with others to create what was at first called a Lay Advisory Group, I didn't hesitate. I saw it as a genuine attempt to carry this thinking forward, to provide a way of articulating the concerns of the community and of interested independent non-police parties towards improving the police response to racial and violent crime.

I would say that the early meetings of the IAG were probably some of the most exciting moments of my career involvement in 'public criminology', for want of a better phrase. I've since been on all sorts of high-level committees, but I was only starting out then. Actually, I had done various kinds of voluntary work before; I had been a lay visitor to police stations in the mid 1980s in one of the early pilot schemes and I had been a voluntary associate in the Probation Service. So I had always been involved in the criminal system as a volunteer, but this was the first time, as a published author and with a university lectureship at King's College, that I was in a position to make a contribution to making policing fairer and safer for all Londoners. That was how I, and I think others on the IAG, saw it.

Those early meetings were enormously exciting. The Metropolitan Police's sternest critics being invited into the briefing room by the Deputy Assistant Commissioner with the specific remit to make radical proposals for reform 'make my eyes water', I think you said. You don't get invitations like that every day of the week. It was exciting because it brought together people who had made contributions to the Inquiry, who I knew already had some profile in their role as activists or commentators or critics or whatever; people like Lee Jasper, Mike Franklin, Heidi Mirza and numerous other people who I only got to know later. It was exciting because the working groups sat down together, activists, police officers, policy-makers, trainers, to ask 'What are we going to do and how do we do it?' – anti-racist policing, improving the response to racist violence, recruitment and retention, stop and search.

I remember being with one subgroup and sitting at a computer on one of the upper floors of New Scotland Yard, more or less writing a manifesto for how these ideas which had come out of the Lawrence Inquiry would actually be implemented, what we would want people to do. I think the way you put it was, 'Tell me what you want me to do, I will look at what you are recommending and I will deal with what I can. What I can't do I'll tell you, and those things we do take forward, hold me to account at various points in the coming months and years.'

Obviously it was an enormously powerful kind of invitation, I felt that it was the organisation 'walking the talk'. This was real, these were things which we were going to change, independent advisors would sit in on the reviews of cases: Michael Menson, Ricky Reel (see Chapter 3) and of course the Stephen Lawrence case itself. The IAG played a key role I think in the response to David Copeland's nail bombing campaign targeting Brixton, Brick Lane and Soho. You had independent advisors attempting to reshape stop and search policy and practice. We were invited to sit in on training and to look at the statistics on the stop and search practice and go through stop and search forms examining how the power was used, whether the grounds for stop were reasonable. Basically it was like, the organisation is open to you to come in, ask the difficult questions, make sometimes difficult recommendations and evaluate what is done. Obviously, there was an acknowledgement of a sort of vulnerability and I remember Lee Jasper saying something along the lines of, 'We go with this, we do our best to try and make the changes, and when the process of change runs out, when it runs out of energy, we have the ability to move away from it and make the reasons that we moved away from it public. That's a way of keeping the momentum going.'

So I would say that at the beginning of 1999 I felt the IAG was doing really valuable work; the police organisation was changing; we were conscious of the discomfort that was being felt by the front-line PCs and the backlash or 'push-back' as insiders preferred to call it. Assuming that some of the people that I had interviewed in the London Borough of Newham in the early 1990s were still in post, I should think there was an enormous amount of discomfort because basically the signal was that the days of overt racism, or even tacit racism, in the police organisation had now come to an end. I think for a lot of people that would have been enormously troubling because I believe many of the people I interviewed in Newham at the turn of the 1990s couldn't see what was wrong with the open expression of explicitly racist views. Going back to Smith and Gray and the PSI study, it was just like, 'Well, it's just talk, I mean, what the hell, shouldn't we have a right to express our view that Enoch Powell was right and that Britain should be a white man's country?' I mean, the signal went out that the explicit articulation of ideas of that kind had come to an end.

I feel now that initiatives like the IAG have a limited shelf life. Perhaps it's a bit like single-issue pressure groups in the political sphere; they are likened to bees: they sting once then they die. Certainly, by the time we got to January 2001, through various ups and downs, myself and quite a few other people felt the thing had run its course. Obviously the four of us who resigned from the IAG in early 2001 – Andrea Cork, Kirpal Sahota, Jenny Douglas and I – were of the same mind.

I think it had run its course partly because the sense of crisis which existed in the Metropolitan Police, in the briefing room in January 1999, had dissipated. Two years on, the Lawrence

Inquiry was history; the crisis had come and gone really. There were other crises. The rise in street robbery, probably fuelled by the first generation of insecure mobile phones, was I think certainly a part of that, and the way in which the post Lawrence reduction in stop and search was blamed for it by disgruntled police officers who found a mouthpiece in the right-wing newspapers. I have learned that crime control always trumps inequality and justice as motivating forces. Also, by then some of the key people had already resigned for a variety of reasons and the Chair of the IAG had been compromised by her involvement – unknown to the rest of the group – in supervising the internal investigation into Ali Desai. Andrea, Kirpal, Jenny and I got together and decided that we would have to walk away from a group that had become toothless. I don't regret it at all. It was probably also, as I said a moment ago, a sense that the moment had gone.

JG: Could you comment on the 'moment had gone'? Assistant Commissioner Denis O'Connor had gone and Commissioner Sir Paul Condon had gone, but I was still there. Would you just say something more about where you felt it was losing momentum?

BB: Well, I think it's probably what I said at first: the Metropolitan Police was dragged into this change process and even though there was a proactive response to it by Denis O'Connor as the Assistant Commissioner, it was in the context of crisis; 'this has to be done', and in that first six months to a year, it *had* to be done.

JG: Critical incident training, gold groups, small working groups around particular cases, could you say something about those?

BB: Yes, these were very valuable, I felt. Whether it was a borough command or senior investigating officer or people leading investigations, they were being encouraged to think through the consequences of their decision-making through incident logs: 'What have you decided, why are you deciding it, and what happened as a consequence of your decisions?' I understood it as a process to get the decision-makers within the police service to think these things through. I think it was really, really important and that was partly in the moment of actually saying,

57

'Right, OK, what's your decision log entry going to be?', but also then taking it to a sort of public inquiry scenario afterwards and saying, 'OK, now looking back, what were your decisions and why did you take them?' That, I felt – well, it was obvious from the Lawrence Inquiry – was not standard practice; it was not something which was always, or even usually, thought about. 'Why am I doing what I am doing?' The answer was often, 'I'm not really sure why I am doing it. I'm doing this because that's what we have always done.' And I think that was very valuable as a training mechanism for the people who were leading investigations and who were leading policing in the boroughs.

The idea of the gold, silver, bronze command is obviously a management tool in the police organisation, particularly in relation to crowd control etc., but the 'diamond group' was perhaps a little bit like an IAG – composed of people, some of whom could be part of the organisation but also people from outside the organisation, to just ask questions. And hearing the answers to the questions, 'The reason we have done that is this, this and this' enabled members of the community who were interested in policing to understand a bit more clearly. I also think it helped the decision-makers, the senior investigating officers (SIOs) and the borough commanders who might find themselves saying, 'Ah, well, obviously I haven't explained that very well', or 'Now I realise that's not such a great idea, thank you for asking the question.' I'm not sure of the right word: is it governance, is it scrutiny, is it accountability? I would put it under the kind of broad definition of accountability. Accountability is a complex idea, 'account-ability'; an understanding that a public service that has the capacity to use coercive force, including deadly force, and indeed to deny services to some people, needs to be accounted for. I think that with the introduction of these measures, together with the other, more formal statutory mechanisms which have been introduced subsequently – such as the MPA and the IPCC – the organisation did actually become more accountable.

In a way, this makes me wonder, why on earth was Sir Ian Blair not informed that the man shot dead on the Underground on 22 July 2005 was not a terrorist but an entirely innocent passenger until a day later, as he claimed?[10] I would have thought that everything we know about critical incidents and the ways in which you would have people asking the difficult questions should have prevented that from occurring. Probably not the shooting itself, but critical incident training should certainly have prevented his failure to know the truth for 24 hours after the fact. It certainly should have prevented the Commissioner from giving inaccurate information to the media long after it was known that a fatal error had occurred. That was what critical incident training was all about. You know, being clear about what's going on and having people asking the difficult questions. For the question 'Who did we shoot?' not to have been asked and no clear answer given is one of the most troubling things about this. Despite the creation of the Independent Police Complaints Commission, despite the creation of the Metropolitan Police Authority, despite all of the accountability processes that have been introduced post-Lawrence, enabling the police to account for themselves, nonetheless you still have that failure.

JG: Would you see that as a measure of a lesson from the Lawrence Inquiry that hasn't been learned, that goes back to Stephen Lawrence's legacy?

BB: I do. Whether mechanisms could possibly have prevented the shooting of Jean Charles de Menezes itself, I don't know; that is probably taking it too far. But it certainly should have prevented the damage done by police officers, including the Commissioner, making announcements that were factually inaccurate for many hours after the incident. I wasn't there, so I don't know what it would have been like to have been the Commissioner of Police or the top team dealing with the aftermath of 7 July and the failed bombings on 21 July. Maybe the answer is that all kinds of chaos happens in such environments. But wasn't that the point about the critical incident training? That despite all the chaos – there is always going to be chaos – you need to have some way of ensuring that the questions that need to be asked are being asked and answered?

JG: Yes, absolutely. OK then, let's move now to the last bit; you wanted to say something about the experience of being young and black on the streets of London 10 years after the Lawrence Inquiry.

BB: Ten years on, things that were of serious concern, particularly to Britain's African Caribbean communities, like the safety of young people, their experiences of policing and the criminal justice system – some of which managed to find their way into the discussions of the Inquiry and some of which did not – have not improved. Their character has changed to some extent, but in many ways I would say the outlook for an aspiring black teenager growing up in London does not appear better as we approach 2009 than it did in 1999.

Let's take three areas: safety, proactive policing, and criminalisation. Safety obviously was an issue for the Lawrence Inquiry and it was focused specifically on protection from racist violence and action against racist offenders. As I've said, I do think there certainly was a radical improvement in the response to racist violence following the Lawrence Inquiry. I don't know whether that is true now but I think it probably is. I think that with the awareness of racist violence, the improvements in policy in dealing with it, the person reporting racist harassment or attack now is likely to be better served by the police in 2009 than they were in 1999. I think there has been a gradual improvement in the responses in the intervening years. However, it's obvious that the safety of young black Londoners has not improved. I think London is definitely less safe now for young black people than it was in 1999. The risk of being stabbed to death or being shot to death – even though the media exaggerates and sensationalises these issues in a way which is unhelpful, and even though I think it's probably the case that most forms of violent crime are reducing – the risk of becoming a victim of homicide for young people in London has increased and the greatest vulnerability is from internecine violence. That is, the threat, the greatest risk, is no longer from violent racists, but from other young black people. Black young people are *per capita* far and away the most likely to be the victims of homicide in London, particularly knife homicide, and it is most likely that the perpetrator would be another young black person.

Now, I certainly don't lay the blame for that at the feet of the Lawrence Inquiry at all, but nonetheless, since the trigger for the Lawrence Inquiry was the death of an innocent young black teenager, there is no escaping the fact that the deaths of innocent young black teenagers is a more acute problem a decade on. That is something which is troubling; it's distressing; it's depressing; it urgently needs addressing. I emphatically don't see it as a legacy of the Lawrence Inquiry, but it has to be said, it is something which is part of the wider picture of unsafety and injustice – and the causes of it, I believe, are very deep and very complex.

In relation to proactive policing, I am not sure that the discussion around stop and search and its relationship with institutional racism, and all the issues around fairness and justice and inequality, or the role of stop and search in community safety was ever really properly settled. The bottom was never really reached in the Lawrence Inquiry. I don't think the police service was ever really convinced about the arguments in that area. Certainly, the evidence submitted to the Inquiry was never really looked at properly and the conclusion that stop and search should more or less be retained as is, but should be made fairer and more transparent, was I think a kind of compromise which didn't satisfy anybody. It is true that following the Inquiry, levels of recorded stop and search fell away quite sharply and I believe that was a good thing because I think it meant that fewer black people were stopped in circumstances where suspicion was absent and there was no case for stopping them. In other words, the extent of unlawful stop and search was reduced. In the book that I wrote with Coretta Phillips, *Racism, Crime and Justice*, just before the Lawrence Inquiry, we recorded that only one in 17 black people stopped and searched on suspicion of being in possession of drugs was actually found in possession or arrested for any other offence.

JG: What sort of reasoning leads to that?

BB: Yes, exactly. What is the basis for your suspicion and how reasonable is it? One measure must be how frequently does your 'reasonable suspicion' turn out to be founded or unfounded? When I ask people what would count as a reasonable 'success rate' – how frequently should stops 'on suspicion' lead to the detection of criminal behaviour – they usually start off with a figure of around nine times out of 10. When I say the statistics suggest lower, people drop down to 50-50. If fewer than half of stops on suspicion yield wrongdoing, then we have got problems because how can that be reasonable? I then ask how does one 'hit' from 10 stops grab you, or one in 17? In other words, 16 out of every 17 people you suspect of being in possession of drugs and on whom you conduct a search in a public place turns out in fact not to have drugs on them. Most people find this quite shocking.

So, unfortunately, we never got to the bottom of this debate. After the publication of the Lawrence Inquiry, police officers did stop and search somewhat less extensively because the 'reasonableness' of their suspicion and lawfulness of their activity was challenged. Unfortunately, this coincided with a spike in the street robbery figures, a very significant proportion of which were mobile phone snatches. It was the first wave of mobile phones – a highly sexy, desirable, portable, saleable, easily stealable, a classic 'hot product'. So, in the months after Lawrence, we had a sort of 'crime wave' driven entirely by other factors, in my view. However, a number of people blamed the increase in robbery – and violent crime more generally – on the Lawrence Inquiry and said, 'You see, political correctness gone mad, the police have stopped doing stop and search, look at the crime graph.' You know, 'We've de-policed the streets and violent crime has gone out of control.'

JG: 'Blood on his hands.'[11] I remember it.

BB: So I do feel that in the face of the Lawrence Inquiry's relatively weak promise of reforming stop and search practice, the police very, very quickly retrenched and very shortly stop and search was back to its pre-Lawrence levels. Sadly, without having the desired impact on violent crime. I think the use of stop and search remains disproportionate and discriminatory and should be radically reformed.[12] Current practice simply is not good enough.[13] The experience of stop and search contributes to undermining the legitimacy of the police service in the eyes of those people who have been stopped unnecessarily and its claims of deterrence are not really based on the evidence. Its damaging impact on support for the police is very clear. I think it contributes to breaking the bond between community and police, which takes me to criminalisation, which is my final point.

The unlawful and excessive use of stop and search powers has contributed to the criminalisation of black youth. Oppressive policing is carried through into an increasing black prison population, disaffection and criminalisation which also feeds back into the problems of violence in society. So we now have continuing high rates of stop and search which is still not producing the results that's claimed for it, a rapidly increasing number of 'offenders brought to justice' – driven by government targets – resulting in a growing prison population and a black prison population that is growing at a rate which exceeds the growth of the prison population in general. Again, that isn't the legacy of the Lawrence Inquiry; it has happened in spite of the post-Lawrence reform process. So for the black teenager who aspires to be a professional person – let's say an aspiring architect like Stephen Lawrence – they are still today facing twin threats of unsafety and criminalisation.

JG: Is that the context in which some of the other legacy issues that we've talked about occurred?

BB: I think they are issues that have different trajectories but which cross in 1999; the issues of the criminalisation of the black community on one hand and a kind of public response to racist violence on the other. Those issues crossed at the Lawrence Inquiry because of the ways in which the testimony, not just of the police, but of several witnesses, spoke of things like, 'We didn't know it was a racist attack … we thought it was a fight between black youths.' All of those issues – community safety, police effectiveness and accountability, racism in policing, the experiences of black youths – they sort of intersect at the Lawrence Inquiry and then what happens in terms of actually providing safety, providing justice, protecting liberty, becomes much less clear. It probably needed – and still needs – a different kind of process, a different kind of engagement. Maybe what was needed was a kind of Royal Commission or some more thoroughgoing inquiry that would really get to grips with the problems of inequality, insecurity and injustice facing people of colour in British society.

Notes

1 Bowling, Benjamin (1998) *Violent Racism: Victimisation, Policing and Social Context*. Oxford: Oxford University Press.
2 Saulsbury, William E. and Bowling, Benjamin (1991) *The Multi-Agency Approach in Practice: the North Plaistow Racial Harassment Project*. Home Office RPU Paper No. 64. London: Home Office.
3 Sibbitt, Rae (1997) *The Perpetrators of Racial Harassment and Racial Violence*. Home Office Research Study 176. London: Home Office.
4 Graham, John and Bowling, Benjamin (1996) *Young People and Crime*. London: Home Office.

5   Stephen Lawrence was murdered on 22 April 1993 and the first reports were published the next day, 23 April, St George's Day.

6   Hesse, B., Rai, D. K., Bennett, C. and McGilchrist, P. (1992) *Beneath the Surface: Racial Harassment*. Aldershot: Avebury.

7   Smith, David and Gray, Jeremy (1983) *Police and People in London*. London: Policy Studies Institute.

8   Graef, Roger (1989) *Talking Blues: The Police in Their Own Words*. London: Collins Harvill.

9   *Violent Racism*, page 294.

10 Sir Ian Blair said that he was not informed that the dead man – Jean Charles de Menezes – was an innocent tube passenger until 10.30 the following morning. The IPCC report found it 'somewhat surprising ... that nobody sought to inform the commissioner of the evidence of error that was in the hands of his closest colleagues as early as the mid-afternoon on the day of the shooting'.

11 Editorial comment, *Daily Telegraph*, 13 October 1999.

12 Bowling, Ben and Phillips, Coretta (2007) 'Disproportionate and discriminatory: reviewing the evidence on stop and search', *Modern Law Review*, 70 (6): 936–961.

13 Bowling, Ben (2007) 'Fair and effective police methods: towards "good enough" policing', *Scandinavian Studies in Criminology and Crime Prevention* Vol. 8/S1: 17–23.

Chapter 3

Police engagement with communities post-Lawrence

Jeff Brathwaite

This chapter examines the establishment and development of a unique form of engagement with communities which emerged as a result of the Stephen Lawrence Inquiry and the concerns about the police's relationship with minority ethnic communities. The formation of the first Independent Advisory Group (IAG) in UK policing was in many ways ground breaking and opened the way for minority communities to directly contribute to police governance. Drawing in part from my own doctoral research, which included semi-structured interviews with a range of key players in the field, the chapter explores the reasons for the setting up of the group and describes the context in which independent advice was developed. To an extent, it relies on the words and opinions of a number of independent advisors to describe the motivating factors that caused members to join the group. It sheds light on what IAG members thought they could contribute to policing and highlights the uncharted and dynamic nature of the advisory process. Power, influence, and the jockeying for advantage preoccupied the activities of the IAG in its early days. The chapter gives an analysis of this struggle and the subsequent relationship that the IAG established with the police organisation, despite the group's agenda for changing some police practices. The chapter also acknowledges that the author was a key player in the development of the group and its subsequent processes and personal reflections are also contained in the narrative. The chapter concludes by giving a critical analysis of contemporary IAGs and a prognosis for the future of this form of community and police engagement.

Background

On 22 April 1993, Stephen Lawrence, an 18-year-old black man with a promising future, was stabbed to death in a racist attack in south London. The experience of Stephen's parents, Doreen and Neville Lawrence, was one of institutional racism both in the investigation and in the support that they received from police throughout the investigation. In particular, they were concerned about the lack of information that was reaching them and the insensitive manner in which they were being dealt with (Macpherson 1999: 26:17). They considered that they were being patronised and were not given the sympathy that a grieving family should receive, as noted by the Inquiry:

> inappropriate behaviour and patronising attitudes towards a black family were the product and manifestation of unwitting racism at work, coupled with the collective failure of the investigation team to treat Mr and Mrs Lawrence appropriately and professionally, because of their colour, culture and ethnic origin. (Macpherson 1999: 26:37)

The Lawrences had to struggle through a judicial system that failed them time and time again until finally, on 31 July 1997, the Home Secretary, the Rt Hon. Jack Straw MP asked Sir William Macpherson to chair an inquiry into the matters arising from the death of Stephen Lawrence (Macpherson 1999: 3:1).

A vast number of individuals and organisations submitted written evidence to part one of the inquiry. Police officers, past and present, who investigated the initial and subsequent murder investigation, gave evidence throughout the hearing. This was a very low point for the police service as the inadequacies of the investigation were laid bare to public scrutiny. The very public judicial investigation into the Metropolitan Police (MPS) culminated on 25 June with an Assistant Commissioner attending the Inquiry to offer a personal apology to Mr and Mrs Lawrence (Macpherson 1999: 30.1: 218).

Part of the police service response to the Stephen Lawrence Inquiry was the introduction of independent advice to the policing sector. A striking feature of the first Independent Advisory Group is its unusual origin in so far that it only came into existence because the Metropolitan Police deliberately set out to create a group of people who would critically appraise its operating ethos. The individuals, who were external to the police service, had no idea that such a group was possible given the traditionally closed nature of policing. The police saw lay involvement as the means of reaching out to minority ethnic communities in order to secure their confidence.

Out of that strategic approach was developed the *lay advisory group*. This name was later changed on 17 December 1999 by the group's membership to the 'Independent Advisory Group' (IAG).

At the end of July 1998, I became the Deputy Director of the Racial and Violent Crime Task Force (RVCTF) at New Scotland Yard. Deputy Assistant Commissioner John Grieve, the director of the task force, said to me, 'Jeff, you are responsible for forming the advisory group. This is my gift to you.' I thought, 'thanks, where do I go from here?'

I tackled the challenge in two ways. I formed the hypothesis that if we were able to work with and satisfy the concerns of our severest critics, then we would be getting it just about right for our communities. Secondly, because of John Grieve's farsighted and winning strategy of attending every Inquiry hearing across the country, I was able to listen to the experiences of many different communities across the country. One member of the panel asked of the police, 'What mechanisms have you as a police service to listen to the concerns and perceptions of minority ethnic groups?'

The composition of the first group's membership and the ethos that we sought to instil within the group were rooted in the hypothesis and in minority ethnic communities' experiences. The police sought to develop a relationship with the group based on openness, honesty and transparency. There was no precedent for such a ground-breaking process, no template to follow. Police Community Consultative Groups were altogether different in their formation and processes and were arguably not a good comparator. Needless to say, achieving those ideals involved a difficult and painful process. The director of the Racial and Violent Crime Task Force was later moved to say:

> It has been extraordinarily painful but my conclusion remains that independent advice was a necessary and possibly sufficient condition in the broadest sense of our recovery from the shock of the finding of institutional racism in the Stephen Lawrence inquiry. It has also been totally uplifting. I have long wanted to be part of a police renaissance, a rebirth, a new enlightenment about the nature of power in society… (MPS 2000f: 6–7)

Despite many difficulties, the group was determined to constructively challenge police. The evidence showed that a significant number of

IAG members felt that they had something positive to bring to the process of addressing racism in the police, as made clear by one interviewee:

> It was an opportunity to actually push the Met to actually do something differently because their failings had been documented throughout all the public hearings. Having given evidence myself at the public hearing, it was quite evident that if the Met was going to set something up that was really going to challenge them, then I had to be a part of that really. (NC1)

Such individuals were considered vital for the credibility of the group. The Metropolitan Police Service (MPS) also identified individuals who had been in this area of work for some years, people who had been telling the police for a long time that they were getting things wrong and that the MPS was not delivering an equitable service to the black communities, as other interviewees put it:

> I don't know but I think there are individuals who are really in for the long journey and they're in it for the long term benefit of changing what happens in the police, and I think there are some that are in it for the quick fixes and lots and lots of high profile media interest. But I think it's those individuals that for a period of time sustain and develop and consolidate the work of the group, who give time to do it. And it is about having that additional commitment to it. (NC9)

> I saw it as an opportunity to influence fair and open policing practice with particular reference to minority ethnic communities ... Because I was persuaded that the MPS wanted the IAG to be more than just a PR face. (LP1)

Some of the reasons for joining the IAG were more deeply personal whilst others reflected a previous relationship with the Metropolitan Police Service:

> I think what essentially drives me are two things, it's about a personal thing, it's about having a 17-year-old black boy, and being frightened every time he's out with his mates; you know, is he going to come back to me in one piece, not because I see him being attacked by other young people, I fear him being

pulled into something by officers on the streets, so that drives me. (NC10).

The evidence also suggested that others joined from a strong ideological position and a basic desire for fairness and justice:

I think all the members of the IAG, in my experience of the IAG, do have a genuine passion for equality. I think most of them are involved in some way in equality issues. That seems to be where we are all from, one way or another, whether it is at academic level or caseworker type people. (AS1)

My ideological position to all forms of racism and my professional skills can benefit the MPS. (CT1).[1]

In many ways, the first members of the IAG felt that the Lawrence Inquiry presented an opportunity not to be missed in so far that for the first time there was a convergence of agendas which made the likelihood of long-term change more possible than ever before. The police were at a loss as to how best to win the minority ethnic community's confidence. The government agenda was one of social reform and social inclusion. The determined campaign for justice by Stephen Lawrence's parents forced the government to initiate a judicial hearing into the failings of the Lawrence murder investigation.

Most worryingly for the police, public opinion was against them. For the first time in policing history, a significant number of people from minority communities were in a position where they were desperately needed by a police organisation that they perceived had traditionally discriminated against them.

The IAG, as a group, did not have a cohesive strategic plan on how to influence the police organisation. In its initial dealings with the police it relied on the police to give direction, but individuals soon began to apply their personal agendas and expertise to the issue at hand. The issue primarily was that of institutional racism as defined by the Stephen Lawrence Inquiry. The police organisation was attempting to survive this period of challenge in the full glare of the media and was seeking solutions.

There was no precedent in any police service for seeking out its severest critics and inviting them into the organisation with a mandate to critically appraise all current and future practices and policies. In the early days of the group's existence and in the heat of the ongoing public debate, their criticisms and concerns frequently made media headlines.

Independent advice initially focused on race alone but events in April 1999 were to widen the issues from minority ethnic communities to all minority communities. Nail bombs were detonated in Brixton, Brick Lane and Soho by David Copeland. Copeland's intention was to start a race war in the UK. He extended his hate to the lesbian, gay, bisexual and transgender community. This was all unfolding while the Lawrence Inquiry was still taking place.

Shortly after the first explosion at Brixton, an IAG member was bravely sitting alongside a senior police officer at a televised press conference, imploring the minority ethnic communities to remain calm. Six hours after the Soho bombing, members of the lay advisory group and the RVCTF were briefing key members from the lesbian, gay, bisexual and transgender (LGBT) communities at New Scotland Yard, reassuring and giving advice. This was unprecedented and was effectively the birth of the first LGBT advisory group. Copeland is now serving six life sentences for the atrocities which resulted in three murders.

Between 1998 and the end of 1999, policing in London faced an onslaught of high-profile critical incidents. It was a very testing period for the police in London. Amongst the usual policing demands were incidents that ran and ran in the national press throughout the year:

- the Stephen Lawrence Inquiry;
- the Menson murder investigation;[2]
- the Ricky Reel investigation;[3]
- nail bombings in Brixton, Brick Lane and Soho;
- the Paddington rail disaster.

IAG members were involved in all of these incidents, giving independent advice and insight to police. This was not an easy process because the idea of 'unaccountable' members of the public giving direct advice to police was an oxymoron: very difficult for some individuals to accept at the time.

Key achievements of the IAG

Arguably, the IAG's span of influence through its network is an important strength. However, it is clear that the group's members clearly believed that its very existence and survival in the policing environment was a key achievement. When asked about this, respondents said:

I suppose the fact that it's still there. And the fact that despite the fact we started off with lots of individuals that there is still a core number of individuals who have not lost energy, have not lost interest and who have continued to plug away at some of the issues. You know, as you said at the beginning, two and a half years on the Stephen Lawrence Inquiry Report is still around but it's not the high-profile media interest any more. And to be fair there have been a number of improvements in the Met so you know the need to have adverse discussions around things that perhaps we had when we started. So I think the fact that we're still there is a major achievement. I think also the fact that we can be assured now that in terms of critical incidents that it is second nature to call in a member of the IAG, be that localised or strategic, and if nothing else there is an acceptance in local boroughs that you can involve communities in operational treatment and you don't have to just deal with them at the consultative group, you can involve them in your operational policing, you can take them into your confidence and I think for me that is a massive achievement. Because we can all have consultation meetings, but the opportunity to actively be involved in live cases must ensure, you know, black communities are going to get a service. (NC8)

Survival, learning how to work together. Finding common ground with the MPS and helping with case reviews. (WA3)

I think that's a difficult one. I'm not being awkward, but let's look at the word achievement because the fact they they're here in the organisation is an achievement. The fact that they have the direct ear of the Commissioner is an achievement. The fact they have the ear of the Home Office is an achievement. (AS5)

Community Safety Units (CSU) in the MPS are at the cutting edge of its effort to deal with hate crime. The IAG has had a history of assisting CSUs to develop and innovate. Moreover, the IAG has helped in the training of CSU staff, giving a community perspective on how policing should be delivered. Twenty-five per cent of the recommendations that came out of the Stephen Lawrence Inquiry had some connection with victims, families and communities. Therefore, the training of Family Liaison Officers (FLO) is vital in the effort to gain the confidence of communities. Independent advice in this area was seen as fundamental and the IAG had been working closely with the police on this:

> If you're looking at pieces of work, this is where I have difficulty, you know because I would argue that the work they did around Virdi [see below] is an achievement, but the organisation has yet to acknowledge that. But pieces of work that have influenced the organisation, there I struggle. I suppose that's a bit unfair, we can look at IAG involvement in CSUs, CSU training. They sit on the steering group and their influence there helps the organisation look at, have a better understanding of, the issues. (AS5)

The reluctance of the police hierarchy to make best use of perspectives and ideas of its minority ethnic officers was criticised by its black officers. The IAG was seen to bring a black perspective to the debate at the highest levels in the organisation:

> I suppose one of the problems of the organisation is we look at the academic viewpoint but there is a deficit in the organisation of black people. Therefore, when we look at any group aspect of policing, there tends not to be a black perspective. I'm not saying any black person's going to give a black perspective but what I'm saying is that perspective is always going to be missed. And that's one of the problems with the organisation anyway. The real decisions in the organisation are white middle-class male, so that is going to influence the decision. If we're going to then put some black people in that arena, that's going to influence a decision. So that's an achievement. (AS6)

A number of respondents viewed the Virdi case as a success for the Independent Advisory Group. The group rigorously examined the circumstances of the discipline hearing of Police Sergeant Virdi, an Asian officer who was cleared of wrongdoing.

Against all odds, the IAG managed to observe the process of the discipline hearing and wrote a damning report of its observations, making a number of recommendations. The MPS was slow to respond to the recommendations but events moved on. Sergeant Virdi was found guilty and dismissed from the police service. He eventually won an industrial tribunal case for unfair dismissal and was cleared of any wrongdoing. Virdi was reinstated to his previous rank of police sergeant. What was interesting about this case was the subsequent Metropolitan Police Authority Inquiry into the case which vindicated the findings of the IAG.

The Virdi case showed that the police's internal investigators were not sufficiently attuned to the various manifestations of racism and to deal with cultural differences. It was perceived that even the most enlightened officers had some difficulty in addressing the Virdi issues because of inter-organisational conflicts:

I mentioned Virdi earlier when we mentioned achievements. Virdi is an achievement although it's not recognised by the organisation. It invites the IAG to give critical comment, and when we do, then they'll say thank you but goodnight. This defeats the object of having us there. There's this gloss thing. I would argue that the police behaved appallingly over IAG's involvement in Virdi. The police was almost criminal in that they looked at the report, report goes up to a senior officer to respond and doesn't respond, and when he does it's dismissive and so on and so on. And we look at the 28 points of recommendation that have come out of it, how many have been dealt with; I don't think any, even now. It's incredible. (AS5)

I mean, I think we quietly said we told you so because we wrote a report on our views on Virdi which we gave to the service and tried very hard to influence the process, and it wasn't until the process had been gone through and they found to their cost that we were right all along, that they were able to regroup and say well, you know, we should have listened to you, so in some way you could say that Virdi was one of our finest hours, but I mean for some of us, I think Virdi was just one of a variety of issues that we were dealing with at the time and I think in that sense, Virdi just compounded the issue. (KR9)

More and more frequently, the IAG was being given access to cases that had the potential to have an adverse effect on minority ethnic communities as well as attracting unwelcome publicity for the police. In the main, these cases arose on boroughs and were investigated and resolved locally with the help of independent advisors. These advisors were not necessarily from the main advisory group at Scotland Yard, but rather, were members of locally set up arrangements. The fact that independent advice had now caught on in the police was testimony to the value being placed on the community perspective:

You know, the cases that I'm talking about were on a local division, that are not high profile at that stage, [but] could easily become high profile and being able almost to now be absolutely assured that there's always going to be IAG involvement at local level ... I think it is much more powerful than the high-profile cases, because that says it's gone wrong and it stops certain things from going wrong in the first place. (NC9)

Effective advice comes through involvement in the initiation of policy or, for that matter, police operations. It was initiation, not validation of previously decided policies, which was the key to successful partnership and collaboration:

Obviously, the occasions when we go to management board and now, you know, chair and vice chair, I'm invited to all the management board meetings, I think is a key issue and an achievement because in essence I think if we're going to influence policy, we need to be around a table, not outside the room and being told about it afterwards. And so I think in times of strategic development that is the key achievement. I think also in the chair, the IAG process in the main has become part of policing, I think, particularly in the Met anyway, because I don't think any strategic issue takes place now without IAG involvement, and maybe I'm being naive. Anyhow, most strategic developments don't take place without IAG's involvement. I think also in some weird morbid way, Copeland contributed towards that because I think the IAG process, including the lesbian and gay, bisexual, transgender group keep ... because of Copeland. And because the advisory process worked so effectively because of Copeland, I think a lot of issues now, when people are thinking strategy, they automatically include the IAG in that strategic development process and so you could say that again it's a key achievement. (KR10)

Critical incidents

The area of critical incidents (see also Chapter 7) stands as one of the group's key successes. In many ways, the IAG had enhanced its standing in the police through the added value that it brought to the recognition and handling of critical incidents. Critical incidents have been previously defined. What can be further said is that a key success factor in this area is the ability to approach incidents with an open attitude and accountability, especially in the following key areas:

- communication with the family;
- communication with the community;
- the investigative process;
- issues of disclosure.

The benefits derived from such an approach are likely to include:

- open dialogue with families and communities;
- better understanding with families and communities;
- improved confidence in the investigative process;
- better community intelligence;
- improved investigative opportunities (MPS 2002b: 3)

Critical incidents and independent advice tended to go hand in hand. It was very rare in the MPS for such incidents to be investigated without some involvement from the community, either in the form of an independent advisor or a community representative. The IAG considered itself well able to impact on such incidents through influencing the mind-set of senior investigating officers. Advisors were able to give a critical appraisal of the lines of inquiry and the likelihood of success in gaining the confidence of the affected community. This perspective is valued by the senior investigating officers (SIO) as another aid to their decision-making. Police value this new approach:

> I think, talking to SIOs, it makes a difference. I think one of the things about advisors is having that community input into that investigation. One of the criticisms about the police is this whole thing about how we communicate. What are we doing outside the organisation? I think one of the things the advisory process brings is lots of things that we as an organisation, because of the nature of our job, take for granted. The advisors are saying, 'Why are you doing that?' If the advisors are saying 'Why are you doing that?' you can bet the community are saying, 'Well, why are you doing that?' We just take it for granted. (AS5)

The early successes of the IAG with critical incidents have had a profoundly positive effect on the police organisation. Senior officers were anxious to ensure that the group was involved, especially in high-profile cases. In fact, operating procedures in the police now advocate their use (MPS 2002b). If we look at a further view from the police, it is clear that the benefits of independent advice are readily recognised:

> I think probably again it's a bit proof of the pudding syndrome. We look at Lawrence, we look at having people in to critique, to have a look at what we are doing, then realising that there is a contribution that could make a difference. Might make us look at things a different way. And I think that's worked in a couple of places. I think that part of it is to do with success. So if you've got advisors involved with the SIO, and the SIO then reports, actually although it pains me to say this, I found it valuable for various reasons. Some of the reasons, like I said, are about the community perspective and wow, is this the way they're looking at us? Why have they interpreted what we've done like that, that's not how it is at all. People realise the value and it's growing. (AS5)

The Lawrence Inquiry concentrated the police's effort on early recognition of incidents that, if not handled properly, might result in public concern. Through the efforts of the RVCTF, the term critical incident was developed and is now in use in forces across the country. Likewise, the involvement of independent advisors had proliferated across forces. What started in the MPS has now been adopted as a concept of community involvement:

> Oh, yes, IAG involvement in critical incidents has gone well beyond the Met now, and we see lots of forces now looking at the use of independent advice in critical incidents and other spheres of policing. The audit that ACPO have done, which is hot off the press ... the ACC, West Yorkshire say that 12 forces haven't got an IAG, which is interesting – 12 out of 43 haven't got an IAG of any kind. The others have an IAG of sorts, whatever that is. Some forces have critical incidents panels, they use their community advisors. (AS5)

> Well, independent advisors in critical incidents? If you do some comparison in editions 1–4 of the critical incidents guidance and look at what we've learnt from the process we were going through, and read how it changes and in particular the lack of

defensiveness around the nature of independent advice, then there's the 1,400 calls on the hotline, things that might have been critical incidents but never were, of those 1,400 you probably get 80 or so might have gone critical, but for the intervention ... might have gone more critical than they were, but for the intervention of IAG, FLO, CSUs, critical incident thinking. (CJ3)

Critical incidents have been a success for the IAG. It is through the practical application of its expertise and skills in serious crime investigation that the IAG gained respect and acknowledgement from the investigators of serious crime. Nevertheless the group has weaknesses as well. These will be explored in the next section.

Above all, the support given to the IAG by the Home Office was useful in concentrating the minds of senior police officers. That interest ensured that the MPS and other forces invested significant resources and energy into redressing the failures of the Lawrence case. Investment in the IAG was arguably seen as a means of attaining success in winning the confidence of minority ethnic communities. Failure of the IAG process was not an option for police.

Weaknesses of IAGs

There is a view that the activities of the IAG are not widely known by those who have a campaigning interest in race issues. Its influence may therefore not be as potent as it otherwise might be. One reason for this relative obscurity may be the decision taken very early in the IAG process not to reveal the identity of its members. This decision was taken for the best of reasons at a time when there was concern about 'right-wing' interest in the group, as well as a bombing campaign in London. However, in time, the more prominent members of the group began to enjoy press coverage, their identities coming into the public domain. On the one hand, the IAG had always argued that it represented the issues and did not represent any particular community:

... But I think people need to know who they are because it's about the organisation also making clear that we are taking into account other perspectives. If we don't tell anyone or we don't show that we're taking in other perspectives, when a decision is made, it's not about blaming someone, because it could be we're not going to take the advice, but we've taken into account other perspectives. Who knows that we're doing that if they don't know we've got another advisory group. (AS4)

The danger with such prominence is this: if the IAG was publicised on a frequent basis, then it might begin to change its shape and respond to issues as a group of mediation, on individual cases, rather than having a critical strategic overview of policing. IAG members are unable to devote all of their energies to policing matters simply because it is not their full-time occupation. Some members have left the group because they felt that it was losing its critical edge. Others simply could not give the commitment that the group's increased involvement in critical incidents demanded. Their widespread acceptance in the police meant that more and more demands were being placed on members:

> The important thing about this, the people involved in the process, it's not a full-time job, they're doing it in their own time. There comes a point when you say, well, hang on I'm spending x [sic] amount of time a week doing this, is it really worth it? Then, clearly, they decided it wasn't. (AS9)

Internally, in the group, the issues of power and leadership caused splits to appear, leading to changes in the membership of the group. This left a core of four or five members to provide the actual leadership of the IAG. These were determined individuals who recognised that immediate changes were not always possible and that credibility and a good record of accomplishment were valuable assets. Of course, there was a weakness in having so much invested in so few. Like most issue networks, these individuals arguably gained influence at the expense of others, some of whom resigned, allegedly in protest at actions of the leadership cadre in the group:

> What the IAG still needs to watch out for is the fact that at the moment the success of the IAG is still dependent on too many personalities. It is dependent upon personalities within the organisation and within the IAG. And so in a sense they need to have structures, and some systems and some mechanisms for ensuring that the IAG continues to be challenging. And that it is there to provide advice because otherwise it would be very easy for the Met to say, oh, we'll do something different. (NC3)

Changes within the IAG triggered concerns about the future of the group in the event that senior officers from the RVCTF left the department for other posts, as is inevitable. The IAG feared that if there were to be a change of senior officers in the RVCTF then there was a real danger that the group's continued existence would be threatened. The members believed that there was already a tendency for the organisation to attempt to subsume the group into its systems and practices:

Simply because one person's commitment is not another person's priority. So I think it would suffer very, very badly. It would suffer if there was a change at the top of the tree and it would suffer when there is a change in the director of the Racial and Violent Crime Task Force, it has already suffered since you left, and that is where as IAG we are having to be very alert to the fact that your successor has a different belief and view of IAG. Completely different. And it is very much more about it becoming part of the structure, it becoming part of the system and so tagging us on to police existing structures and systems. (NC3)

This respondent was of the view that as the original senior officers who set up the Task Force moved on to other duties, the focus of the RVCTF was shifting to such a degree as to cause alarm amongst some of the IAG membership. They feared that the group might become subsumed by the police organisation. It can be argued that their insecurity emanates from their outsider status and recognised that, ultimately, the police had the power to radically alter the relationship that the IAG enjoyed with the MPS. This was a reality that exposed the vulnerability of the group. Other respondents referred to particular incidents where they perceived some damage was done to the integrity of the group. The most noticeable of these incidents was the Paddington rail disaster.

Respondents viewed their involvement as advisors in the Paddington rail disaster as a failure because the role of the advisors in the incident was not clearly defined:

I think the most interesting out of those for me has to be Paddington because it was early days for the IAG, people clearly didn't know who they were or what they were about. So I think there was a lot of misunderstanding around Paddington. They felt that the advisors were just interfering, and that it was probably the police that allowed the advisors to have direct access ... maybe the access should have been through a third party, maybe DCC4, rather than being able to have direct contact with victims, police officers, etc. because the feeling back there was it was all new, events took over. (AS11)

I think Paddington was a failure. (NC12)

Paddington was symptomatic of the uncertainty that existed around the use of independent advice. It was apparent that there was a gulf between what the IAG members thought they were there to do and the perception of the police, to whom this was an untried and untested partnership. Inevitably, some members found it difficult to understand the processes within the MPS and therefore were not as adept as others at getting things done. Some members were frustrated that others were lagging behind and not pulling their weight. This led to real frustration amongst the leaders of the group:

The mistaken assumption is that because it's voluntary involvement you can do it badly, and I think sometimes the weakness of the group is the knowledge of some of its members basically about a system of where it needs to get to and a naivety that some members have of how things get done. And because of that naivety it actually means that progress can be very, very slow sometimes because it will never ever be in the MPS's interest, so that to me is a weakness, that if you don't understand the system and how to interact with each other and how it all overlaps and who is responsible for what, that I think is a weakness. I think some of the other failures, I suppose the group hasn't been able to grow and develop in the way I think it should, to me that is a failure, it should have grown. (NC12)

It was evident that not everyone was contributing to the process in a tangible way. The group seemed incapable of working with structures and having a plan was an anathema to most individuals. This caused a degree of frustration in the group and with the police who were used to working to more rigid formats.

A work programme from the group's Bournemouth seminar[4] was developed, as the result of the energy and commitment that went into the conference itself, but the follow through was patchy, with some individuals failing to carry out agreed actions. Nevertheless, there was a clear agenda for change after the Bournemouth seminar (MPS

1999c). The seminar was considered a success by most participants. The first meeting after the seminar saw the group reorganising its processes and changing its name from 'Lay Advisors' to the 'Independent Advisory Group' (MPS 1999h). The IAG produced dozens of documents in its endeavour to assist the police. Examples include recommendations from the subgroups as well as documents in response to crises such as the Virdi discipline hearing and its development plan after the lifting of its boycott following difficulties that some members experienced at the Paddington rail disaster.

There was, however, a view that the group's reluctance to embrace a tightly formalised structure was a weakness that needed addressing:

> I think there were some individuals that didn't think it needed that kind of formality ... why should it be their responsibility, they are there to facilitate something for us, in a sense it was almost ... we'll blame somebody else for our inadequacies. So I never felt that people took it very seriously. I think that, for me, has been a real failure of the group because there were still individuals that would turn up to meetings, say nothing and never ever do anything, just taking up space. Sorry, they just needed to disappear. So, big failure. (NC13)

Typical replies from respondents gave an indication of how the IAG operated and was perceived by its members. Replies mentioned the lack of integration in the group and the limited degree of interdependence between the actors in the group. There was evidence of a low degree of consensus amongst the actors although meetings and the conference were rather formalised by an agenda and were well attended. The following illustrated the characteristic of the group:

> We talked too much and did too little. We have failed to develop a clear and coherent agenda. (WA4)

> The group members tend to work as individuals more of the time than perhaps they should. Thus little work has been done to create an 'IAG view' on major issues – the communication within the group and between chair and vice-chairs and minds. But not sure whether this is a strength or weakness. (LP4)

> Extremely immature, basic political analysis of racism. Basically, political correctness to a stupid extent, self defeating for many. (CT4)

Power was in the hands of a few. This is a problem that results in some failure. People have day jobs and other commitments that exclude them from doing a better job. (SL4)

Some IAG members were impatient and even critical of the lack of action emanating from the various groups and subgroups. This in some way mirrored the police's hesitancy in taking up some of the 'big issues'. Other members saw power in the hands of a few who they believed communicated well at the chair and vice-chair levels but did not effectively communicate with the wider membership. There were serious questions about the style of leadership, how the group was represented by that leadership and the nature of the collaboration with the police. This all leads to the question, given the nature of the set-up of the IAG, its unequal distribution of power and its reliance on resources from the police organisation, can it truly lay claim to be 'independent'?

How independent is the IAG?

This discussion on the independence of the IAG should start with a definition of the word 'independent' as described in the Collins Thesaurus: 'Self-governing, autonomous, non-aligned, self-determining, self-sufficient, liberated, self-supporting' (Collins 2003). The question of independence is therefore pertinent to the IAG and its future relationship with the MPS and its police authority, the MPA. This relationship and whether the IAG can be said to be truly independent will be discussed later.

It was earlier established that independent advice was endorsed by key actors in the policing sector. A survey by the MPS in 1999 also established that borough police commanders found it of use because between the 32 boroughs, there were 103 different groups providing a 'lay involvement' function.[5] The term 'lay involvement' or 'lay advice' evolved into the current and widely used term 'independent advice' (see Chapter 8). At the Holly Royde Conference[6] in March 1999, the following definition of lay involvement was developed and later endorsed by the Advisory Group Conference (MPS 1999c). The definition stressed the independence of advisors (i.e. not police officers or employed by the police). It also stated that whether or not the police acted on the advice given, the advisor had no responsibility for the outcomes. It will be shown later that this assertion was difficult for the IAG to embrace on a number of practical and moral grounds.

The evidence over the years supported the general assumption that advisors '... are free to make observations both within the service and to the broader community'. However, it then goes on to reassure the police that lay involvement is helpful and that '... it poses no threat to operational independence of the constable or the chief constable as it does not affect the particular powers, responsibility or formal accountability of either'.

If this definition is further deconstructed, a number of anomalies begin to emerge. It could be argued that there is a moral ownership and responsibility by advisors for the outcome of their advice. This must be so even though, in law, there is no accountability on their part for the decisions and actions of police, providing that those actions were lawful and there was no evidence of a joint endeavour to act outside of the law. Secondly, although in practice the advice given by the IAG is mostly helpful to police, if the police choose to ignore that advice, there is then an implied degree of negligence on their part if the advice proved to be sound.[7] Seeking independent advice is one of the important items on the police's 'check-list' when investigating serious crime or other matters that may affect community confidence. There is therefore the threat of a public backlash, if such advice was not sought or was ignored and a harmful outcome resulted from such inaction.

It is therefore clear that despite the stated intention of the definition of lay involvement, in reality there is a close operational working arrangement with the police. If advice is not acted on or considered, there is then an expectation from advisors that an explanation would be given by police as to why the advice was not taken up. The new police imperative on winning the confidence of minority ethnic communities has compelled chief officers to embrace 'new' knowledge and experience from minority ethnic communities. This new enlightenment only goes so far, however: involvement with the IAG is always caveated with the notion of 'operational independence'. Operational independence is jealously guarded by police, a fact that is clearly spelled out in the definition of lay involvement. The definition marks out what is out of bounds to the IAG. As outsiders, they are clearly required to acknowledge that operational policing is the property of the police. For further reading on how 'constabulary independence' functions as a means of 'furthering professional closure' and of 'marking out disputed territory' see Savage, Charman and Cope (2000: 196–197). Nevertheless, because of the interconnectedness of these pressure groups with the police and the very nature of police governance, even the Chief Constable's

'Constabulary independence', can be viewed as 'a doctrine which is sailing against the wind' (Savage, Charman and Cope 2000: 207).

If we go back to the assumption that advisors have no responsibility for outcomes and visit the case of Solly v. the Crown 2002,[8] an independent advisor was required by the court to give an account of his actions in a case, which tested whether or not those actions had contaminated a key witness's testimony. The actions of the advisor were exonerated but a precedent was established. Independent advisors are accountable for some outcomes. It is clear that they may be questioned in court as to their involvement in criminal investigations. This fact is recognised by the MPS which gives the following guidance to advisors:

> The presumption must be that disclosure will take place of all potential evidence and may include Gold strategy group minutes and of any liaison between police and Independent Advisors/ Mediators. (MPS 2002b: 12)

So, are independent advisors truly independent? The evidence suggests that advisors give an independent view from their perspective, which is usually insightful and helpful to investigating officers. Any advice thus given can be said to be 'independent advice'. However, at a different level, the closeness of the advisor's relationship with the police may have a tendency, at least to the objective observer, to undermine that independence. Furthermore, it is arguable whether such an interdependent partnership can be said to be truly independent. This position has prompted concern amongst some members about the drift of the group to a more 'inner group' position and the fear that it will be subsumed by the police:

> I think much again is going to depend on how the IAG transforms itself into a body that remains independent but influential and has the right approach to tackling the MPS and to working in conjunction with the MPS. That will be absolutely crucial. Unfortunately much of it is still going to depend on personality, about who is there to make those transformations, make the links and the liaison, so technically it should be a very positive way forward in terms of the IAG remaining almost on the shoulder of the MPS and asking, 'Why are you doing this?' The day that we stop asking 'Why?' then I think that is when we do not have any kind of critical edge. (NC13)

Like the Black Police Association, the IAG believed in the importance of maintaining a 'critical edge' in its dealings with the police. It would appear, now, that there is an established relationship with the police, it is becoming increasingly difficult for the IAG to maintain that condition. This is especially so since the Stephen Lawrence Inquiry is now some 10 years ago and police corporate memory as well as the public's memory of the events is beginning to fade from the mind and from the political agenda. The police crisis, though not ended, is arguably receding. The challenge for the IAG, as is common with pressure groups, is to either evolve or face disintegration when the present policing crisis over race is perceived to be over.

The future of Independent Advisory Groups

Five years after its inception in 1999, there was evidence to suggest that the IAG process was evolving and positioning itself for the future in two important respects. The group was working with most of the high-profile departments in the MPS, where its involvement was seen as an important part of business. Murder investigation was a very good example of this collaboration, which has now spread nationwide as critical incident training becomes part of the national training agenda. That kind of activity was a strong base for sustained longevity. The second advantage was the apparent willingness of two key actors in police governance, ACPO and the Metropolitan Police Authority (MPA), to embrace the philosophy of independent advice as an important form of public consultation and public accountability:

> I think the MPA themselves are very keen for there to be an IAG that can provide a view of policing which is outside all of the political parties or approaches, and that can actually provide them with a well-informed, non-political, practical view about their concerns about policing. The MPA with the best will in the world are going to be largely governed by politics. So they are not in the same way as us independent in anything, they have a remit which they have to work to which is not like the IAG, and it doesn't have a remit in terms of its set up by a statute, it must be there. This is the way we support, we don't have those kind of structures, but we operate in a way that we do have them. Then people take the advice that we give them seriously. (NC14)

It will be interesting to see whether the IAG is 'co-opted' by the Police Authority. The IAG's relation with the police has settled down but may well continue, rather low key, indefinitely. (WA4)

However, a simmering danger for the group was its reliance on a few high-profile individuals to maintain its strategic position and credibility. These key actors were likely to move on, leaving the group devoid of talent and withering on the vine:

I think some of this goes back to this thing about us losing our edge. And the characters, when you realise half the [IAG] members have been with the organisation the last five years, in people's minds they'll start to ask questions ... the value and their position with the organisation. I think that's why it's important that we try and get some kind of turnaround of advisors. (AS10)

The drive to revive the group with new advisors met with some success. However, there was still a reliance on a few experienced advisors, as the new intake tried to assimilate the ethos of the group.

There were additional concerns about where the police organisation was going with the diversity agenda. The IAG saw the trend for a greater and greater emphasis on diversity as a threat to the 'race agenda'. It feared that 'race' would be sidelined in favour of other diversity issues such as gender and disability. When this concern was coupled with the then Home Secretary's (2002) perceived lukewarm approach to the Stephen Lawrence issues, respondents feared that the Lawrence agenda was no longer being seen as a political priority and that 'race' was gradually being marginalised by both the Home Office and the police hierarchy:

The likeliest outcome is that it becomes ever more marginalised as key strategic issues are achieved, principally by diversity, and details of police practice get bogged down into procedural morass. (CT4)

As long as pressure from the current Home Secretary to push race off on to the edge of the agenda is assisted by the top echelons of the MPS, we should have a reasonable relationship. We have support in the form of the new boss ... together we think we might turn back a current trend to push race down the list of important policies and actions. We cannot escape the fact that the MPA would love to control us and the Mayor's advisors are hostile. (SL4)

Though some respondents feared control by the police authority, and therefore loss of 'independence', others saw a development where the group could benefit from a closer relationship with the MPA and the MPS:

Of course, when we came we had a different agenda and a different view, I mean I'm not sure if it was planned or not but we've gone over and over and invited the whole of the service, and I think we now see ourselves as part of that permanent process. Personnel will change but, you know, independent advisors, I think, will remain as part of the MPS – permanently, I think. (KR13)

It was clear from the analysis that the IAG had evolved and would continue to evolve as the nature of its relationship with other key actors altered. Whether it remained an 'independent' group or became part of the police organisation was in part dependent on the group's maintaining the capacity to give critical appraisals of police policies and practices. In turn, this ability relied on the key actors within the IAG being able to sustain strategic influence within, as well as outside of, the police organisation. The group was in danger of losing its effectiveness if the 'personalities' were not replenished:

I think the IAG will have a dip then it will re-emerge again. (NC14)

It was feared that should the IAG dramatically change its focus, then some of its membership would decide that the group no longer satisfied their interests and might well depart. This is not an unknown feature of pressure groups:

I think they will continue to be critical partners, the organisation will see them as such. I wonder if they will lose their edge, their efficacy if they become stitched into the fabric of the organisation? Then, I think they should be disbanded. (AS10)

It may now be extremely difficult to have a police force where there are no minority staff associations or some form of independent advice. As long as there is a dearth of minority ethnic officers in the police service, there will be a need for an IAG type of group to bridge the gap between minority ethnic communities' perception of the police and the police's interpretation of the needs of those communities. Moreover, the problem might still exist even if the police in London attained its target of 5,000 minority ethnic officers by 2010. It can be argued that not all minority ethnic police officers are aware of the needs of all minority ethnic communities. They are just as likely to need formal development in this important area of policing. They are as susceptible as their white colleagues to the organisational norms of the police service. Inspector (now Superintendent) Paul Wilson's comments about black officers and how they may succumb to the police occupational culture bears out this point (see Macpherson 1999: 6.28).

If the IAG is to remain 'independent' and influential, it must ensure that it maintains a credible networking base. We know that it relies on personalities who are capable of networking into a variety of powerful government and non-governmental organisations. The real danger is that some of its key actors may adopt some of the norms of the police, thus reducing their ability to critically review the working arrangements of the police. This process may come about through over-exposure to the operating practices of the police, whereby the group is subsumed by the organisation and members stop asking the 'difficult questions' because they are no longer 'naive'.

On the whole there are real benefits for the police in having minority ethnic influences on police governance. It has been shown (Brathwaite 2005) that minority ethnic associations and the IAG have influenced police governance to a remarkable degree, for example in the handling of critical incidents; the inclusion of multi-perspectives in their thinking and the consideration of policing from the minority ethnic communities' viewpoints. Overall, the respective memberships are optimistic about the future relationship with the host organisation, recognising that such a relationship will be bothered by conflict from time to time. Only in time will we know whether this balanced and considered approach will come to dominate both groups in the future.

Where are we now?

The growth in the number of IAGs reflected a recognition of the need for local mechanisms to help deliver a police service according to need. The Stephen Lawrence Inquiry hearing questioned the effectiveness of the police service's consultation processes. IAGs have a responsibility to ensure that effective engagement takes place and should be constantly asking themselves a number of key questions:

- Do we truly understand our role and is that understanding common to all of us?
- Have we remained focused, have we retained our critical edge?
- Are we a reactive group, or are we one that is capable of pre-empting issues, thus helping to shape the policing agenda?
- Do members really feel freed up to give genuine critical analysis and make recommendations?
- How much power has the police given up? (Giving up some power is not a weakness but rather a sensible and necessary organisational strategy resulting in more challenges which generate more original thought and innovation.)
- Are we as a group still fit for purpose?

Independent advisory groups and independent advisory networks are not just consultation groups. They should, they must, go far beyond that. They are active and vibrant (or should be). They breathe in and taste what is happening now in the policing environment. If there is something slightly off, they should detect it, critically analyse it and make recommendations. IAGs and independent advisory networks (IANs) should be capable of agitating for change.

Their relationship with police should be a working relationship; not too cosy but one of mutual respect and a desire to move the policing agenda forward. What do I mean by that? I believe that most if not all police forces strive for excellence within their given resources. This is the very nature of 21st-century policing. IAGs and IANs have a vital part to play in achieving this ideal in respect of community engagement. If IAGs behave as if they were consultation groups, then they are not adding full value to the process. The fact is, police do not need another consultation group; they have lots of them. They do not need IAG members to be experts in policing; they do that very nicely themselves.

What the policing sector is hungry for are new perspectives on what they do and what they plan to do. That is the added benefit of IAGs and IANs. Even if advisory groups are not asked for their perspectives they should still find some means of contributing a viewpoint that is helpful. IAGs should be scanning the local policing environment for issues that may impact on local communities. That is part of their role! Fast-time participation in critical incidents, as well as slow-time in policy development – that, in many ways, should be the strategic approach of IAGs.

Nationally, there appears to me to be a drift towards commonality, driven by ACPO. In order to achieve commonality there is usually a strong dose of prescription. In my view, that would take away from the ethos of independent advice.

IAGs and IANs must not be restricted by bureaucratic strait-jackets – that is a sure means of killing off initiative and creativity. They must be allowed to be free-thinking and flexible in their approach. Yes, they must have some fundamentals in place to enable the groups to manage themselves. It should be noted that I said to manage themselves, not be 'managed by police'. The latter may be more comfortable for the police but results in less beneficial outcomes.

But there is a sense that IAGs are resisting this drift towards sameness. IAGs and IANs must remain locally focused. This is one of the fundamental messages that came out of the Lawrence Inquiry, 'understanding and addressing the concerns of minority communities'. IAGs and IANs remain relevant to policing. However, the challenge for these groups today is to ensure that they are moving forward with the new policing agenda. What is their relationship with Safer Neighbourhood Teams, Police Consultative Groups and Local Strategic Partnerships? Networking with these groups at the local level is crucial if IAGs are to remain relevant.

Advisory groups make a unique contribution to police governance. Critical incidents, their ability to focus on specific long-term issues and their impact on strategic matters are all testimony to the added value of IAGs and IANs. However, advisory groups now need to network into other strategic groups locally, drawing part of their membership from those groups.

There is a strong argument for IAGs to evolve into independent advisory networks. Networks recognise all the strengths that the current IAGs have but also acknowledge that groups need to take up more encompassing roles if they are to keep pace with the shifting policing agenda and remain relevant. Some groups are working towards that end already, if only by default.

With strong, insightful and courageous leadership, together with certainty about their sources of authority, IAGs and IANs will continue to add significantly to police governance and provide a voice for those who remain 'hard to hear'. There are, however, some serious concerns about what the passage of time is doing to members of Independent Advisory Groups. The next section examines the IAGs' drift towards the policing norms and the apparent enculturalism of the groups.

Independent Advisory Groups: a critical review of contemporary groups

When the first Independent Advisory Group (IAG) was formed some very senior officers hoped that it would fade away after six months. IAGs are still around but there is a problem. Some have forgotten (or only vaguely remember) the reasons why they were formed in the first place, becoming consultation groups in all but name; they have lost their critical edge, unable to function with the conviction and focus that distinguished the original group. They have in effect evolved from being 'critical friends' to just being friends; they are unable or unwilling to give rigorous critical appraisals of policing issues that affect local communities.

On the other hand there is growing suspicion that some senior police officers and police staff who are responsible for effective coordination of IAGs and the synthesis and dissemination of learning from the groups are less engaged than they were previously. In defence of this position, some allude to the positive changes that have taken place since the Stephen Lawrence Inquiry, to justify the drift away from active critical engagement of IAGs. Others point out that they are now able to get the views of thousands of people through computer surveys and questionnaires. To use these arguments misses the point. It is in the 'white heat' of a face-to-face debate that connections are made and perceptions are honed and learning takes place. The face-to-face emotional element can never be replaced by remote contact.

Working with independent advisors who are actively focused can be trying for police. It is therefore not surprising that some forces actively shy away from potential areas of conflict. But it is during these periods of conflict that the best learning can occur, enhancing the quality of the police service being provided.

There may be a number of reasons for this lack of application; a significant reason is a need for emotional investment in the issues. If senior managers view IAGs as a necessary evil then that emotional connection will be missing. IAG members will notice that the IAG process is simply a mechanical management necessity and will respond in a lacklustre manner. Engaging in the IAG process must take place in an active spirit of openness, trust and transparency. Without these ingredients the relationship will falter and never reach its full potential.

Many IAGs need to go back to basics and refresh their knowledge and awareness of the key issues that forced the police sector into finding an effective means of listening to the concerns of minority communities; working collaboratively with those communities to deal with the issues in a way that benefited everyone. This is a fundamental first step if IAGs are to function anywhere close to their full potential.

The race agenda, which was endorsed by government and to some extent embraced by the public, paved the way for other minority groups to lay claim to a process that addressed their concerns. In particular, the Lesbian, Gay, Bisexual and Transgender Advisory Group, the Disability IAG and Gypsy and Travellers IAGs began to gain prominence across the country. The process of collaboration and engagement became a common theme across all the various types of advisory groups.

It is meaningless for IAG members and the police to simply state that IAGs were formed as a result of the Stephen Lawrence Inquiry if there is only a partial awareness of the key issues that the Inquiry addressed. Failure to deal appropriately with these issues over a decade ago led to a flawed murder investigation and inappropriate treatment of a grieving family.

The principle of individuals from communities working collaboratively with police in order that local policing is delivered according to need was adopted by ACPO and HMIC as best practice. However, what was missing from the piece were two factors: an understanding of the intrinsic factors which determine the quality of the IAG advice and a commonly held understanding of the role of IAGs and their sources of authority. This has, in some cases, led to IAGs being used as clearing houses for every conceivable community issue.

What is becoming increasingly clear is that a number of IAGs are functioning as consultation groups; even some of the long-established IAGs are beginning to lose their 'critical edge' by acquiescing more and more to the directions of police. The result is a loss of momentum by the groups, slowing down the process of challenge, innovation and new approaches. The ideal state is an equilibrium of proactivity on the part of IAGs and input and requests from police.

IAG chairpersons have a role to play here. They should use the talent within their respective groups or seek support from across forces to achieve this balance. Senior police officers should also recognise that it is in the service's interest to have searching and inquisitive advisory groups that challenge police to deliver even better and more appropriate local services. Police forces should actively welcome this challenge.

At the heart of every group should be a number of significant fundamentals. The group should:

- have a truly independent view which it is free to exercise, courageously if necessary;
- be aware of its sources of authority. Only when certainty about its role is properly established can the group begin to effectively give critical analysis and independent advice which is relevant and impactive;
- be involved in critical incidents and strategic policy development at the earliest possible stage.

These underlying minimum requirements are dependent on police remaining sensitive to the needs of local communities, including those newly emerging communities that are a result of the expansion of the European Community. IAGs have their part to play in remaining alert to policing issues affecting local communities. They should robustly seek to include local perspectives into the police management of those issues that potentially have an adverse effect on communities.

IAG members should know that at times their views will be at variance with those of the police. This is a legitimate position to have. This is where added value originates; not in giving more of the same but in providing a different view, a different approach that not only increases the quality of policing but satisfies the needs of local communities.

Above all, IAGs are not consultative groups. Their engagement with police should not become a matter of routine but should be an active furtherance of the police/community relationship. Passive IAGs are not adding benefit. They should not be 'nodding dogs', as the first IAG Chair famously stated at the group's inaugural conference in 1999. Members must be selected for the added benefit that they could potentially bring to the advisory process.

In today's policing environment, there is a need for a robust selection method for IAG members. IAG members should be selected by an independent mechanism that is open and transparent. Such a mechanism, which has been successfully applied in one or two forces as well as the Prison Service, should not exclude those with 'grass-roots' community experience but should aim for a mix that reflects the diversity of the issues in the policing sector.

This is a critical time for policing and communities. Society is on the cusp of potentially serious polarisation as a result of extremist terrorist activities. Predictably, the policing agenda has refocused to reflect this preoccupation. However, it should be remembered that there is an IAG history of nearly a decade with a wide range of experience to draw on.

Undeniably, the current policing approaches to murder investigations and other serious incidents are light years away from where they were 10 years ago. However, with the passage of time lies the twin danger of complacency and organisational amnesia. This danger applies equally to police as well as advisory groups. There has been little evidence that this danger has been acknowledged across the police sector despite the proliferation of IAGs across the country. Whether it is acknowledged or not, failure to get to the race issues right is a greater risk to policing and the fabric of society than the other important minority issues. There is ample evidence to qualify this position such as the race riots of 1978, 1981, 1985, 2001, the Scarman Inquiry, the Stephen Lawrence Inquiry, the Morris Inquiry, the Virdi Inquiry and most recently the inquiry into race, religion and police culture, which was ordered by London's Mayor, Boris Johnson (2008).

Conclusion

This chapter sought to link the relationship between police and minority ethnic interest groups, campaigning for change within the police sector. The focus of the chapter embraced race and policing issues, whilst at the same time recognising that other similar forms of engagement exist for other minority groups. However, there is an acknowledgement that the race IAG group led the way in developing this form of interaction with police and represents the locus of this unique form of community engagement.

There is clear evidence that IAGs have had a significant influence on policing policy. Most notable is their involvement in critical incidents. This involvement has resulted in an apparent paradigm shift in the policing of minority communities and in the operational 'mind-set' of the police. The focus is moving away from a police-centred approach to one that is more community centred, where families and communities are important first concerns, rather than the police processes and the maintenance of the status quo.

The Police Reform Act of 2002 now places an emphasis on citizen-focused policing which means that the IAGs are well placed to assist the police in achieving this new approach. IAGs, however, will have to review their working practices and prevent the drift towards malaise and ineffectiveness. This is particularly important in light of the new policing model which emphasises neighbourhood policing. Neighbourhood policing and IAGs are complementary approaches to community engagement. Police should not be tempted to choose one over the other but should be encouraging the building of links between the two approaches.

Independent Advisory Networks (IAN) are the favoured model at the local borough level for a number of practical reasons. The membership of an IAN can represent the diversity in local communities, including the business communities. In this way, local commanders can have a strategic overview of local concerns as well as having a diverse number of people from whom critical appraisals could be had.

It is argued that even though IAGs should maintain their lay status, there is a compelling view that they would benefit from independent guidance and support on how to develop their role and critically appraise the issues at hand whilst at the same time retaining perspectives that are reflective of local communities.

Fundamentally they must be more robust at linking current societal issues with the policing responses to those issues. Furthermore, IAGs should, as a matter of policy, develop more sustainable networks with 'grass-roots' community groups. Most IAGs have now reached the stage where they need to refocus and again embrace the core principles that sustained the first group during the turbulent early years of its existence.

Ten years after their inception, some reworking of IAGs is imperative if they are to remain relevant to the evolving policing agenda.

Notes

1 All quotes from an unpublished PhD thesis entitled 'Hard to Hear Voices: A Comparison of Internal and External Ethnic Minority Pressure Groups within the Policing Sector', J.O. Brathwaite (2005).

2 An alleged suicide that on reinvestigation subsequently turned out to be a murder.

3 A major investigation into the death of a young Asian man who was reported missing and whose body was later found in the River Thames.

4 Bournemouth seminar, held on 12–14 November 1999, was meant to map the way forward for the IAG.

5 *Lay involvement: an analysis of the MPS Borough Commanders' Survey* (MPS 1999d).

6 The Holly Royde Conference is an annual event sponsored by the Home Office to discuss race and discrimination in the Criminal Justice System.

7 In the Virdi discipline case, the IAG's involvement and advice on the process of the hearing was not heeded. A subsequent MPA Inquiry report questioned the inflexibility of the then Discipline Regulations and made 18 recommendations. See *Beyond Words*, IAG Report June 2000; The Virdi Inquiry Report (MPA 2001).

8 The independent advisor's involvement did not affect the outcome of this case. It is of interest to note that I, as the Scotland Yard senior officer who was responsible for developing the ethos of independent advice in the MPS, was required to submit written evidence of the nature of independent advice to the courts. This was a new arena for the courts as well!

Part Two:
Lawrence and Operational Policing

Chapter 4

'Practical cop things to do': the Stephen Lawrence Inquiry and changing the police mind-set

John Grieve

This chapter examines a range of police operational developments which have reflected various dimensions of the legacy of Lawrence. It draws, from amongst other things, personal engagement with the immediate policing response to Lawrence, not just subsequent to the publication of the Inquiry Report but responses which emerged as the Inquiry was still deliberating. In particular, it addresses the menu of tactical options that was developed during the last weeks of part one of the Stephen Lawrence Inquiry (hereafter SLI) and the opening weeks of part two during the late summer and autumn of 1998. I attended several weeks of part one and five of the six travelling sessions for part two. Out of these tactics were developed elements of the new Metropolitan Police (hereafter MPS) Anti-Racist Policing Strategy (18 December 1998) and later elements of the Diversity Strategy at a Strategic Conference later in 1999. The argument here is one I have developed elsewhere (Grieve 2004: 26) and concerns the critical role of 'street-level' officers in generating police leadership. There is an old military adage that by and large 'strategy is tactics talked through a brass hat', or rather in the police case through silver braid. This is both an upward and downward flow of leadership ideas and experiences from the workers on the streets to senior staff in the boardroom. More specifically, police leadership comes within the sound of the click of the handcuffs.

The tactical menu described here was intended to be mapped on to existing good police practice. In this sense it is an example of incrementalism in policy development (see the Introduction to this volume), where initiatives at any point in time tend to build on existing trends and tendencies. In the context of the tactical menu in question this was to become part of a bedrock of what was to emerge as Anti-Racist Policing. After outlining the tactical menu, the chapter goes on to look at the SLI recommendations, the Home Secretary's Action Plan and the creation of the Stephen Lawrence Steering Group, and finishes with some assessment of the balance of both successes and failures relating to the SLI.

In developing this discussion I have tended only to deal with those issues with which I had direct involvement. I am conscious that this account does not go into, in any depth, the important roles of many other groups and individuals, officers, the Association of Chief Police Officers (ACPO), Her Majesty's Inspectorate of Constabulary (HMIC) or the Home Office (HO). For what it is worth, this chapter is to an extent a former practitioner's journey through the discourses emanating from the SLI.

The Racial and Violent Crime Task Force (CO24) Action Plan: Operation Athena

I had been shortlisted to be Deputy Chief Constable of the Royal Ulster Constabulary when Sir Paul Condon asked me to lead the response to the Stephen Lawrence public inquiry, then in its last weeks of specific hearings for part one. Things were not looking good for the Metropolitan Police.

The Racial and Violent Crime Task Force (CO24) was created on 6 August 1998. Included in my terms of reference, drafted in the first few hours, was 'To set and develop operating standards for investigation, the use of intelligence and victim care'. In response to this we prepared, in consultation with a range of actors and stakeholders, a tactical action plan called Operation Athena.

The plan had reached 'Version 6' six weeks later on 18 September 1998 (Metropolitan Police 1998a). It was written using the management and planning systems and changes introduced by Commissioners Newman and Imbert during the previous 15 years (see Savage 2007: 136–138). All the initial 16 members of the task force were involved supported by an early-morning strategy group (see Chapter 5). It was implemented and amended continually (*Police Review* 11 September 1998) up to the publication of the Home Secretary's Action Plan on 24 March 1999 (Home Office 1999) and one month after the publication of the Inquiry Report. These investigative plans were driven and largely created by the active and committed street and detective officers and police staff first recruited and their contacts. Their role supports a contention argued below of the precedence of tactics in the arrival at strategy and the importance of the street officer (Grieve 2004); that by and large 'strategy is tactics talked through silver braid'. In fairness to the 'silver braid', Denis O'Connor as Assistant Commissioner had, prior to the arrival of the RVCTF, appointed three remarkable Superintendents (with silver braid), Sara Thornton, Mark Simmons and Bob Quick, to both monitor what was being heard at the SLI and prepare our responses in part two. Indeed the Inquiry Report itself acknowledged the prior existence of the action plan when they wrote:

> Already by the establishment under Deputy Assistant Commissioner John Grieve of the MPS Racial and Violent Crime Task Force (RVCTF) the signs are that the problem is being recognised and tackled. (Stephen Lawrence Inquiry 1999: 30, para. 6.47)

The three Superintendents were already recognising and tackling the problems; our investigative tactics were mapped on to some of their solutions. There were five objectives designed to support the RVCTF Mission Statement of the new task force, which was 'To ensure that racially motivated and violent crime is recognised, investigated thoroughly to agreed quality standards and reviewed objectively to enable lessons to be learned'. The objectives, together with the tasks associated with their potential achievement, were as follows:

Objective 1: 'To improve the investigation of racial and violent crime by setting minimum quality standards and creating a review process'

Task list:
- Critical incident management;
- Crisis intervention teams;
- Multi-agency task force;
- Developing a manual for the investigation of racial and violent crime;
- Implementation of quality assurance;
- Duty officer and help line;
- Minimum standards for community safety units;
- Review Lawrence recommendations;
- Court presentation;
- Racial motivation definitions.

Objective 2: 'To identify training needs through the review process and to contribute to the development of training in investigating racial and violent crime'

Task list:
- Review Lawrence recommendations;
- Cadre training for critical incident management;
- Investigation training.

Objective 3: 'To raise awareness and understanding internally and externally of the racial sensitivities in tackling racial and violent crime'

Task list:
- Marketing strategy;
- Internal forum representation;
- Presentation packages;
- Briefing and debriefing;

Objective 4: 'To improve communication with the communities we police in order to develop successful strategies to tackle racial and violent crime'

Task list:
- Active and rigorous fora;
- Advisory group;
- Community feedback;
- Communication of our strategy;
- Prevention package;
- Proactive operations.

Objective 5: 'To develop an integrated intelligence model to improve our response to the prevention of racial and violent crime'

Task list:
- Create a strategic and tactical intelligence cell;
- Propose intelligence initiatives for force-wide implementation;
- Develop community intelligence;
- Develop open-source intelligence;
- Supply information on prevention and proactive operations.

(Metropolitan Police 1998a: 13)

Although we had put together a seemingly comprehensive list of objectives and the tasking to achieve them, what was missing from our analysis and these lists was what was to be the essence of recommendation 1 of the SLI and which underpins and underlines the overall philosophy and broad context of Lawrence. Recommendation 1 read:

> that a ministerial Priority be established for all police services: to increase trust and confidence in policing amongst minority (ethnic) communities.

We had concentrated on racist crime – recommendation 1 was about a much broader concern. The Labour Home Secretary was to use his powers under section 37 of the Police Act 1996 (passed interestingly under the previous Conservative government) to create a ministerial priority for the police along the lines of recommendation 1. Recommendation 2 showed how this broad aim was to be measured. It included racist incidents monitoring and prevention, record keeping, family/witness liaison, multi-agency cooperation, training, stop and search, recruiting minority ethnic officers and complaints.

The Stephen Lawrence Inquiry and the Home Secretary's Action Plan

The then Home Secretary, Jack Straw – who had of course pledged in Opposition to the Lawrence family to call for a public inquiry when in office – republished the 70 recommendations of the Stephen Lawrence Inquiry (Home Office 1999). This put the Inquiry back on the front pages. For each recommendation he published an outline of some activity, even where his agreement with the recommendation was only partial. His action plan coincided with a full day's debate in the House of Commons on 29 March 1999 (Hansard 29 March 1999). There was an interesting foreword to the action plan. Each recommendation showed an outline of the work required, who would lead (the police had the lead in 26 of the 70 recommendations – not including those led by the Home Office or ACPO), what the milestones for progress would be and how the outcomes would be reviewed, assessed and monitored (Home Office 1999: para. 2:1). He also drew attention to the *links* between different recommendations, linkages which I illustrate later in the discussion on family liaison. In addition he set up a steering group comprising independent members, representatives from race relations fora, the Council for Racial Equality, the Black Police Association, ACPO, the Superintendents' Association, the Police Federation, Her Majesty's Inspector of Constabulary, the Metropolitan Police and the Crown Prosecution Service. This was to become effectively an oversight body. Also included in this foreword were four principles, which can tell us something about the Home Secretary's and Home Office's thinking on the Inquiry.

The four principles in the Home Secretary's action plan were:

1 *Partnership and involvement*: There will be involvement and consultation of minority ethnic people and their representative bodies as well as the police, relevant local and public authorities and other organisations at all stages to ensure that there is genuine partnership running throughout the programme.

2 *Policing diversity*: The work must help and support police officers to enforce the law in a multicultural and multi-ethnic Britain, better to serve the community. We need to be sure that changes will lead to real improvements. That would involve pilot projects and assessment where necessary.

3 *Recognising and rewarding success*: We would encourage all those involved to strive for the highest standards. We would acknowledge and praise achievement. Equally those who tolerate bad practice could expect to be identified and called to account.

4 *Raising standards and promoting professional competence*: The investigation of serious crime of all types, whether racist or not, must be conducted to the highest possible standard. Strong leadership, high-quality intelligence gathering and good organisation are all crucial. (Home Office 1999: 1)

What follows is an account of our early tactical development, but I will start with one notable exception, which may or may not be considered the most important and prove the rule.

Institutional racism

The SLI was to be best known for its discourse on *institutional racism*, the core of which was the way in which institutional racism was to be *defined*:

Taking all that we have heard and read into account we grapple with the problem. For the purposes of our inquiry the concept of institutional racism which we apply consists of:

The collective failure of an organisation to provide an appropriate and professional service to people because of their colour, culture or ethnic origin. It can be seen or detected in processes, attitudes and behaviour which amount to discrimination through unwitting prejudice, ignorance, thoughtlessness and racist stereotyping which disadvantage minority ethnic people. (Stephen Lawrence Inquiry 1999: 30, para. 6.34)

The finding that captured most attention was that of institutional (not institutionalised) racism in the police service, and beyond. This finding was leaked in the *Sunday Telegraph* (21 February 1999), days before the Inquiry Report was published (24 February 1999) and was the only finding in its format that came as a shock; in fact it was argued for some hours within the MPS that the leak was wrong. One way to view this failure to predict the wording and consequences of the finding is to see it as a strategic intelligence failure. The evidence of the Inquiry hearings was heard by myself and others, I had the intelligence cell to my hand and yet was persuaded by other more palatable evidence that we would not be found guilty of any form of racism, institutional or not, however it was to be defined. There was a minority on the team though who *did* believe that finding, in the form that it did, would occur, but the majority view prevailed at the time.

The argument exploring this as an intelligence failure is discussed more fully in Chapter 6. In this context we can note that officers had travelled to the USA to research the concept of 'institutional racism' and its current standing, and had concluded that on that basis it was outmoded, had little academic or practical standing, and as such was not particularly useful. The argument was that we could deal with all the issues arising by redefining what we were doing as Anti-Racist Policing – a positive, as opposed to the negatives emanating from the Inquiry. The finding of institutional racism required that we arrive at a tactical doctrine to come to terms with the strategic dilemma of how to deal with this finding. In other words, what we were doing to respond to other identified issues was make a start dealing with institutional racism itself.

After some initial doubts expressed at his appearance at the public hearing on 1 October 1998, the Commissioner Sir Paul Condon decided that the published definition could be 'lived with' and that 'the practical cop things to do' would address the problem. At the Inquiry he had said:

I am not denying the challenge or the need for reform, but if you label, if this Inquiry labels my service as 'institutionally racist' [pause] then the average police officer, the average member of the public will assume the normal meaning of those words. They will assume a finding of conscious, wilful or deliberate action or inaction to the detriment of ethnic minority Londoners. They will assume the majority of good men and women, who come into policing to serve their fellow men, go home to their families, go to their churches, go to their voluntary groups, go about their daily lives with racism in their minds and in their endeavour. I actually think that use of those two words in a way that would take on a new meaning to most people in society would actually undermine many of the endeavours to identify and respond to the issues of racism which challenge all institutions and particularly the police because of their privileged and powerful position. Racism is a feature throughout society. Racism is a feature of policing. (Stephen Lawrence Inquiry transcript, part 2, day 3, page 290, line 16 to page 291, line 11)

The following day (2 October 1998) he wrote to the Inquiry to reiterate his concerns but also to tidy up his thoughts. He wrote:

Racism as you pointed out can occur through a lack of care and lack of understanding … almost unknowingly, as a matter of neglect.

In the antepenultimate paragraph of the same letter he wrote:

Notwithstanding my caution over labels, you could overcome a number of my genuine, deeply felt concerns by establishing the standard for the police service, if not for public life, that could apply from now on. This would point up the peril of 'unconscious' or unintentional racism. Countering that would require the Met and others to have a demonstrable and compelling programme at every level to avoid racism occurring unwittingly.

That 'unwitting, lack of care, lack of understanding, neglectful, unknowing' was what we had set about working towards eliminating

– the shock when it came was that together they were defined as 'institutional racism'. However, we did not wait for the Inquiry Report but got on with the Commissioner's 'demonstrable and compelling programme'.

Despite that narrowing of an intellectual gap, the Inquiry concluded that it did not accept 'the contention of the Commissioner of the Metropolitan Police' that:

> ... if this Inquiry labels my service as institutionally racist, the average police officer, the average member of the public, will assume the normal meaning of these words. They will assume a finding of conscious, wilful or deliberate action or inaction ... (Stephen Lawrence Inquiry transcript, part 2, day 3, page 290, line 16 to page 291, line 11)

In reply the Inquiry retorted:

> We hope and believe that the average police officer and average member of the public will accept that we do not suggest that all police officers are racist and will both understand and accept the distinction we draw between overt, individual racism and the pernicious and persistent racism which we have described. (Stephen Lawrence Inquiry Report, para 6.46: 30)

Champions, within and beyond the MPS, were therefore needed to support the changes required to reverse that 'unwitting, lack of care, lack of understanding, neglectful, unknowing'; (to become the opposite of the final definition as 'unwitting, ignorant, thoughtless and stereotyping' – aware, knowledgeable and sensitive and understanding of diversity). Senior officers were required to sign up and had no choice. What we also needed were (volunteer) committed agents on the ground floor of the organisation to come forward. Beyond that, we needed to get to grips with the discourses surrounding the notion of institutional racism, some of which were presented as evidence to the SLI.

Institutional racism: evidence to the Lawrence Inquiry

Although Lord Scarman had rejected the term 'institutional racism' in the context of his inquiry into the Brixton disorders (Scarman 1981: 64), a conclusion which the Kent Police had also reached in the context of the Lawrence case (SLI 1999: 2), the SLI heard from Professor

Simon Holdaway that officers failed to 'reflect on the implications of their ideas and notions, negative relationships between the police and ethnic minorities are created and sustained' (SLI 1999: 23). They also heard from the Black Police Association spokesperson that:

> ... institutional racism ... permeates the Metropolitan Police Service. This issue above all others is central to the attitudes, values and beliefs which lead officers to act, albeit unconsciously and, for the most part, unintentionally and treat others differently solely because of their ethnicity or culture. (SLI 1999: 24).

The Black Police Association went on to say that institutional racism:

> ... should be understood to refer to the way the institution or the organisation may systematically or repeatedly treat or tend to treat people differentially because of their race ... We are not talking about the individuals within the Service who may be unconscious as to the nature of what they are doing ... Much has been said about our culture, the canteen culture, the occupational culture ... Given the fact that the majority of police officers are white, tends to be the white experience, the white beliefs, the white values ... Predominantly white officers only meet members of the black community in confrontational situations, they tend to stereotype black people in general. This can lead to all sorts of negative views and assumptions about black people. (SLI 1999: 25)

Two academics offered further support for this view to the Inquiry. Dr Robin Oakley referred to a generalised tendency towards different and less favourable treatment of BME communities than to the white majority. He also thought that institutional racism in this sense was pervasive '... throughout the culture and institutions of the whole of British society and is in no way specific to the police service' (SLI 1999: 26). This is resonant of MP Paul Boateng's remarks of five years previously (see below). Professor Ben Bowling drew attention to a distinction between uncritical and unconscious racism:

> ... some discrimination practices are the product of *uncritical* rather than unconscious racism. That is, practices with a racist outcome are not engaged in without the author's knowledge, rather the actor has failed to consider the consequences of his or

her actions for people from ethnic minorities. Institutional racism affects the routine ways in which ethnic minorities are treated in their capacities as employees, witnesses, victims, suspects and members of the general public. (SLI 1999: 27 – emphasis in original; see also Chapter 2 of this volume)

Police exposure to 'institutional racism' pre-Lawrence

The problems subsequently identified as 'unwitting, ignorant, thoughtless and stereotyping' had been recognised, at least implicitly, before. Lord Scarman's inquiry into the Brixton disorders, as has already been noted, wrestled with the issue (Scarman 1981: 59–64). The problem of racism in its various guises was also one of the central concerns of the study by the Policy Studies Institute Report on policing and people in London (Policy Studies Institute 1983, Part IV: 109–162). A decade later, a huge conference held on 24–26 February 1993, two months before Stephen Lawrence was murdered, which was initiated, designed and organised by Sergeant trainers at Hendon, and attended by over 600 police, community and CJS workers, made 'Fairness, Community and Justice' its central focus (Metropolitan Police 1993). Paul Boateng, then Opposition MP but later to become a Home Office Minister, appeared at the conference and identified racism as a key problem for society and policing in the 1990s. He concluded it was a major police management issue that required monitoring, and presciently put his finger on a key issue for half a decade later – 'Why the police, why us?':

These challenges have to be set within the broader context of a society that has far to go in dealing with the issues of racism, sexism and homophobia. A society that possibly has little right to put the police in a pillory in relation to any of those aspects of discrimination until it has put its own house in order but that inevitably, because of the power that it vests in you, is still entitled to expect the highest possible standards from every individual police officer. (Metropolitan Police 1993: 12)

Being put in the pillory or the stocks is exactly what it felt like later as the SLI unfolded.

The issues were revisited in the *London Beat*, a new overarching mission and policy statement which on 18 June 1998 had identified the same challenge for us, possibly emerging from the Inquiry, but also from other broader sources. It stated that:

We also recognise that sections of the minority communities are especially vulnerable to crime and those crimes that are racially motivated are particularly abhorrent ... we believe that the most effective way to win back confidence is by protecting vulnerable communities ... this will be achieved by investing in partnerships, developing systems to monitor the integrity and impact of our tactics and by focussing on the reduction of violence. All divisions will use an intelligence system to build up a picture of the vulnerability of their various communities (Metropolitan Police 1998b: 18)

That year the MPS Strategy *The Policing Plan for 1998/9* included 'the development of performance monitoring on racial incidents and racial crime at a local level' (Metropolitan Police 1998c: 5). For these reasons, to some extent we were pushing at an open door with the tactical doctrine and menu we were about to offer, and the champions needed to carry them forward would soon identify themselves. They were the intelligence officers, the investigators who were to staff the Community Safety Units which were in the process of being set up, trainers, communicators, minority members of police staff (the MPS was the largest employer of minority ethnic staff in London), anyone who was engaged in any form of family liaison (including traffic officers) or community liaison in any role and all those who believed in reducing violence and protecting the vulnerable. This was a sizeable and varied pool of champions.

Coming to terms with 'institutional racism'

Even before the SLI Report was published officers monitoring the emerging evidence had noted the significance of Ben Bowling's submission to the Inquiry, drawing as it did from his own research (Bowling 1998a), and had consulted him on possible policing responses to the problem of institutional racism. Bowling organised workshops on 12 November 1998 and 2 December 1998 which led to a large conference on 18 December 1998. This produced a plan and a concept – Anti-Racist Policing – into which our tactics were fused.

David Wilmot, then Chief Constable of Greater Manchester Police, another major metropolitan police service, publicly accepted the institutional racism label as applying to his own organisation on 13 October 1998. Two letters to *The Times* (19 October 1998: 21) illustrate degrees of support but also the confusion that would persist over the concepts of 'institutional' and 'institutionalised' racism. One letter, under the heading of 'Institutionalised Racism' written by Richard Wells – then Chief Constable of South Yorkshire Police – explored the development of the concept of racism in terms of the, at times, inadvertent policies and practices that resulted in outcomes which disadvantaged BME communities. Wells pressed for a leadership response and solution. The other letter, by Keith Hunter, another senior officer, identified a 'few racists' in the service who 'acutely embarrassed' the rest of the service and identified as a form of institutional racism the tolerance of such racists within the police culture; he also called for a leadership response.

Although some other police leaders did not agree with such judgements, many duly accepted both Sir Paul Condon's initial and amended position on institutional racism within the police service, as explained above. However, some other senior officers, including some very thoughtful members of the service, could never fully agree with this position. Brian Paddick, the most senior openly gay officer, although hugely supportive of the 'practical cop things to do' stance, the whole Anti-Racist Policing movement and the emerging hate crime agenda (Paddick 2008: 111–114), felt that the finding of institutional racism let the overt racists and bigots in the police off the hook, and was misunderstood by our colleagues in doing so (personal communication). Nevertheless he loyally worked at the agenda we had prepared. More worryingly, Bob Lambert, an intelligence officer in Special Branch, who again was hugely supportive of the agenda, and in particular the community engagement, impact and critical incident dimensions, was also not convinced:

> Although, I should say, I never bought into the notion of 'institutional racism', it seemed like an evasion of the real issue. The Met, like most other public employers in London, had a minority of officers who were racist or incompetent or both. They should have been dealt with firmly or sacked where appropriate ... to label the entire service racist was a mistake, bad for morale and misleading. (quoted in Jackson 2008: 8)

In the light of all the above, and the core finding of the SLI, it is interesting to note that the words 'institutional racism' do not appear in the recommendations, nor in the Home Secretary's action plan. The unqualified term 'racism' does, however; although it can be argued that many of the recommendations (for example, recommendation 29) are about the police as an *institution* and their efforts to deal with racism. Hence institutional racism can be inferred. Foster,

Newburn and Souhami (2005: 96) also drew attention to the absence of the specific words 'institutional racism' in the action plan they were evaluating. They noted that institutional racism was 'the single most powerful message officers received from the Stephen Lawrence Inquiry'. Many officers, they argue, did not receive advice or guidance on how to eradicate or even consider its 'collective and systemic aspects' (2005: 96).

Whatever the internal and external debate over the application of the label of institutional racism, our responses to the finding of institutional racism were to progress in the form of 'practical cop things to do'. In this regard we knew that effective *communication* of our aims and work was of the essence. From the outset we had a full-time media and communications specialist as a full member of the team. Carol Bewick wrote a detailed strategy for a dual purpose that addressed both external and internal audiences. In terms of *external audiences* we made ourselves available to any part of the media. We had full-time 'fly-on-the wall' TV crews recording two documentaries over our first two years, one to be shown on the publication of the SLI, the other on the first anniversary of publication. No week went by without media coverage or interviews. Slowly the positive column inches began to emerge. Carol did a remarkable job. As part of an unusual methodology Carol designed a Londonwide roadshow with Sarah Brown. Together with Jeff Brathwaite, we criss-crossed the capital and later went to other parts of the country (Parekh 2000). We aimed to influence several thousand influential thinkers, communicators, politicians, majority and minority community members, some of whom we invited more than once so that they could be exposed to our debates with various audiences. We would always visit the local police station, talk to the officers, sometimes going out on patrol with them. We would seek their advice on whom to invite, and explain that this was part of an 'outside looking in' and 'inside looking out' strategy. These experiences were frequently exhausting – we were often subjected to much criticism – but always stimulating.

In terms of our *internal audiences* we drove the 'let's nick some racists' agenda (*Police Review* 11 September 1998 and *The Observer* 31 January 1999). From autumn 1998 we also prepared a series of posters around the theme of 'intelligent intelligence', identifying what sort of intelligence would help arrests, plus a menu of things to do called Operation Athena Spectrum, emphasising different options – one for each letter of the alphabet. We held conferences and workshops for community safety officers, intelligence officers, family liaison officers and trainers.

Unfortunately, as we worked through our responses we encountered ill will within and outside of the service. A number of people felt it necessary to send me, as a senior lead for a number of the responses, abusive emails – usually sent on their last day in office. One even went so far as to send me thirty pieces of silver (unfortunately, fake). However, I always felt they were in a small minority, and those who were 'practical cops' (like Bob Lambert and Brian Paddick) felt there were practical things to do even if they did not agree with the route by which we had got there. We examined where we were going and came up with the strapline: 'everybody benefits'. As policies and practices unfolded under this banner, it was clear that although many of the changes drew from or built upon existing practices, it was the potential *linkages* between them which the SLI had exposed and that we were to address. Perhaps even more importantly, what the Inquiry at the very least furthered were more fundamental transformations in the police 'mind-set', the community of ideas or 'thought world' of policing (Sheptycki 2004: 328), or what was referred to in the Introduction to this volume as a *paradigm shift*.

In the remaining sections of this Chapter I will identify a number of operational and policy areas which embodied the policing response to the SLI, focusing on two areas in particular: *family liaison* and the *investigative response* to murders and other serious crimes, both of which, I would argue, capture the 'paradigm shift' brought about by the SLI.

Lawrence and the practical policing response

Family liaison

I have chosen to focus in depth on family liaison because of its deep significance to the whole Lawrence agenda. Over one quarter (at least 18 out of the 70) of the SLI recommendations relate directly or indirectly to families. Although underappreciated prior to Lawrence, families are of critical importance to policing. On the one hand, consideration of family needs, concerns, priorities and preferences is an absolutely central element of what the provision of policing services should be about. On the other hand, families can themselves play a key role in criminal investigations, as witnesses, sources of information, in helping to conduct surveillance, provide observation posts and so on. Families are also a critical link between the police and the communities they police when investigations are under way

(Savage, Poyser and Grieve 2007; Roycroft, Brown and Innes 2007). However, the critical role of families, and therefore of family liaison, was not fully articulated or appreciated at the time of Stephen Lawrence's murder and in the years following that event.

This is not to say that 'family liaison' was not adopted by murder squads as part of their functions in the past. It was seen as an investigative task but not a *specialism*. Some records were kept of family liaison activity but there was little uniformity in practice. The Anti-Terrorist Branch (ATB) had highly experienced family liaison officers (FLO) but there was neither specialist training nor specialist command structure in the Metropolitan Police, or so we believed. There had indeed been 'family liaison officers' in the original Lawrence murder inquiry and those concerned were given a hard time under cross-examination during the Inquiry under Macpherson.

Five weeks after the sixth version of our developing strategy, on 27 October 1998 (four months before the Inquiry reported), I was persuaded to go and hear a presentation by Ron Cuthbertson. It will be noted that the sixth version made no mention of family liaison although it was relevant to many aspects of our work. Ron was a working detective operating a totally unofficial course in north London for murder squads. It was based on a course already being run by the Avon and Somerset Police (we owe a huge debt to Avon and Somerset for sharing their expertise not only in the work they had done with families, but also in the way in which they had combined it with their innovative community awareness programmes.) What Ron told us that day challenged our thinking, and changed the way we dealt with families, how we looked after our own officers who were fulfilling liaison roles, and how we were prepared for the Inquiry's final report.

Ron Cuthbertson identified the current ambivalent attitudes and requirements of MPS management for the deployment of FLOs; he went on to describe the complexity of the FLO's tasks, both investigative and information giving. In relation to murder enquiries, 'Don't lie to them [families],' he said. 'Even if they are suspects they will see right through you with their heightened emotions.' 'What if it's likely that they could be suspects?' 'Even that is not an excuse for telling them nothing.' He described the training required to reach judgements; the necessity of record keeping, liaising with lawyers, other groups, victims' representatives and supporters, and dealing with media interest; the tightrope act required at court with family as witnesses; and overall a description of the distinct 'thought world' occupied by trained FLOs. Ron subsequently worked as a course director responsible for the training of over 1,300 family liaison officers in London, as well as nationally and internationally. He also worked on the training of senior officers in managing family liaison officers and handling critical incidents (see below and Chapter 7). In short he wanted family liaison to be a *specialism* as important as firearms, hostage negotiation or exhibit-taking.

Family liaison became a core issue in our developing tactics in response to the Report, and my role was expanded to become the MPS professional lead in this area. The family liaison officers were trained with the assistance of the programme designed by Avon and Somerset Police. This was developed in London, supported by the hospice learning programme, specifically that of the St Christopher's Hospice founder Dame Cecily Saunders (Grieve and French 2000). After the attacks on New York on 11 September 2001, family liaison officers were deployed to support the families of British victims, winning praise from both the families and the Prime Minister. Ron helped set up family liaison coordinators and later he carried the national flag at the 9/11 memorial service at Westminster Abbey. He was awarded the Queen's Police Medal for his work.

Nevertheless, as Ron was always the first to admit, it was undoubtedly the efforts of Mr and Mrs Lawrence and their experiences that gave rise to the massive increase in the recognition of the importance of effort and resources in respect of police family liaison. The SLI had identified, as the third of twenty issues, that they wished to question and consider the following in relation to family liaison:

- first contact with the family;
- properly and sensitively handled;
- what happened at the hospital;
- appointment of liaison officer;
- appropriateness of selection (training?);
- conduct of liaison officers after appointment;
- did the relationship break down – if so, why?;
- extent of guidance/direction/supervision by senior officers;
- effect, if any, of intervention by others on police/family;
- role of supporters of the family;
- role of family legal advisor.

> (Stephen Lawrence Inquiry Statement of issues and witnesses for public hearings and Stephen Lawrence Inquiry Miscellaneous documents).

The Inquiry, after questioning the witnesses in parts one and two, and travelling to Bristol where it heard from Avon and Somerset Police about their projects, subsequently included the following recommendations, which are summarised here in tabulated form, related to other recommendations as a case study of linkages with notes on what has gone before.

From Table 4.1 it can be seen how family liaison officers (FLOs) were central to the response to key parts of the SLI and why they were to become champions of the Lawrence agenda (I have long been of the opinion that FLOs should be known as 'Lawrence officers' in recognition of the role played by Stephen's parents). Family liaison, as a result of Lawrence and in due course, had risen in status within policing operations to the level of a genuine specialism.

Murder and the investigative response

The impact of the SLI on the management of murder investigations is dealt with in detail in Chapter 5. In the context of this chapter a number of issues can be raised in relation to the investigative response to murder and other serious crimes. The efficacy of investigative processes within policing had been challenged much earlier, most notably as a result of the highly critical and much debated 1981 'fly-on-the-wall' television programme, based on the Thames Valley Police, which included most controversially the 'interview' by detectives of a woman who had made a rape allegation. The debate that the programme provoked in itself led directly to changes in the investigation of sexual crimes, for example through the creation of Sexual Offences Investigation Techniques Officers (Blair 1985). The SLI was to raise even more fundamental questions about the investigative response.

Recommendation 20 read:

> that MPS procedures at the scene of incidents be reviewed in order to ensure co-ordination between uniformed and CID officers and to ensure that senior officers are aware of and fulfil the command responsibilities which their role demands.

Recommendation 21 went on:

> that the MPS review their procedures for the recording and retention of information in relation to incidents and crimes, to ensure that adequate records are made by individual officers

and specialist units in relation to their functions, and that strict rules require the retention of all such records as long as an investigation remains open.

In response to this, documentation which already existed to record police decisions was enhanced and expanded to include the rationale for the decision, the context for the decision and available knowledge or areas of ignorance pursuant at the time of the recording. In relation to this, specialist loggists and decision-makers were trained during the critical incident management exercises (see below). Another new concept to emerge in relation to the investigative response was the 'golden hour'. This was a concept borrowed from accident and emergency unit procedures employed by practitioners such as paramedics, which stressed the importance of action in the first hour after (in their case) an accident or emergency and (in ours) the discovery of a crime. There was, in addition, a re-emphasis of the responsibilities of individual officers and commanders to be carried out as the initial steps at the scene.

Another key area of the investigative response was the process of *review* of ongoing or past investigations. The RVCTF were early advocates of self-review systems and later of independent systematic, objective review, again based on a medical consultative model. These had been commonplace outside London but the Inquiry had turned up systemic failures in the MPS application of them (SLI 1999: 195–207). Paragraph 28.61 of the Inquiry Report was particularly damning. It condemned the review that had been carried out in the Lawrence case, but did *not* find that 'its inadequacies were the result of corruption or collusion'. It *did* find that '… unquestioning acceptance and repetition of the criticisms of the Lawrence family and its solicitor are to be deplored.' This wording is eerily prescient of a similar criticism in the Victoria Climbié Public Inquiry (Laming 2003: 322) which stated that 'unquestioning acceptance of information … is unacceptable in a police officer'. The process of review is considered in more depth in Chapter 5.

Another area of investigative response to be shaped by the Lawrence agenda was that of *community concerns and impact analysis* (discussed in depth in Chapter 3). The significance of the local dimension and community impact of murders and other serious crime investigations had long been formally recognised, at least as long ago as the Scarman Report (Scarman 1981). Furthermore, and much undervalued by many of us at the time, community impact issues were already informing the decisions and practices of the RUC,

Table 4.1 Key recommendations relating to family liaison

SLI recommendation number	Summary of primary recommendation from Stephen Lawrence Inquiry	Home Secretary's and Police Action Plan and linkages to the SLI	Notes
23	That police services should ensure that at a local level there are readily available designated and trained family liaison officers	All the primary recommendations were accepted by Home Secretary and ACPO. ACPO undertaking a complete review. Recommendation 1 underpins everything that follows 'to increase trust and confidence in policing amongst minority ethnic communities'.	Huge programme of work undertaken given added impetus by the Copeland case the following year – see chronology in Appendix. Based on Ron Cuthbertson and Avon and Somerset Police
24	That training of family liaison officers (FLOs) must include racism awareness, cultural diversity according to the family's needs	As 23 above, recognising the centre of excellence in Avon and Somerset. Rec 20 that refers to recording and retention of information, what are now called decision logs, clearly applies to FLO logs of their activities	Ron Cuthbertson's aspiration of specialist FLOs was reinforced and his training regime recognised
25	Appointed FLOs to be dedicated primarily, if not exclusively, to that task		As 24 above
26	SIOs and FLOs be made aware – good practice/positive duty, satisfactory management of family issues, providing all	This was a core recommendation and can be related to: Rec 9 Appropriate Harm Test with respect to withholding disclosure	As above at 24, became a veritable mantra for police thinking: 'An issue for the family is an issue for us.'

118

possible information about crime and investigation	Recs 35, 36, 37, the duties of CPS to the family Recs 40, 41, 42, 43 which further outline the family's role as civil parties to the proceedings, private prosecutions, coroners and legal aid Rec 29, that there should be a manual of guidance for all witness and victims dealing; clearly FLOs were central to that Rec 30, local contacts in minority communities to assist with training Rec 31, extending expertise to other victims and witnesses particularly in racist, young or vulnerable victims; this latter also relevant to Rec 44, intimidation of witnesses	Rec 20 which is the basis for critical incident training for leaders and senior officers ensuring co ordination and understanding always involves FLOs
27 Good practice to provide for SIO recording and consideration of request or complaints by the family by line command	Rec 21 refers to all records and their retention	The subject of records keeping in decision-making was central to critical incident training; loggists and decision-makers were trained
28 Use of Victim Support Service, their local contacts in minority communities	Local contacts in minority communities to assist with training Rec 24 above is relevant	Victim Support workers were involved in our Independent Advisory Group and other fora.

in relation to public order policing and, of course, counter-terrorism. The draft Murder Manual developed in 1998 had begun to lay out ways of sharing the work between specialist and local officers, and therefore to enable investigators to benefit from local insights into the community impact of both serious crimes and the policing responses to those crimes. As Chapter 6 makes clear, the SLI was to affirm community impact analysis as the core feature of the investigative response to serious crimes, together with an emphasis, as already made clear, on the importance of families and their interaction with communities to the intelligence-gathering and handling process.

As Chapter 6 also makes clear, this was subsequently to lead to refinements to public order *risk assessments*, including those relating to counter-terrorism. It was clear from the Inquiry that failure to understand the risks apparent to the community was part of the systemic failure of our investigation into Stephen Lawrence's murder. The Human Rights Act 1998 had just been introduced, and the Health and Safety Act was becoming increasingly influential within the police mind-set. As far back as 1983, and later as a delegate on the Senior Command Course at Bramshill, I had prepared a method of risk analysis to deal with the harms that had emerged from a series of stated cases and *causes célèbres* (Harfield and Harfield 2008: 148–150). This covered physical, psychological, political, legal, economic and moral risks and threats. Once again, Lawrence would bring these themes into sharper focus and ensure their institutionalisation within the investigative response to serious crimes.

Linked to this would be the whole area of *critical incident comparison, analysis and management*. The rise of 'critical incident thinking' – of how to recognise, identify, interpret and act upon events which had at least the potential of becoming critical incidents – within the British police service, and its homage to the Lawrence agenda, have been discussed elsewhere (Grieve, Griffiths and Crego 2007; Alison and Crego 2008; see also Chapter 7 of this volume). Following on from work undertaken in the immediate aftermath of the SLI, a workshop was organised by Professor David Guest in May 1999 for Denis O'Connor and myself leading to a subsequent critical incident working party, which would eventually drive our critical incident thinking towards a 'seven-tool' approach to the management and analysis of critical incidents (Alison and Crego 2008: xxvii):

1 CCA (comparative case analysis), which has now been at the heart of my own thinking and analysis of intelligence work for over 40 years.

2 PLAN BI (proportionate, legal, accountable, necessary acting on best information), derived from the Human Rights Act (see Harfield and Harfield 2005: 196), a risk management decision-making instrument for the assessment for police activity that interferes with anyone's rights.

3 EEP (experience, evidence, potential), another method of analysing a risky decision.

4 SAFCORM (situation, aims, factors involved, choices, option, risk, monitoring), a briefing and preparatory model borrowed from the military.

5 STEEPLES (social, technical, environmental, economic, political, legal, ethical, safety and health), a context scanning model that, when explored with measures of the likely impact to anyone or/and potential outcomes or consequences, temporal/urgency/ importance, vulnerability, high/medium/standard measures of possible risks, or financial details, gives the capability to reach the next tool which is:

6 RARARA (record, analyse, remove, accept, reduce, avoid/averse), a way of making decisions and considering possible consequences/ outcomes, whether functional or dysfunctional (Richards 2006; Harfield and Harfield 2008: 153).

7 3PLEM (physical, psychological, police/community; political, legal, economic and moral risks) (Harfield and Harfield 2008: 149).

This seven-tool framework has informed critical incident leadership training in recent years (Grieve, Griffiths and Crego 2007), but essentially builds upon the momentum generated by the SLI, in the way outlined in Chapter 7.

Conclusion: from practical failures to practical successes?

In this chapter I have sought to examine the legacy of Lawrence in terms of, firstly, the impact on the organisation itself of the finding that the MPS was 'institutionally racist' and, secondly, the 'practical cop things to do' which followed alongside and in the wake of Lawrence. Is it possible to conclude that the police service has moved from evident practical failure as epitomised by Lawrence to practical successes? First it has to be said that Stephen's killers have not been brought to justice, at least at the time of writing. That is a measure of our failure. Second, the most wide-ranging assessment of the impact of the SLI (Foster, Newburn and Souhami 2005: 97) concludes and argues with a mixed message that there were substantial changes in policing in the five years after the SLI, but that this was not uniform across police forces. Significantly, the greatest difficulty has been for police to understand the problem of 'institutional racism' and to design responses; the police service, they argue, has addressed many of the issues attached to Lawrence but not the main one! Foster later concluded on the basis of her research that detectives overwhelmingly believed that the Stephen Lawrence failures were born of incompetence not racism. This did not mean that they had not embraced and recognised change, just that they had not accepted institutional racism (Foster 2008).

Eighty-one per cent of police respondents agreed with a statement offered by Foster *et al.* that they felt under greater scrutiny than four years before. As one officer stated: 'I have to be more accountable for my actions' (Foster *et al.* 2005: 29). They had anxieties about allegations being made during stop and search or investigating racial incidents which could now embrace their own actions. An interesting table in Foster *et al.* (2005: 28) looked at assessment by police of their own performance at the time of the review and four years before, measured by a percentage improvement in categories of work that they considered to be 'excellent/good'. There appeared to be a general recognition of learning and improvement, except in their confidence during stop and search. Some improvements seemed substantial, such as the 70 per cent improvement in police behaviour in respect of racial incidents (see also Chapter 10). Other areas of apparent improvement also relate to the Lawrence agenda, including a 27 per cent improvement in family liaison, 26 per cent improvement in the management of major crime, 17 per cent improvement in the quality of murder investigations and 42 per cent improvement in responding to critical incidents (Foster *et al.* 2005: 28). Some of the things we did can be considered useful: it is for others to decide if they amount to success. Much of any improvement can be directly related to the SLI and act as evidence of a positive legacy.

There are additional measures of the positive impact of Lawrence. The Inquiry Report itself, as noted above, twice endorsed the MPS plans as a move in the right direction (SLI 1999: para. 6.47 and para. 6.50). In three separate HMIC Reports some improvements were noted. In the four Home Secretary's Action Plan Annual Reports on Progress (the fourth in March 2003), steady activity was noted. Bob

Lambert, formerly of the Special Branch Muslim Contact Unit at New Scotland Yard, revealed in an interview how influential had been our thinking in response to the SLI, specifically about communities and their role, for the community aspects of the government's counter-terrorist prevention and prosecution strategy post 9/11 (Jackson 2008). The more general spread of critical incident thinking and training, not just nationally but internationally, also stands as some measure of impact and legacy, as does the spread of the thinking about family liaison into areas such as counter-terrorism.

However imperfect and incomplete, I suggest that the suite of 'practical cop things to do' outlined here as policing responses to Lawrence amounts to a legacy which is substantial. Some of those responses reflected 'street-level thinking' which went far beyond the actual recommendations of Lawrence; others acquired a momentum of their own without a specific steer for the SLI. In both cases it was the SLI which either helped launch new initiatives or gave momentum to initiatives and developments already emerging. In these senses I believe the strategy we arrived at to achieve 'trust and confidence' and tackle the finding of institutional racism was indeed 'tactics talked through silver braid'. Whether the skills developed as a solution are applicable to all or any other crises remains to be seen.

A note on references: It was the request of Sir William Macpherson and his advisors that the report into the events surrounding the death of Stephen Lawrence should be known as the 'Stephen Lawrence Inquiry Report'. Whilst most continue to refer to the Inquiry Report as 'Macpherson (1999)', I have chosen to follow that request.

Chapter 5

Doing the right thing: a personal and organisational journey of change in homicide investigation in the Metropolitan Police Service

Bill Griffiths

At the funeral of his murdered son Damilola, in January 2001, Richard Taylor said to me, 'I am depending on you'. With these words I was reminded of the privileged role that I held as a police officer empowered to investigate the death of another human being and of the trust that he, his family and his community placed in me to deliver justice for Damilola. This, therefore, is my personal story, and the story of how the Metropolitan Police Service faced the charges made by the Stephen Lawrence Inquiry of professional incompetence, failed leadership and institutional racism, and embarked on arguably the most significant change in its history.

The Stephen Lawrence Inquiry

The Stephen Lawrence Inquiry will be best remembered by many for its finding of 'institutional racism' in the Metropolitan Police Service. The term was defined as:

> The collective failure of an organisation to provide an appropriate and professional service to people because of their colour, culture, or ethnic origin. It can be seen or detected in processes, attitudes and behaviour which amount to discrimination through unwitting prejudice, ignorance, thoughtlessness and racist stereotyping which disadvantage minority ethnic people ... It persists because of the failure of the organisation openly and adequately to recognise and address its existence and causes by

policy, example and leadership. Without recognition and action to eliminate such racism it can prevail as part of the ethos or culture of the organisation. It is a corrosive disease. (Macpherson 1999: para. 6.34)

As a serving senior officer at the time of publication in February 1999, I both observed in others and felt within myself the full range of emotions that are commonly associated with bereavement and grief: shock, denial, anger and guilt. The Inquiry had identified collective failure and I know I am not the only one who hung my head in collective shame. I looked inside and asked of myself whether I am or could be perceived as racist, albeit through unwitting prejudice, ignorance, thoughtlessness and racist stereotyping behaviour. Once aware of this possibility, I began to question how could I, my colleagues, and the Service change?

However, our immediate focus was the more tangible issue that led to the institutional racism charge, the systemic failure of the investigation into the racist murder of Stephen Lawrence on 22 April 1993, as clearly spelled out in the concluding chapter of the Report:

The conclusions to be drawn from all the evidence in connection with the investigation of Stephen Lawrence's racist murder are clear. There is no doubt that there were fundamental errors. The investigation was marred by a combination of professional incompetence, institutional racism and a failure of leadership by senior officers. A flawed MPS review failed to expose these inadequacies. The second investigation could not salvage the faults of the first. (Macpherson 1999: para. 46.1)

Having served mainly as a detective, this too provoked professional shame, challenging personal emotions and significant introspection, but I could not claim to be surprised at this analysis because, the finding of institutional racism aside, which came relatively late in the deliberations of the Inquiry, I knew in both my head and my rapidly sinking heart that this would be the conclusion of the Inquiry.

My anticipation had been acquired over a journey that started long before the Inquiry itself and was reinforced as the compelling evidence of failure emerged. These failures and omissions were revealed by individuals as they provided evidence to the Inquiry but blame clearly rested with the organisation that had failed to put in place a supporting environment, proper training and sufficient resources to help those individual officers to provide a professional service. They were in the main dedicated and well-intentioned colleagues giving of their best but they were not operating to good and acceptable standards. Major investigation and the necessary infrastructure, including training and best practice, had been starved of investment over many years.

In the ten years since the Inquiry, a large part of my professional life has been spent in leading many of the changes that had to be brought about to remedy the failings, together with developing an understanding of what remains to be done. Therefore, the following account is very much a personal one, not least concerning significant internal challenge and turmoil, but hopefully also of interest to the reader because it is the story of how the Metropolitan Police embarked on a massive and wide-ranging cultural change programme.

To bring clarity to the change journey, I have mapped it on to the 'progression of competence model'. We begin the journey in an organisation that was unaware of shortcomings in its service provision: *unconsciously incompetent*. Slowly the organisation becomes aware of its shortcomings and the scale of the challenge ahead: *consciously incompetent*. Adjustments and improvements are tried, tested, trained and introduced to the mainstream as the organisation becomes *consciously competent*, and gradually *unconsciously competent* as the changes are embedded into systems, processes and behaviours within a new culture.

Looking back, I can also see how the essential awareness and adjustment to that which has to change proceed at different pace for individuals, teams, departments and, indeed, the entire organisation. For example, at the point in February 1999 when the Report was published, I and many others were conscious of organisational incompetence, whereas the great majority of my colleagues appeared to be confronting the scale of it for the first time. Combined as this was with the impact of the judgement of institutional racism, the Met collectively went into shock and then denial, before experiencing anger and disappointment and then finally acceptance that it had to change.

A programme for change

Phase I – unconsciously incompetent

On appointment as Commander (Crime) for the newly formed 4 Area (South East) in August 1994 under Assistant Commissioner Ian

Johnston, one of my first briefings from his Deputy, Perry Nove, was on the attempt that had been mounted to secure evidence against the suspects for the racist murder of Stephen Lawrence in April 1993 (referred to below as 'the second investigation').

Among the many things I recall from that briefing was that Ian Johnston, upon taking over command of the Area earlier that year, had called a family meeting to try to salvage the relationship that had broken down between the police, the Lawrence family, and their supporters. The most telling confirmation of the breakdown in this relationship had been in the ironic remark by Mrs Lawrence upon meeting the senior investigating officer (SIO) several months after the murder: 'We meet at last!'

The innovative and proactive second investigation produced clear evidence of violent racism exhibited by some suspects that, famously, was later published in the *Daily Mail*, but did not provide sufficient additional evidence for the Crown Prosecution Service to bring a prosecution.

Ian Johnston then acceded to the family's request to support a private prosecution, which would be led by Michael Mansfield QC, instructed by Imran Khan Solicitors. This courageous decision resulted in an unprecedented disclosure to the family of all the material available to the police. Working with the incisive brain of Michael Mansfield, we soon discovered there were many unanswered questions from the original investigation.

Nonetheless, following an 'old-style' committal (meaning evidence was examined before a magistrate and legal arguments heard), a number of the suspects were sent for trial with a case to answer. It was strongly felt that the evidence of racism the investigation team had covertly secured would be very influential with a jury. That was not to be and, on a 'Turnbull Ruling' (identification evidence from an eyewitness to the stabbing ruled unsafe to go before the jury) at the Old Bailey in April 1996, the suspects were acquitted with no case to answer.

Phase 2 – consciously incompetent

The Inquest into Stephen's killing held in February 1997 proved to be the turning-point for both my personal awakening and the beginning of the organisational shock waves that were to follow.

In evidence to the coroner, Mrs Doreen Lawrence spelled out her clear view that Stephen and her family had not received an appropriate service from the Met. Moreover, they had been the subject of racist stereotyping. Her position is set out in full in the Inquiry Report (paragraphs 42.13 and 42.37).

On a professional level, I reflected hard on her words and could clearly see how she could form such a view. The investigation had not stood out as particularly competent and had been beset by errors, missed opportunities and missed communication. However, it had been reviewed by a respected senior detective with experience outside of the Met and all of us senior officers had hoped against hope that his review would suggest that everything that could have been done had been done, and that in any case some investigations simply do not have the breakthroughs that others do.

At an emotional level, I was devastated. Having read for myself the same evidence that Mrs Lawrence was alluding to, I had simply not understood her perspective as a bereaved mother and person of colour. My mind-set began to change from that moment and I have never stopped challenging myself to understand other perspectives, what they tell us of their actual experiences of policing in London, and what needs to change to ensure an appropriate professional service at all times.

March 1997 saw the appointment of Kent Police to a Police Complaints Authority (PCA) investigation into the Met's investigation with me as its liaison officer and involved in recovery of material that was to demonstrate even more errors and omissions than were known hitherto. Then in July, Home Secretary Jack Straw announced on behalf of the new government that High Court Judge Sir William Macpherson of Cluny would chair a public inquiry into the matters arising from the death of Stephen, particularly to identify the lessons to be learned for the investigation and prosecution of racially motivated crimes.

In October 1997, I was invited to Kent Police HQ for a presentation, not about their PCA investigation, but on their discovery of 11 'lines of enquiry' that had been missed by the original investigation and the shocking revelation that, in their opinion, the review that senior officers had depended upon for quality assurance was completely flawed. Their report was published in December and:

> ... roundly and severely criticised many aspects of the MPS investigation and specifically blamed individual officers. (PCA 1997: para. 3.3)

April 1998 found me at Simpson Hall in the Hendon Training Estate addressing the most senior 120 detectives in the Met on the findings from the PCA Report. Facing this audience was not for the faint-hearted. They were a massively experienced group of investigators and famously sceptical.

However, I considered myself no less experienced as a detective and had been given a new role that very month – Director of Crime Management with responsibility for all Met crime policy – with a specific remit from Sir Paul Condon, then Commissioner, to take forward the issues arising from the PCA Report.

I set out to the assembled group the PCA findings which were at that stage concerned with the efficacy of the investigation and the errors and omissions by individuals involved in it. The Kent team had concluded that there was no evidence of racism, which was at the heart of Mrs Lawrence's complaint, so my presentation at that time was chiefly concerned with systems, processes and training, about which there was very little positive news.

Nonetheless, there was a clear mandate to commence the work that obviously needed doing in anticipation of the public inquiry findings and I proposed to the assembled colleagues as a starting point six working groups, and received volunteers to lead each. The six groups were:

- initial response and scene management;
- exhibit handling;
- major incident room (MIR) skills and procedures;
- policy files;
- family liaison;
- training.

The groups comprised practitioners and they were to report back to me and a small policy development team headed by Detective Chief Inspector Ragna Tulloch, who also did a sterling job in supporting the Inquiry itself day to day. I was also introduced to the concept of programme management through the work of Derrick Norton, who was assigned in support. As the Inquiry unfolded in the following months, so too the other components of change started to become obvious, for example, the poor professional awareness of senior officers and the lack of coordination between departments (later referred to in recommendation 20 of the Report).

In addition, the negative impact of the Inquiry on the Met's reputation grew exponentially throughout that summer with the revelations of error, omission and incompetence from witnesses at the Inquiry, many of them our own staff. It was clearly a crisis and other players joined with the response, notably my fellow Deputy Assistant Commissioner and friend John Grieve who was diverted from his counter-terrorism work in August to set up the Racial and Violent Crime Task Force (RVCTF) and the Diversity Strategy reporting to Assistant Commissioner Denis O'Connor, and Dr Jonathan Crego who had approached me with the offer to develop specific immersive learning exercises for serious crime investigation. Others, too numerous to mention, were in support and developing discrete projects such as the emergency response improvements, known in the medical arena as the 'golden hour'.

Phase 3A – starting the journey to become consciously competent

The two Assistant Commissioners joined forces to co-chair fortnightly early morning meetings with us and other key thinkers and doers. This 'top cover' provided not only strong leadership but also a mandate for executive action, appropriate governance and, most importantly, impetus for change because bureaucracy was kept to a minimum. This unprecedented arrangement provided a responsive, flexible and scalable reaction to the emerging findings from both phases of the Inquiry and positioned us well to be able to react to the institutional racism (IR) definition when it came and to demonstrate that we had been proactive.

I took huge personal learning from these meetings. They were invariably energised, creative and innovative while often personally stretching, challenging and sometimes grumpy. But it was a fine example of 'teamship' and mutual respect within an organisation in crisis as well as demonstrating selfless leadership as everyone present had vital components of change to deliver.

The products and developments from this surge of effort that were in place by January 1999, the month before the Inquiry reported, may be summarised as follows:

- Front-line response officers had been, and would continue to be, trained in the workplace with an interactive CD-ROM (the best technology of the day) designed by Jonathan Crego to enhance their skills in crime scene assessment and management – 'On Scene and Dealing'.

- A programme of Emergency Life Support (ELS) training for all first responders and their supervisors had been introduced.

- SIOs had been tested in a pilot programme and would continue thereafter in groups of 15 to spend a week immersed in a homicide investigation simulated by HYDRA (again designed and built by Crego's team – see Chapter 7).

- Senior officers (ACPO level) would continue the existing practice of training with Borough Commanders and SIOs in a joint three-day exercise known as the Strategic Management of Critical Incidents (SMoCIT). It included independent scrutiny (from a 'Diamond Group' of senior and outside people), engagement with the professional media, involvement with a bereaved family (in role play) and being held to account for decisions at a public inquiry (again in role play).

- Where possible exhibits would be handled to the standard used in counter terrorism and a specification agreed for building/converting improved exhibit areas.

- The murder response had changed from an approach with core specialists (SIOs, office managers and exhibits officers) supplemented by available but more generalist Borough detectives (as was done with the Stephen Lawrence investigation) to a model of permanent staff dedicated full time to homicide investigation (an overall increase of in excess of 650 staff during 1999).

- Policy files had been replaced by decision logs where all important choices, including any like the controversial decision in the Stephen Lawrence case *not* to arrest suspects, would be recorded with the rationale clearly laid out for accountability and review.

- A project had been commissioned to replace HOLMES (Home Office Large Major Enquiry System), the system that had been so poorly utilised in the Stephen Lawrence case, with HOLMES 2 as soon as practicable (a £5m project).

- Family liaison had been identified as a key area for improvement and, with the initiative and drive of a junior but nevertheless experienced staff member, Detective Constable Ron Cuthbertson, had developed into proper training for the role based on best practice 'borrowed with pride' from Avon and Somerset Constabulary.

- Work had started on a proper system of murder review.

- Met policy on homicide investigation was on the drawing board awaiting the Inquiry findings and in any event to place the Met in line with ACPO policy on Major Incident Room Systems, Procedures and Administration (MIRSAP).

- The intelligence system had already been changed from barely accessible paper records to the interactive electronic system known as CRIMINT.

- The Racial and Violent Crime Task Force (RVCTF) had commenced its work, Community Safety Units (CSU) had been set up to tackle hate crime in all London Boroughs, and the 'Protect and Respect' diversity strategy embracing much of the above had been published.

Of course, very little of this work counted so far as the media and public were concerned – nor should it have – given that on 24 February 1999, the day the Stephen Lawrence Inquiry Report was published, then Commissioner Sir Paul Condon, in his first briefing to senior staff, was obliged to set out the following list on one of his presentation slides, headed 'Incompetence':

- First aid
- Initial response
- Family liaison
- Senior Investigating Officers
- Surveillance
- Incident room
- Identification parades
- Searches
- Informants
- Policy and records
- Murder review

Notwithstanding the combined and intense effort to implement changes and improve processes ahead of the findings, we had to accept public censure and seek to build later on that foundation. Indeed this censure was a helpful driver for change within the organisation, keeping us focused on improvement.

But even by February 1999 (almost six years on from Stephen's murder) my research led me to the opinion that, beyond the Stephen Lawrence case, the general state of murder investigation in the Met was disturbingly dire and overall under-resourced and unprofessional. This was not about individuals and their best endeavours. Indeed the majority of cases were carried out with great dedication and diligence. Nor was it about the results they achieved in spite of the poor support and infrastructure. This was unquestionably a systemic *organisational* shortcoming. Therefore, it was no surprise to read recommendation 4 of the Lawrence Inquiry:

> That in order to restore public confidence, an inspection by HMIC of the Metropolitan Police Service be conducted forthwith. The inspection to include examination of current undetected HOLMES based murders and Reviews into such cases. (Macpherson 1999: rec. 4)

Phase 3B – becoming more consciously competent by addressing the wider picture of unconscious incompetence

In my new role as Director of Crime Management, between June and August 1999, I was the natural host to the inspection team under David Blakey, the HMIC with responsibility for crime. The team comprised experienced detectives from many forces around the country and I am sad to admit this experience to be one of the low points of my service, simply because I knew by then that the 'Scotland Yard' reputation for professional investigation was in tatters, Stephen's case having been linked in the public consciousness with the Michael Menson and Ricky Reel 'failed' investigations that, by now, had been assigned to John Grieve's team for remedial action. The restoration of public confidence would be a desperately hard hill to climb even without the wider professional perspectives of respected colleagues from around the country.

And so it transpired in part two of the HMIC 2000 Report *Winning the Race: Embracing Diversity*, published in January 2000. While acknowledging our earlier attempts to properly resource the Met's new approach to homicide investigation, our innovative training at three levels, our drive on effective family liaison and the adoption by the Met of national policy, the overall tone of the HMIC report on the state of homicide investigation in 1999 can only be described as condemnatory.

Nonetheless, we believed our action plan to be sound and, taking account of the Inquiry findings, published Special Notice 6/99 in April which set out for the first time our clear policy on a number of essential processes for a murder or unexplained death:

1 Crime scene logs
2 Incident management logs
3 Decision logs
4 Family liaison logs
5 Community concern assessments
6 Intelligence-led investigations
7 Arrest strategy
8 Search strategy
9 Interview strategy
10 Identification strategy
11 Self-inspection booklet
12 Review process

The HMIC team had also approved of the published vision for the programme of work on major crime which had been signed off by Sir Paul Condon and his Policy Board:

> To restore trust and confidence in MPS integrity and expertise by ensuring the organisation's response to murder is demonstrably 'world-class'. (HMIC 2000: para. 16.2)

Of the 12 HMIC recommendations, the following was influential in the next stage of my personal involvement:

> Her Majesty's Inspector recommends that the Metropolitan Police Service develops the role of its chief officers within murder investigations in accordance with ACPO guidelines. He further recommends that steps are taken to more clearly define chains of command and accountability for murder investigation. (HMIC 2000: rec. 10)

Accordingly, when in February 2000 Sir John Stevens was appointed Commissioner, he immediately announced the termination of the Area structure (which had in any event been limping along with a temporary joining up of Areas to make three pending the introduction of the Greater London Assembly (GLA) and Metropolitan Police Authority (MPA)). This meant that all homicide investigation, as well as the resources assigned to serious crime not dealt with on a Borough or in connection with counter-terrorism, would be brigaded under one command within Specialist Operations (SO) reporting to Assistant Commissioner David Veness.

Not only was I immensely honoured to be asked to lead the new command of some three thousand staff, almost one third of whom were assigned to homicide investigation, I was both humbled by this new responsibility as 'head of profession' and also excited by the prospect of being able to make a difference to the performance of the Met, in particular to the quality and integrity of service provided. I have believed for some time that the greatest privilege in law enforcement is to investigate the death of a fellow human being, and I felt similarly privileged to be appointed the leader for the officers and staff dedicated to that policing function.

Research into why this (at that time exclusively a police) function is appropriately described as a privilege had been supported by the (relatively new then) Human Rights Act 1998 which came into force in 2000. Article 2 of the European Convention on Human Rights (ECHR), the right to life, sets out that the state must ensure that investigations into the unexplained death of its citizens must be thorough and competent/comprehensive. Advice sought from the Crown Prosecution Service suggested the following criteria should apply:

- The SIO must have appropriate skills and knowledge;
- He or she must be competent to investigate the circumstances and professional in approach;
- There must be an appropriate level of supervision;
- Thorough and complete records must accompany each stage of the investigation;
- There must be an element of review.

Many of the comments in the HMIC inspection of homicide investigation in the Met amount to disbelief that the Met, with its vast resources, appeared so miserly with their allocation to such an important policing function compared with other forces. Examination of case law helped to clarify the legal position on this issue, as in:

> The shortage of resources, illness and so on, are not acceptable reasons to fail to comply with legal requirements. (*R v. Manchester Crown Court* ex parte *McDonald*)

Having been appointed to command what became the Serious Crime Group (SCG) (and been almost immediately ascribed the media sobriquet 'Murder One'), I clearly had a significant opportunity to inculcate a 'profession' within what had been viewed as more of a 'craft'. Given the poor coverage the Met had received in the media during and after the Inquiry, the families and communities of the bereaved, as well as the wider public, had somehow to acquire confidence in the competence of those charged with the investigation into the death of their loved ones and community members. The only way to secure that confidence was through the experience of their contact with the Met and, notwithstanding the trauma of their respective tragedies, it had to be the professional service each of us would expect and demand.

Part of the problem in providing a properly resourced and professional service had been a structural one. Under a devolved Area model, not only had five slightly different systems evolved, workloads were disparate to the point that the North West Area in particular was at breaking point. So seizing the opportunity arising from the dismantling of the Area structure, we analysed the previous three years of homicide data and came up with a subdivision of three commands for murder investigation in the Met which would allow greater resilience within a common standard. In time we also developed a small specialist capability for homicide investigation in the newly formed Child Abuse Investigation command.

In addition, while the overall murder rate in London is very low compared with other major world cities, the analysis showed a disproportional number of homicides within the African-Caribbean community compared with the wider population – at a ratio of about 2.5 times the number of victims to those of White European origin. Racially motivated cases like Stephen's are relatively rare (seven for all ethnic origins recorded in 2000/01), but the picture that emerged was of perpetrators and victims both coming from the African-Caribbean community (50 out of 189 London homicides reported in 2000/01 rising to 77 out of 202 in 2001/02), and a high number associated with firearms, with detection rates of 76 per cent and 73 per cent respectively.

Operation Trident had been in place for some time and was refreshed by Denis O'Connor with its mission to work with the community (and this was the initiative that later informed the wider inception of Independent Advisory Groups under the Diversity Strategy), gather and analyse intelligence, and be more proactive in preventing homicide, particularly those involving guns. Building on the small team of 14 that had been allocated, we initially were able to assign about 60 officers for intelligence and proactive operations. However, we soon embraced homicide investigations as well, and then all the investigations into shootings, to provide an all-encompassing response to the black community. This involved in excess of 300 officers, with the aim of both reducing the incidence of such violence and improving investigative results.

The point of describing the development of Operation Trident by acquiring resources from elsewhere is to illustrate a case study of a truly unique innovation and partnership between police and a specific community, working together towards a common goal. I believe the enhancement of this partnership to have received a positive boost directly attributable as a legacy from the tragedy of Stephen's death and the Met's being held publicly to account for its failings.

Thus, initially brought together on 1 March 2000, the homicide components of the SCG (later in June 2003 to be separated from SO to form the Specialist Crime Directorate under the then Assistant Commissioner Tarique Ghaffur) moved steadily forward. In the following five years while it remained my personal responsibility, and in the three years since, the Met has become unconsciously competent on a number of fronts.

One early benchmark of progress relates to the investigation into the murder of Damilola Taylor, aged 10, on 27 November 2000 in Southwark. While this was not a racist crime, it nonetheless was of massive public interest given Damilola's age and that he was fatally stabbed with a broken bottle by youths not much older than him. It took six years and three trials to achieve a conviction for manslaughter against two brothers. The first trial which failed provoked a media 'blamestorm'. Consequently, the Commissioner invited a review by a distinguished and particularly well-qualified 'oversight panel' consisting of:

- Bishop John Sentamu of Birmingham, a Stephen Lawrence Inquiry panel member when Bishop of Stepney and now Archbishop of York;
- David Blakey, formerly the HMIC who conducted two inspections of MPS homicide pursuant of recommendation 4;
- Perry Nove, formerly Commissioner of City of London Police who as Deputy Assistant Commissioner had initiated the proactive second investigation into Stephen's death.

They published their review in December 2002 and, while they were unimpressed with the handling of the pre-trial work, they had this to say about the police response to that investigation:

The panel also believes that there are demonstrable differences between the police handling of the investigation of this case and that of Stephen Lawrence. In particular, the commitment and effort of those who responded to the incident and those involved in the investigation, the provision of early and sustained family liaison and the commitment and involvement of senior officers will enable the MPS and its community stakeholders to work towards developing higher levels of confidence and trust in the ability of the MPS to understand and respond to crimes of major concern. (Damilola Taylor Oversight Panel Report 2002: para. 6.5)

Phase 4 – achieving unconscious competence by professionalising the investigation of homicide and unexplained death

It is not suggested here that changes would not have occurred without the catalyst of the Stephen Lawrence Inquiry. But there is no question that, on the qualitative level, this extraordinary event has led to an unparallel scale of step change. Unconscious competence suggests that the Met's response to a serious crime, whether racist or not, would be intuitively consistent. What would that response comprise?

I am confident that any response officers and their supervisors arriving at the scene would be trained in Emergency Life Support (ELS) and crime scene management principles as well as understanding their responsibility to conduct a comprehensive search for witnesses and available intelligence regarding perpetrators. The definition of an incident that is 'critical' (i.e. potentially has a significant impact on the confidence of the victim, family or their community) would be understood by them and they would react accordingly. Homicide Assessment Teams that work outside of available hours to the murder investigation teams would attend in support of the local teams and ensure the 'golden hour' principles (in line with the paramedical model, and in addition to ELS, that the best opportunity for recovery of evidence, identification of witnesses and pursuit of offenders sits within the 'grip' by responders on the first 60 minutes) have been applied to the crime scene and any 'fast track' actions that are appropriate. They will remain to advise and brief the 'on call' senior homicide detective who will make the assessment of further action.

A crime scene management log would be opened together with an incident management log to ensure all first steps and supplementary actions are properly recorded and all evidence recovered by dedicated and especially trained forensic teams and handled to the best possible evidential standards within a sterile environment.

A trained and accredited SIO with the major inquiry team would be mobilised and a HOLMES account opened within a purpose-built MIR (major incident room). Family liaison officers would act primarily as investigators for the SIO but also to sensitively, and in line with recommendations 23–28 of the Lawrence Inquiry, meet the needs of the family, a role best described as 'compassionate professional'. Support in turn to FLOs in their demanding role would be available at the local level by trained Family Liaison Coordinators together with expert advice at the strategic level from Family Liaison Advisors.

A Community Concern Assessment would be completed jointly by the SIO and Borough Commander. When appropriate, an independent advisor invited from either, or sometimes both, the local and strategic level would work with the investigation. When appropriate, a staff member who has registered 'life skills' on the Community and Cultural Resources (CCRU) database, will be assigned to work with the particular needs of the family or community concerned.

The investigation would be recorded and auditable on HOLMES 2 which has in excess of 500 networked 'seats' across the Metropolis, which means that all back office functions are accessible from any part of the MPS homicide command and scalable to any investigation imaginable. Every MIR operates consistently with ACPO MIRSAP and all staff have appropriate training and accredited skills. Every SIO assigned a homicide, unexplained death or other critical incident investigation will have achieved national PIP (Professionalising Investigation Programme) level 3 accreditation. Decisions that may impact on the progress of the investigation would be properly recorded in a decision log.

From the training perspective, every SIO, Borough Commander and ACPO officer in London will have attended SMoCIT training (over 70 exercises run nationally since 1999). In addition the Met's Leadership Academy provided Values-Based Leadership, leading people skills and role-based skills (including critical incidents) to Team Leaders (sergeants and inspectors). The Crime Academy has made available training across the board through nine Faculties:

- Criminal justice (interviewing + Achieving Best Evidence);
- Forensic science;
- HOLMES;
- Intelligence (offender, crime and geographic analysis);
- Investigative (trainee detective through to detective inspector);
- Senior Investigating Officer (nationally accredited programme);
- Specialist (risk and public protection, Community Safety Units, family liaison, exhibit handling);
- Covert policing (surveillance, informant handling);
- Counter-terrorism and Disaster Victim Identification.

Because of the 'flawed review' aspect identified by both Kent Police and the Stephen Lawrence Inquiry, every investigation is assessed by an accredited detective superintendent within 48 hours, is subject to a seven-day supervisory review and then a 28-day MADS progress review (the audit trail for all messages, actions, documents and statements is checked to ensure nothing important to the progress of the investigation has been missed) by an independent review officer. No investigation will be closed without a six-month full review prior to closure. Any critical incident or 'category A' (grave crimes of significant public interest such as Stephen Lawrence and Damilola Taylor) investigation may be subject to a full review at any time commissioned by the Gold Commander who will lead, direct and coordinate the service response. All London homicides where defendants have been charged are handled by a Joint Trials Unit (with the police and CPS working together) adjacent to the Central Criminal Court.

It is perhaps worth mentioning here the subculture change that I observed with the introduction of the Met's Murder Review Group (MRG) in 2000. Initially the 'imposition' of a review was seen by SIOs as just that, and somehow a personal challenge to their integrity and professionalism. Within five years, I noticed that SIOs faced with complex investigations where the perpetrator(s) are unidentified would be calling for an early review in order to ensure that nothing had been missed. This shift on the vulnerability continuum, from feeling suspicious at the need for review to seeking quality assurance, equates to a 'second opinion' in the medical world, and a positive indicator towards improved professionalism and maturity.

Furthermore, in order to ensure learning is taken forward, all reviewing officers can make service-wide recommendations that address processes, systems and training needs, strategic review meetings are led between senior MPS and CPS officials and a NPIA practical guide to Critical Incident Management is available (initiated by John Grieve in 2000 and updated annually in the MPS then adopted nationally in 2007).

These are, of course, mostly measures of input and output. What difference may be detected in the high-level outcomes? Looking at the data for 2007/08 we see a reduction in London homicides to 156 (53 of African-Caribbean origin) and a detection rate of 88 per cent. It is strongly felt that this overall improvement in performance can be attributed to the improvements described and the Met's commitment to work for a safer London for all its citizens and communities.

Conclusions

The improvements in the past 10 years towards a more professional service are in my view significant, and the actual policing provided in London in 2008 would have been unrecognisable in 1993 or even 1999. I am confident that the fundamental approach by the Met to any serious incident today would be to seek to meet the needs of the family and the community affected by their trauma. While mistakes and omissions remain inevitable in any human interaction, I also believe that in today's prevailing culture they would be identified and openly acknowledged earlier, followed by swift remedial action and the timely offer of an apology. Moreover, the overall results with respect to serious crime have been improved to, and are sustained at, an impressive level that could indeed be said to be 'world-class'. I am also confident that these changes are now so 'unconsciously competent' that they have become embedded in the DNA of the Met.

However, some observers and commentators have pointed out that a focus on the professional competency aspect potentially avoids or denies the possibility, even probability, that institutional racism remains, whether visible or detectable in processes, attitudes or behaviour. It has been reported that some colleagues remain in denial that IR ever contributed to the failings of the investigation into Stephen's death (Foster 2008). Such views must be respected and embraced if we are to avoid complacency or a sense of 'job done' or to forget that the central challenge from the IR definition is to avoid disadvantage to minority ethnic people. My story of the changes in the past 10 years has primarily addressed the processes surrounding murder and critical incident investigation, but what of attitudes and behaviour?

I share the view with many others that attitudinal change follows required behavioural change. So, for example, seat-belt law is now virtually self-enforced in this country because of widespread belief in its merit, but in its early years there was not universal 'buy-in' and enforcement required significant police attention. Buy-in only occurs with a change of mind-set and motivation. This either happens with a light-bulb type shift (as in my own case when I heard what Mrs Lawrence had to say at the Inquest) or through encouragement and enforcement of a standard of behaviour.

Therefore, I would argue that addressing process change, as we have manifestly done since the Inquiry, has brought about individual and corporate behavioural change which, increasingly over time, will lead to inculcation of underpinning and permanent attitudinal change. The checks and balances now in place that challenge observed or detected attitudes and behaviour, which amount to discrimination through unwitting prejudice, ignorance, thoughtlessness and racist stereotyping include:

- extensive use of independent advisors both in training (senior leaders and for team leaders) and in the operational field;
- access to and involvement of BME staff in specific operations through the Community and Cultural Resources Unit;
- highly developed family liaison arrangements in line with recommendations 23 to 28;
- accreditation of SIOs to the national standard;
- extensive accountability and auditable record keeping and a robust system of review.

The conclusion of the Stephen Lawrence Inquiry referred to failed leadership and the second half of the IR definition specifically lays down a leadership challenge. I have described in my account some of the leadership issues I encountered and many of the leadership examples I observed on the way when directly responsible for some of the changes arising from the Stephen Lawrence Inquiry. The past three years have seen me continue my work in the Met as Director of Leadership Development that has also allowed me to continue with the post Stephen Lawrence agenda, for example by bringing the SMoCIT exercises to Borough senior leadership teams. The former Commissioner, Sir Ian Blair, initiated the cultural change programme

Together that seeks to improve the leadership capability and people skills of the Met based on our refreshed and revised values:

- We will be proud to deliver quality policing. There is no greater priority;
- We will build trust by listening and responding;
- We will respect and support one another and work as a team;
- We will learn from experience and find ways to be even better.

All the leadership programmes provided use the Metropolitan Police Values and Behaviours as a basis for discussion and personal review and the 'Leading Our People' skills modules (TeamMet) flow directly from the recommendations in the Metropolitan Police Authority's Morris Inquiry that examined internal human resource processes (Morris 2004). The setting up of a Leadership Academy which embraces the HYDRA immersive learning suite and provides values-based leadership training to all levels across the organisation is further evidence of the Met's commitment to provide and to constantly improve a fair and exemplary policing service to all London's citizens. Good leadership has had many descriptions and models but can be distilled as a behaviour, namely *doing the right thing*. The 10 years since the Stephen Lawrence Inquiry have, on the whole I believe, seen the Metropolitan Police striving to do so.

Chapter 6

The Stephen Lawrence Inquiry: from intelligence failure to intelligence legacy?

John Grieve

This chapter considers what was referred to in the Introduction to this volume as the *'intelligence legacy'* of the Stephen Lawrence Inquiry (SLI). It examines how alternative ways of dealing with intelligence in the policing context emerged in the wake of the SLI; in particular, how academics were brought in as analysts, mirroring the approaches to intelligence found in the submarine tracking room in both world wars (Beesly 1990, 2000). It considers the role of precursors to the National Intelligence Model (NIM) in police intelligence, including the Force Intelligence Development Steering Committee (see Grieve 2004: 30; Savage 2007: 115–116), Systems for Investigation and Detection (SID) (Grieve 2004: 31), Northern Ireland counter terrorist operations, and operations which predated al-Qaeda. I will then move on to look at subsequent developments and how the learning from the SLI was later applied in policing intelligence operations in respect of community impact assessments (CIA). This will include current intelligence operations against terrorism and the application of intelligence systems by the Independent Monitoring Commission (IMC) (Kerr 2008b: 31 and 2008a: 38), which used both covert and open source intelligence models drawing from academic research and thinking (Bowling 1998a and b; Travis 2001; Stanko 2008), and reflection on the interaction between statutory and street agencies as intelligence tools (Juett, Smith and Grieve 2008). I will offer comment on both intelligence failures identified in the SLI and subsequent intelligence successes, both at tactical and strategic levels. Essentially, the purpose of this chapter is to seek to apply concepts of intelligence and intelligence failure developed outside of the SLI to the lessons provided by, and the organisational response to, the SLI.

The Racial and Violent Crime Task Force (CO24) Action Plan: Operation Athena

I have already considered the background to the Racial and Violent Crime Task Force (RVCTF) in Chapter 4, and made the point that as well as senior management backing, ground floor 'champions' were needed to support the changes required to become the opposite of 'unwitting, ignorant, thoughtless and stereotyping' – that is, aware, knowledgeable, sensitive and understanding of diversity. Some of the problems identified subsequently as 'unwitting, ignorant, thoughtless and stereotyping' (SLI 1999: 20–35) had been recognised in advance of the SLI as well as the potential for intelligence systems:

> ... we believe that the most effective way to win back confidence is by protecting vulnerable communities ... this will be achieved by ... focussing on the reduction of violence. All divisions will use an *intelligence* system to build up a picture of the vulnerability of their various communities (Metropolitan Police 1998b: 2–3 – emphasis added)

This position was derived from a previous intelligence project (Grieve 2004: 21). The MPS Strategy – The Policing Plan for 1998/9 – included 'the development of performance monitoring on racial incidents and racial crime at a local level' (Metropolitan Police 1998c: 4). As noted in Chapter 4, the RVCTF (CO24) was created on 6 August 1998, and included in my terms of reference as senior officer, drafted in the first few hours, was 'To set and develop operating standards for investigation, the use of *intelligence* and victim care' (Metropolitan Police Miscellaneous documents for Stephen Lawrence Inquiry 1998).

It will be recalled from Chapter 4 that there were five objectives designed to support the Mission Statement of the new task force, which was 'To ensure that racially motivated and violent crime is recognised, investigated thoroughly to agreed quality standards and reviewed objectively to enable lessons to be learned'. It is objective 5, which concerns intelligence, in support of that mission that we are concerned with here: 'To develop an integrated intelligence model to improve our response to the prevention of racial and violent crime'. The task list to support this objective was to:

- create a strategic and tactical intelligence cell;
- propose intelligence initiatives for force-wide implementation;
- develop community intelligence;
- develop open-source intelligence;
- supply information on prevention and proactive operations.

(Metropolitan Police 1998a: 14)

The champions we needed to achieve these tasks identified themselves almost immediately; they were principally for the matters I am considering here the intelligence officers, but also those educated customers of intelligence, the investigators who were to staff the Community Safety Units which were being set up, those from the communities we policed who worked with us, communicators and those who were engaged in family or community liaison in any role, and all those who believed in reducing violence and protecting the vulnerable. This ran to many thousands of officers and police staff.

None of these tasks was new. What was new was a strategic *intelligence led* approach to racial and violent crime to support the application of resources to a tactical menu; in other words to encourage and assist officers to arrest those offenders as a priority. Although we had been looking at numerous models of intelligence for the SID steering group and implementation team, for example Sun Tzu and Sims 'Information Designed for Action' (Grieve 2004: 21 and 2008; Sims 1993), the intelligence officers we worked with had already been exposed to different kinds of thinking.

We had been particularly attracted to the role of analysts and academics attached to the U-boat tracking room of the Admiralty and the way their analysis had been converted in quick time by training of wartime crews in effective operational tactics (Beesly 1990 and 2000; Baker 1972 and 1999). It was a precedent to introduce academics into the heart of the police strategic and tactical cell. We were encouraged in this at an early stage of the task force's evolution by exposure to Ben Bowling's work on violent racism (Bowling 1998a and 1998b) which we classified as 'open source intelligence'. This thinking about the role of academics was not unproblematic and was obstructed by those who considered academics unsuitable for security clearances to work in and listen to police operational decision-making, particularly when the service was facing a barrage of criticisms. Yet this scenario was exactly what Beesly (1990 and 2000) had described as taking place during the Battle of the Atlantic – the one military campaign that Churchill said kept him awake and worried at night. If it was good enough for him, it was good enough for us.

Consequent to that thinking, the Operation Athena action plan objective 5 for an integrated intelligence model came, in time, to include all hate crime, including racist incidents, and the techniques developed were applied to other forms of crime. Amongst the tasks for that objective were:

- to create a strategic and tactical intelligence cell within the task force and close to the leadership (another important lesson from the Battle of the Atlantic (Beesly 1990 and 2000) – later my more operationally inclined colleagues tried to wrench the book from my hands!);

- to propose intelligence initiatives for force-wide implementation including training and a menu of intelligence-driven tactical options (what became known as tactical doctrine – another concept borrowed from the military);

- to develop community intelligence (an idea taken from anti-drugs strategies, and especially drug related violence which had become a specialism of Operation Trident);

- to develop the related concept of open-source intelligence and open supply of information on prevention and proactive operations (which became a three-monthly strategic digest with some practical tactical best practice). (Metropolitan Police 1998a: 14; *Police Review* 1998b: 17)

The Stephen Lawrence Inquiry and intelligence failures

During the course of the SLI, Michael Mansfield QC, a frequent critic of policing in general and in particular police 'intelligence' that may have contravened human rights, repeatedly pursued with a number of police officers during their evidence the adequacy or otherwise of their use of intelligence about the perpetrators of hate crime. During his closing speech to the Inquiry, he said:

> In summary, there plainly has to be a compendious and effective local intelligence gathering operation in existence that can be accessed quickly by officers at any time, day or night, especially when those officers may not be familiar with the locality. The information itself should be categorised in such a way that

it can be called up by reference to name, or description, or address, or offence, or modus operandi, or vehicle, or associates. Computerisation must clearly have made this possible for the future ... Where the offence occurs in the hours of darkness over a short space of time and the perpetrators disappear on foot into the locality, it then behoves investigating officers to act with speed and intelligence. Time is of the essence. (Stephen Lawrence Inquiry transcript, Michael Mansfield closing speech, page 11055)

There were at least 11 occasions when intelligence – in these cases intelligence failure – was considered in the SLI Report. A few examples will help illustrate this point. At paragraph 12.31: '... officers ... did nothing to extend at once and energetically ... the collection of intelligence and information which might have been used'. At paragraph 14.4 there is criticism of the failure of systems to record intelligence received in connection with the investigation. From paragraph 14.4 onwards and in Chapter 18 of the SLI report, the surveillance operation is questioned. In paragraph 19.36 is noted '... the failure to follow up intelligence' and as Harfield and Harfield (2008: 28) have noted, this was a classic example of the intelligence gap matrix categorised 'under the label "don't know what we do know"' (2008: 28). At paragraphs 35.11 to 35.13 the Inquiry questions the recording, retention and card indices of both local intelligence and specialist intelligence. I want to analyse that intelligence failure and consider why (although hugely important for police learning, tactics and training) this was not a specific recommendation of the public inquiry. To my mind intelligence was one of the most important keys in tackling the dilemma of institutional racism. Intelligence could potentially provide the knowledgeable, thoughtful, sensitive, specific response which the finding of institutional racism cried out for.

What kind of intelligence failure is in question here? Sheptycki offers a lexicon and framework for analysis of police intelligence pathologies (Sheptycki 2004 and Sissens 2008). Although written in relation to the National Intelligence Model (NIM), this framework is applicable to the world that the Inquiry was seeking to understand. Sheptycki describes the organisational problems of intelligence sharing in a multi-agency setting. One of the basic concerns of the SLI had been the failure of the police to understand or appreciate the context of multiple partners in the community when investigating violence; this framework can be usefully applied to the intelligence failures exposed by the SLI (see Table 6.1).

Table 6.1 The Sheptycki lexicon applied to the Stephen Lawrence Inquiry

Number	Sheptycki's lexicon	Stephen Lawrence Inquiry findings	Notes
1	Digital divide, the inability to search and communicate across different systems	Suspect information was held in a number of paper systems and databases across several investigations	SID (Systems for Investigation and Detection, see Grieve 2004) began repair process in 1993. RVCTF introduced new categories of search engines across several databases. NIM provides potential for ultimate response
2	Linkage blindness	Suspects were subjects in several investigations. Insufficient early notice taken of repetition of suspects' names (but in fairness see note 3 below)	RVCTF analysts from a variety of disciplines working in all data sets, new social science disciplines and analytic techniques
3	Noise – pertains to the value assigned to different sections or pieces of information to the exclusion of others	Failure either to act quickly enough or to assign intelligence resources, e.g. full surveillance	Compare spontaneous applause given to Mellish's second investigation at the SL public inquiry, which had made full use of resources (Cathcart 1998: 18 and Cathcart 1999: 356). But also compare Cathcart 1999: 210 who very fairly writes that Mellish had 'levels of [intelligence] support which [first inquiry] could only have dreamed of'

Table 6.1 continues overleaf

Table 6.1 continued

Number	Sheptycki's lexicon	Stephen Lawrence Inquiry findings	Notes
4	Intelligence overload, compulsive data demand	HOLMES 1 system set up after Byford Report into Yorkshire Ripper series of murders notorious for overloading of relatively straightforward inquiries	Solutions had already been designed in HOLMES 2
5	Non-reporting and non-recording	See below for the great increase in racial incidents reporting – a measure of improved confidence in the police and criminal justice system	Programme of work for Intelligence Cell Analytic System (ICAS) described below
6	Intelligence gaps particularly between different categories of criminal and their behaviour	Suspects and relatives were known to a number of investigating teams and agencies for a number of crimes including robbery, drugs, corruption as well as extreme racist violence	See above rows 1, 2 and 3
7	Duplication, data held by several agencies	See categories 3 and 5 above	See above rows 3 and 6
8	Institutional friction	SLI rec. 2 (iv) – monitoring trust and confidence – includes 'information exchange' and 'multi-agency cooperation'. Although not strictly within the framework Sheptycki is describing, 25 agencies in National Criminal Intelligence Service (NCIS), this category is relevant to other agencies	Although there had been earlier examples of good police practice e.g. NORIS (Bowling 1998a and b: 171) this was more broadly addressed by RVCTF working with academics and Council for Racial Equality (CRE), Racial Equality Councils (REC), Economic and Social Research Council (ESRC), representatives of street

		and partnerships working against racism, e.g. the failure to access information held by street agencies, for example Greenwich Action Committee Against Racial Attacks (GACARA), Racial Equality Councils (REC), or academics or to listen more broadly and learn from critics	agencies on Independent Advisory Group (IAG) to the RVCTF and later to the MPS as a whole. When we visited some of these street agencies (e.g. the Monitoring Group in West London) we found information about suspects which was the envy of some of our intelligence cells
9	Intelligence hoarding and information silos.	Information silos relevant; see 2, 6 and 8 above. Some racial incidents seen as minor	See rows 1, 2 and 8 above
10	Defensive data concentration	Focusing on themes to the exclusion of other concepts, i.e. the denial by some officers that this was a racist incident	Programme of activities, menu of options by RVCTF to raise the awareness of the pernicious, debilitating nature of all racist incidents; the removal of the adjective 'minor'; the growth of the local CSUs and their role in all hate crime
11	Occupational subcultures	Goes to heart of the finding of institutional racism.	RVCTF as a whole, though not at least two of its members, taken by surprise as much as anyone

151

Sheptycki goes on to look at the context in which the pathologies identified in his lexicon take place using the concept of the organisation as a 'thought world' where members or officers think along the same lines. A version of this 'thought world' is almost exactly what the public inquiry came to describe in Chapter 6, pages 20–35 as 'institutional racism'.

Another model of strategic intelligence failure can be derived from the seminal work by George and Bruce (2008). Table 6.2 uses this model which was largely but not exclusively derived from strategic analysis of failures of intelligence concerning Iraq weapons of mass destruction and the 9/11 attacks on New York. What I want to draw attention to here is my own intelligence failure to identify the arguably key strategic finding of the SLI, that of institutional racism in the form in which it was defined in the SLI, despite the presence of our intelligence cell next door to my own office and dissenting voices from our own 'thought world' which pointed to the possibility that institutional racism would indeed be the issue for the SLI.

I do not want this to be read as a self-indulgent *mea culpa*. Instead my desire is to outline the importance for the intelligence legacy of the SLI of the methodology and creative thinking that the intelligence team applied to the problems we sought to solve. The mere presence of any or all of these derived elements does not make of themselves an intelligence failure. Jack Davis (2008: 158) concludes that having 'well-credentialled practitioners of intelligence ... who have earned seats at the drafting table for assessments [is] a prerequisite for turning instances of estimative misjudgements into an intelligence failure'. In the case of our estimative misjudgements, we had a seat at the table, but were failing to acknowledge the likelihood of the strategic finding of institutional racism and its implications until it was leaked, the week before the Inquiry reported, just in the nick of time. It gave us some preparatory space but not much.

The presence of analysts with different disciplines, background and training, or police officers who have been given different tools, experiences and training, including how to think objectively but creatively about a problem, makes a real difference to an intelligence-led strategy. This is particularly true when they have power or access to the leaders or commanders with power (Evans 2008, Sissens 2008 and Beesly 1990 and 2000), as the U-boat tracking model had shown us. Counterfactually, if these resources had been made available to the original Stephen Lawrence investigators things might have been very different. But then as Cathcart pointed out these assets were beyond their dreams (Cathcart 1998: 18). It was the role of analysts

Table 6.2 George and Bruce (2008): intelligence failures as applied to the Stephen Lawrence Inquiry

Number	Type of failure	Stephen Lawrence Inquiry and evidence	Comments – RVCTF response
1	Estimative misjudgement, relying upon matters which are substantively uncertain, have fallible assumptions and inconclusive evidence (Davis 2008: 158)	In balancing evidence given to SLI (e.g. SLI1999: 23/26 transcript) against our own research as essentially inconclusive, we misjudged the respective weight to be accorded, did not recognise uncertainty	Bowling (1998a and b) had formed this judgement despite our own failure to do so
2	Analysts co-ordinating judgements with subjective judgements of their managers and bureaucratic agendas (Davis 2008: 158)	See above	Some analysts and staff officers offered the opposite judgement i.e. we would be indicted for institutional racism. Other views prevailed
3	Failing to confront organisational norms whilst trying to manage uncertainty (Davis 2008: 158)	Not taking sufficient account of the uncertainty indicated by Holloway – failed to 'reflect on the implications of (police) ideas and notions (SLI 1999: 23)	Relates to cultural issues (see below)
4	Failure to understand political and cultural contexts (Lowenthal 2008:	Failure to appreciate the evidence of the Black Police Association '... institutional racism ... permeates the	We developed open-source intelligence, a library of academic references and supplied information

Table 6.2 continues overleaf

Table 6.2 continued

Number	Type of failure	Stephen Lawrence Inquiry and evidence	Comments – RVCTF response
	267). Related to seeking to assist those professionally mandated to advance a political agenda (Davis 2008: 158)	Metropolitan Police' (SLI 1999: 4). View supported by Dr Robin Oakley (SLI 1999: 26) and Bowling (Bowling 1998a and b; SLI 1999: 26 and 27)	on prevention and pro-active operations (which became the three monthly strategic digest with some practical tactical best practice). (Metropolitan Police 1998a: 14; *Police Review* 1998b: 17)
5	Failure of management to understand analysts' task of predictive warning (Smith 2008: 267)	See 1 above	We strengthened the analysts' role by introducing new tools and academic members of the cell (Travis 2001: 12–14)
6	Emphasis on short-term products (Lowenthal 2008: 267)	Failure to hear the resonance with Paul Boateng's remarks of five years previously (Metropolitan Police 1993: 12). See Chapter 4	We emphasised the long term by building a library of three-monthly strategic digests. (Metropolitan Police 1998a: 14; *Police Review* 1998b: 17)
7	Uncritical acceptance of established positions and assumptions (Lowenthal 2008: 267)	See 4 above	
8	Over reaction to previous errors (Lowenthal 2008: 267)	Previous errors and miscarriages of justice had been ascribed to incompetence	See also Butler (2004)

9	Absence of breadth of research – intellectual savings account that provides the capital that accumulates and builds knowledge (Kerr 2008a: 36)	See 6 above; Paul Boateng (Metropolitan Police 1993: 12), Holdaway, Oakley and Bowling (SLI 1999: 23/27)	We developed wide-ranging open-source intelligence-supplied information on prevention and proactive operations (Metropolitan Police 1998a: 14; *Police Review* 1998b: 17)
10	Absence of long-term assessments of major trends (Kerr 2008a: 36)		Three-monthly strategic digest included tactical best practice. (Metropolitan Police 1998a: 14; *Police Review* 1998b: 17)
11	Absence of competitive analysis or devil's advocate. (Kerr 2008a: 47)		See also Butler (2004) on dissent. The introduction of independent advisory groups, 'critical friends'. See Chapter 3

which was to be at the core of the subsequent work of the RVCTF and its employment of an intelligence cell.

The creation of the Intelligence Cell Analytic System (ICAS) cell

Analysts were to be at the heart of the intelligence operation of the RVCTF. However, it was to have other forces at its disposal: it was to have detectives, uniformed officers, police staff and academics as fully integrated members. Among the first 16 members of the RVCTF we recruited exhibits and evidence detectives, intelligence officers, murder and anti-terrorist specialists and community-conscious officers I had worked with in previous units within the MPS. Teamed with communication advisors they formed a powerful team, the engine of which was to be the Intelligence Cell Analytic System (ICAS). We were fortunate to be able to utilise initially the skills and experience of Joe Chowdrey and Barry MacDowell, who, together with Carol Bewick, Dave Field and Steve Kavanagh, created the means of integrating different kinds of information, from the literature, the media, existing police data banks, covert intelligence sources with open-source intelligence (*Police Review* 1998b: 17).

They were joined soon afterwards by many others whose contribution was invaluable but I want to pick out the late, greatly lamented Ron Woodland, who took the intelligence cell work into a new craft form, almost a renaissance of intelligence, in the form of Community Impact Assessments (CIA) (Bhatti 2008: 177) and who, with others, eventually applied the learning to the counter-terrorism arena. There are many things to note about the new-format CIA, not least that they pioneered the three parts Weekly Tactical Assessment, raw material from the community, and material from police and related systems; the content of these was compared so that their potential could be estimated. Thames Valley Police carried Ron's work forward with his '7Cs model' of where CIA fitted into the whole notion of critical incidents:

- Catalyst – possibly an event that may have a reaction;
- Confrontation – where one group may view things in a different way to another;
- Causality – looking at causes and effects;
- Community (Concerns and) Impact Assessment – the record of the police attempts to understand and tackle the issues;

- Crystallisation – where attitudes on any side or in any group, including statutory agencies become hardened;
- Communication – how information is shared about potential, impact or action;
- Critical incident – asking the questions: has this become critical: how will this have a significant impact on a victim, a family or a community? (Bhatti 2008: 173–176)

It is easy to see where this kind of thinking can help avoid the sorts of conclusions the SLI reached and why it was adopted by counter-terrorism analysts when considering how to respond to information. The intelligence products that came out of the cell were remarkable: advice based on best practice from across London on successful methods of prosecuting hate crime; forensic evidence potential; patterns of crime; arguments to deal with issues like data protection concerns, housing law, posters and sources of open and covert information. Probably the most useful product was the three-monthly strategic assessment – comparisons of racial incidents, arrests and prosecutions year on year but also on a monthly basis, broken down to local levels right across London and illustrated with best practice.

Alongside these movements the RVCTF was fortunate that the Economic and Social Research Council (ESRC) already in 1998 had an existing programme of research into all violence, under Professor Betsy Stanko at Royal Holloway, University of London. After attending an ESRC workshop in the autumn of 1998 we quickly realised the benefits of working together with this team and, increasingly closely, following the U-boat tracking model of operational research (what Stanko called 'playing battleships' – more like playing intelligence, U-boats, aircraft and corvettes!). Together we applied for and received funding from the Home Office Targeted Policing Initiative and set up the Understanding and Responding to Hate Crime project. Our work was based on the ESRC previous studies and what we had learned from the public inquiry (Travis 2001). Unlike other research partnerships we insisted that the postgraduates Stanko brought with her were identified as analysts and full members of the intelligence cell. Stanko introduced us to new methods of mining and analysing; she taught us to see the benefits of routinely gathered data using social science research information technology (itself a difficult concept to explain to those controlling the budget for the purchase of police software). This in turn led to ways of thinking about dangerous people, dangerous places and degrees of risk and methods of prevention and investigation (Travis 2001; Stanko 2008).

Supporting local intelligence cells and Community Safety Units

Both the learning about patterns from the data and learning about the way intelligence could support hate crime investigations at local stations were promulgated to all parts of London by the RVCTF. Officers from around the country also visited the intelligence cell. A poster campaign under the general title of 'Let's nick some racists' was circulated to local intelligence and investigating officers (*The Observer* 31 January 1999). One poster in particular illustrates what we were doing. Headed 'Intelligence for action ... make intelligence work for us. Think intelligence. Think evidence', it then went on to describe database tools, sources, community concerns and evidence. It was illustrated by two hate crime scene photographs, one from Germany in 1945 (courtesy of the Imperial War Museum) and one from London in 2001.

Every three months the local teams and their leaders were given an update on the local statistics and patterns, and the arrests and intelligence reports rolled in. Arrests tripled year on year to over 300 per month and authorised clear-ups (crimes solved) quadrupled to nearly 500 over the winter of 1998/1999. In the same period racial incidents reporting went up 300 per cent to over 2,000 per month but the real measure of the commitment of staff on the ground was the massive eightfold increase in intelligence reports submitted (Metropolitan Police Operation Athena three-monthly reports 1999).

Of course, the improved data capture and flagging of the reports played a significant role, but somebody has to see and hear something that is worthy of a report and report what they have seen or heard. This was exactly what Howard Vincent, head of an earlier reformed Criminal Investigation Department (CID), had wanted in 1881:

> Police work is impossible without information, and every good officer will do his best to obtain reliable intelligence, taking care at the same time not to be led away on false issues. Information must not be treasured up, until opportunity offers for action by the officer who obtains it, but should be promptly communicated to a superior, and those who are in a position to act upon it. Not only is this the proper course of action to take, in the public interest, but it will be certainly recognised, both by authorities and comrades, promoting esteem and confidence, which will bring their own reward. (Vincent 1881: 202)

That 'esteem and confidence' was exactly what we wanted 120 years later; intelligence working in the gutter as a 'practical cop thing to do'. Interestingly and reassuringly a number of very experienced ex-Robbery/Flying Squad officers concluded that they would not recommend anyone for service in their former branch until they had served in their local Community Safety Unit. One reason was that they would be exposed very clearly to the sensitive nature of their job; another that they would work at the nexus of operations and intelligence both tactical and strategic.

The nexus of strategic and operational intelligence in respect of specific cases

Strategic intelligence, the wider views of the context of hate crimes as an overview to inform our thinking, helped us when we came to arrest the killers of Michael Menson and gave evidence at the inquests of the MacGowan cousins who died in West Mercia in tragic circumstances, causing considerable family and community distress, and Ricky Reel (see Chapter 3). We were handed responsibility for the Stephen Lawrence murder investigation on 28 January 1999 but we had already had a mentoring and resourcing role for a number of years. In 1995 I had authorised the release of the technical kit to Bill Mellish's investigation into the murder of Stephen Lawrence, and I had recommended release of the product for use in the private prosecution in the Lawrence case. Other series of hate crimes were prosecuted both by us and by teams we advised.

The arrival of the National Intelligence Model

The introduction of the National Intelligence Model (NIM; NCIS 2000) was both a boost to the work of the intelligence cell and also a complication. The introduction of NIM Codes of Practice respecting confidentiality required considerable effort when dealing with our independent advisors and academic analysts in order to maintain their continued role. The NIM processes for monitoring, evaluation, promulgation and security increased the workload and slowed down development of the intelligence products which were themselves new and required changes in language and presentation. Similarly, the resource allocation procedure, tasking and coordination required rethinking.

Community concerns and impact as threat analysis

Much of the work on critical incident management (CIM) had grown out of our thinking from the Provisional IRA mainland campaigns and where the Royal Ulster Constabulary (RUC) had got to with risk and threat analysis. We had applied this thinking to precursors of al-Qaeda, where we had used 'Dream' or 'Diamond' teams as external advisors for wide thinking groups to aid decisions. Following the Copeland racist bombings in London in 2000, and then 9/11 in the USA, ICAS came into its own as a key strategic player through its strategic and tactical community intelligence contacts and analysis skills. The cell produced constantly updated, evolving community impact assessments. Kerr (2008a and 2008b) considers how this is applied by the Independent Monitoring Commission (IMC) in Ireland and more widely how the intelligence/security world is relevant to police intelligence thinking. Sadly, that was also to be the cause of ICAS's eventual demise as it was too valuable in a world of different priorities and, as often before, London surrendered its toolbox to national agendas, first to ACPO then to the Home Office. 'Impact' nearly became 'threat' analysis. Fortunately the elements I have described above (see also Bhatti 2008) were recognised as not just being part of the 'Pursue' elements of the UK Government's P strategy for counter-terrorism, but also part of the 'Prevent' elements (see HM Government 2008: 42 for example; the other elements are 'Prepare' and 'Protect'; see also Bhatti 2008: 181–182).

Conclusion

A number of elements came together to support the drive for intelligence-led policing of racist and eventually all forms of violence. Human rights and health and safety legislation contributed to the growth in importance of risk analysis and in turn to its specialised offspring, the Community Concerns/Impact analysis and assessment. The National Intelligence Model, whilst administratively a complex fit with the SID-inspired ICAS model, in turn became a cultural driver. Finally, intelligence has always been a much-prized specialism in policing and its practitioners are respected; this helped further the intelligence agenda.

What did we learn from this jolt to 'intelligent policing' which the Stephen Lawrence Inquiry gave? I would pick out three lessons in particular (others may choose different 'lesson learning'). First, that there is no substitute for an all-purpose intelligence cell, as opposed to one concerned only with covert investigation, for any kind of major inquiry, including responses to a public inquiry. Despite the desire to mainstream or centralise, specialist intelligence investigators, researchers, analysts and field intelligence investigators are priceless when they are juxtaposed close to the leadership.

Second, the more diverse the spread of analytic advice and activity, including academic intelligence, the less likely is the chance of missing a major strategic challenge, such as the finding of institutional racism; and the more likely is the possibility of uncovering tactical or operational creative intelligence solutions to seemingly intractable problems. The value of a tactical doctrine, the menu of operational opportunities prepared by such a team, is enormous. Third, intelligence can be community friendly and have a positive effect on the trust and confidence in which the police are held.

Chapter 7

A story of Hydra,[1] public inquiries and Stephen Lawrence

Jonathan Crego

I first met John Grieve in 1990. He was assigned the role of Commander (Training), and I was fresh into the world of policing, having come from teaching in further education. His first words to me went something like this: 'I have no idea about why you are here. You know little about policing, I know little about training. Go and find out what you should be doing, and when you know come and tell me.' This was to be the start of an enduring relationship.

Those early few months in the Metropolitan Police Service were magical. I did wonderful things, rode in the back of police cars, and travelled down the Thames with the river police. I watched prisoners being processed in custody suites, and observed police officers working inside football stadia. The whole experience was one eye-opening moment after another. Frankly, it was hugely exciting and the officers who gave me an insight to their world were highly committed, professional and intensely proud of what they did.

I met John Grieve again and talked through my experiences and he asked me to look more closely at the police management of football events. He was concerned about the recommendations emanating from the Inquiry by The Rt Hon. Lord Justice Taylor into the Hillsborough Stadium Disaster[2] and their implication for police training. My focus was then decided and I met a most colourful character, Chief Superintendent Douglas Hopkins, who was policing football matches at Arsenal. Douglas taught me much about the mechanics of the match, police leadership, and the tensions that operated between the fans, the clubs and the police. He was fascinated by crowd behaviour and tried to explain the incongruous nature of the event. He explained that normal people started to behave very differently when they entered the stands at each end of the ground. He studied their routes to and from the ground, and showed me that the supporters were ritualistic. They would enter using the same turnstile and, in his words, 'step on the same bit of pavement', and he demonstrated that he could control 10,000 people by the placing of thin plastic police tape and that these screaming fans were unbelievably compliant to police. He was master of the circus, and his team understood him. On the very first match that I was with him, the police radio system failed due to a fault in the transmitter system. Douglas was unfazed, not even concerned by the fact that his local radios had a reduced range; he simply created a relay system. He posted officers at the end of each radio's range and they passed messages to the next transmittable stretch. The solution worked perfectly, the stadium was full and the officers completely on top of the problem. What was remarkable to me as a novice observer was the calm and slow-time nature of the solution. Douglas definitely ran a well-oiled machine. This, I was to discover later from Peter Sarner, a police chief from the United States, was the difference between a team and a group of strangers.

I realised that a way of training police officers was to recognise this notion of team. The team was everything and to look at the decision-making and leadership without dealing with the whole team was a reductionist approach doomed to failure. In short, if we're looking at complex, real-life events, teams should be the basic unit of analysis (Kozlowski et al. 1999).

There was some pioneering work at the Scottish Police College funded by the Department of Trade and Industry, examining the use of computer-controlled video disks, which simulated the football match. Douglas Hopkins and I visited and saw it running; it was unbelievably impressive. The world of computing was so primitive in those days, to see video running from inside and outside a football stadium and police commanders communicating with radios was fascinating. As soon as we got back to London, I met John Grieve again and asked him for £20,000 to buy the equipment. He found the money and then spoke some chilling words, the real meaning of which I was only to discover far later on. He said, 'At the next public inquiry, I want you to be gripping the rail and describing what you did to learn from the mistakes at Hillsborough.'

Stephen Lawrence was murdered in 1993 and in the years leading up to the public hearings in the Public Inquiry on 24 March 1998, the meaning of a public inquiry was brought to me in breathtaking realism. Since that comment John made about imagining it was me 'gripping the rail', I have witnessed the public inquiries relating to Gulf War Illness, Victoria Climbié, Harold Shipman and E-coli; even today, I am writing this chapter in the middle of the coroner's inquest into the death of Jean Charles de Menezes. All have had an impact on my own work and that of others as we endeavour, as a team, to learn the lessons and incorporate the recommendations they bring.

John Grieve often recalls a cold and frosty morning at the training college and me shouting through his door, 'If you pay for my PhD, I will be able to create a solution to immersive learning'. This actually happened. His response was simply, 'Bring me your professor and give me the plan'. That professor was James Powell, a professor of architectural technologies working at the University of Portsmouth. We met, James discussed the places the research could go, and John then negotiated on my behalf with the Assistant Commissioner for Personnel for the funds to be released. The sum was £5,000 and the Assistant Commissioner predicted that as soon as I finished, I would leave the organisation. He was wrong. I am still here and the 18 years have been unbelievably stimulating and utterly consuming.

Minerva was an evolution from the learning technologies I had developed in my work with college and university students. I had developed a portfolio of solutions working with challenging students and promising engineers. These solutions gave me a strong platform for the development of a team-based approach to simulation. Now I was to become obsessed with generating a simulation of a football event where police commanders could manage the incidents for real. I learned in the course of my research the terms 'environmental' and 'process fidelity'. My teacher here was a man called Ed Salas. I met Dr Salas at the Naval Air Warfare Centre (NAWC) in Florida where he was then working as Senior Research Psychologist and Branch Head. He pointed out to me three men sitting in a 'T' shape in the back of his office. They were looking at computer monitors strapped to the backs of office chairs with black tape. They had on headsets and were taking the roles of flight crew on a mission, two pilots and one navigator. The software on the monitors was the first version of Microsoft Flight Simulator, and the men were trying to find a place to land when their chosen airfield had been bombed. What I found amazing was that they were running the simulation in the middle of a busy office environment. The physical reality that was the office surrounding them did not intrude on their alternative world. They were flying, they were completely immersed in the problems, and their shirts were transparent with sweat. Ed explained to me that the environmental fidelity of the simulation was far less important than the process fidelity. The naval commanders believed that they were on a mission and that belief or suspension of disbelief was pivotal to the learning. I found myself at the Nirvana of simulation and training.

Prior to visiting Ed, I had been given a demonstration of the Army Tank Simulation System at the same base. Here I had been shown a room the size of a football pitch, with dozens of tank pods, simulating a tank regiment in the theatre of war. The room had impressed me. However, once I saw Ed's immersion, I understood that the tank simulator – however technologically impressive – was just a computer game. The fancy high environmental simulations failed to provide the sense of presence that was being provided by Ed's office chairs and sticky tape. When I returned to England, the search for presence in simulation became my holy grail and has driven my work since.

As my PhD research progressed, Minerva became a laboratory, where I could try out new ideas. My supervisor, Professor James Powell, and I argued like cat and dog. He wanted to control the variables in the experiments; I wanted to develop the simulations; and the football exercises grew more and more complex. The pod representing the control room received the focus of my attention. As many as six different conversations would be running at once: the radio, the video feeds, the conversations between the commanders, the calls to the loggists, and so on. It was here that tensions were high, the officers got angry with each other, slammed phones down, and threw pencils across the room. In one simulation, a press officer entered the room to help with the press lines. She was screamed at by the commander, who yelled, 'Sit down, missy, and when I need you, I will call you'. Later, during the debrief, she described this as the 'normal behaviour' she experienced operationally. I knew I had really reached immersive learning when one Chief Inspector was thrown out of the room, and told to leave the event.

Research has shown that one of the difficulties that emerges when communication is mediated by computer technology is that human interaction is not replicated as it exists in the real world (Baltes *et al.* 2002). Put another way, computer teams do not bond; real teams do. It has become a strength of Hydra that the syndicates who are placed together in a room and tasked with understanding and making decisions in relation to complex events work as real teams do, arguments and all. The behaviours towards the press officer were a useful insight into the behaviours and culture of the organisation at that time. The role of press officer, later to be renamed *communication advisor*, very much along the lines of firearms advisor, was to become a key component in the investigator's toolkit, especially associated with family and community engagement.

I was given accommodation to develop this system in the old police section house in Beak Street, London, which lay in the heart of Soho at the end of the famous Carnaby Street. This old Victorian accommodation was awful. I had the basement all to myself. Hanging from the ceiling were enormous soil pipes which carried the toilet waste from the whole building. These pipes were rusted, old and damp. I slung plastic sheets around them to stop this oozing waste from dripping on to the equipment. That building was to be my home for two years. I ran over 50 simulations with Police Football Commanders.

My original research looked at some 80 years of public inquiries and came to the conclusion that the recommendations were repeated time and time again. The inquiries would focus on:

1 training;
2 equipment;
3 policy;
4 inter-agency working arrangements;
5 communication;
6 new legal frameworks.

These recommendations were repeated in all of the inquiries I reviewed, raising serious questions concerning the extent to which 'lessons had been learned'. The inquiry into a security breach at Prince William's 21st birthday party, ordered by Home Secretary David Blunkett in June 2003, led by Frank Armstrong from City of London Police, had a specific recommendation (rec. 23) which simply read: 'review all the recommendations from previous inquiries and implement them'.

As I worked on in the Beak Street office, I built more sophistication in to the simulations. I started to read more and more of the recommendations from the public inquiry into the Hillsborough disaster, which culminated in publication of the Taylor Report (Taylor 1990).

Like all inquiries I was studying, it was scientific in approach, describing what actually happened, timelines of events, decisions made, and so on. Inquiries take time to gather information, to collate different views and investigate the many accounts of what happened. They are necessarily *post hoc* and, thus, have to describe the past and, as the English writer Leslie Poles Hartley (1895–1972)[3] said, 'The past is a foreign country; they do things differently there'. The present and the future, however, may turn out to be hugely different. The Taylor Report did not foresee the impact of Sky TV on the football game, or the increasing independence from the police of the football club for crowd and safety issues, and one of the unintended consequences of all-seating stadia was that the whole dynamics of the game, fan and ground would change. Taylor drew up new policy and procedures that changed the rules; for example, the 'stands' were abandoned to all seating stadia on the grounds of public safety and the impact on the potential for violence. By legislating that all grounds would need to have allocated tickets and that the placing of home and away fans would be managed by the football clubs, the intention was that the ground would be easier to police. What was not considered – because it was impossible to know at the time – was the impact satellite TV would have on the whole ethos of the game. Now fans from far distant places would be able to participate in the game via their TV sets. The additional cash injected into the game by the TV companies meant that the role of the police changed. It was now the responsibility of the club and its paid stewards to maintain safety inside the ground. The police were there as invited agents should any criminal matters arise, but the responsibility for safety now was not a police matter. The original problems designed into my original simulations became redundant.

I remember building into a Hydra exercise (Hydra is an immersive simulation system used both for research and for training practitioners in preparation for the real-life emergencies they will face as professionals) a problem whereby police had to decide whether or not to delay the kick-off for a match because of late-arriving supporters (a key component in the Hillsborough disaster). The decision was entirely a police matter in the old world. Suddenly the decision was not whether to delay but more about what persuasive skills the police commander needed to convince the football club officials to delay the match bearing in mind the revenue impact from the satellite companies. With the face of football crowd management moving from a criminal matter to one of safety and revenue, the context for police leadership was changing.

The whole context of policing communities was very much at the forefront of the police psyche when Stephen Lawrence was murdered. The Metropolitan Police Service was in real difficulty with its concept of policing diverse communities. Brixton had been a particularly difficult area to police because the community was of the belief that police action was disproportionate and gratuitous. I remember going to Brixton and watching a police 'stop' in the street. Immediately, the police officers were surrounded by an angry group and they required back-up just extricating themselves from an angry street altercation. In the encounter I watched, the peers of the arrested young man managed to drag him away from the arresting officers before the back-up van arrived, and on arrival the van was used much more to protect the officers on the street by adding to their numbers than to effect the arrest of the young black man.

With my experience of the development of senior leaders in football crowd management, it was a natural progression to put all that learning towards training solutions after Stephen Lawrence's murder. The situations, the circumstances, and the incidents were very different but many of the required skills transferred from the policing of football to the policing of diversity. I can say with absolute certainty that the following five things happened as a direct result of the trauma of Stephen's murder and the subsequent public inquiry:

1 The creation of the term 'critical incident';
2 The creation of a programme of learning called 'On-Scene-and-Dealing';
3 Hydra (SIO) Senior Investigating Officer Training;
4 Hydra Strategic Management of Critical Incidents (SMoCIT);
5 Hydra Operations and the National and International Research Programme.

The chronology of the murder of Stephen Lawrence and its subsequent inquiries, private prosecution, and Police Complaints Authority (PCA) investigations will be covered elsewhere in this book. My perspective, having lived through them, was that the Metropolitan Police Service was in 'meltdown'. I was invited to attend the morning Critical Incident meetings. This was a place for the Assistant Commissioners to meet and consider their responses to the Inquiry. The key decision-makers at these meetings were Assistant Commissioner Ian Johnston, Assistant Commissioner Denis O'Connor, Deputy Assistant Commissioner John Grieve, and Deputy Assistant Commissioner Bill Griffiths, among others.

The meetings were full of tension, extremely serious, and one left with a set of tasks that had to be completed. I presented to Denis O'Connor a set of 'solutions'. Indeed one would become a CD-ROM called 'On-Scene-and-Dealing' that would be sent to all front-line supervisors. The technology was in its infancy and even cutting the

CDs was problematic. The CD was an e-learning product that looked at the definition of 'critical incident', and the 'golden hour' of police activity, involving the search for witnesses, preserving the scene, and responding to family, victim and community issues. In its day it was at the edge of the achievable, there were no computers inside the organisation capable of playing it and so special computers were purchased and taken to police stations.

I look back fondly at that project. It was the 'killer application' that provided the business case for learning technologies. I ran a small unit called the Centre for Applied Learning Technologies (CALT). The success of the CD was huge and it was given freely to other police agencies across the country. The Centre for Applied Learning Technologies, with its innovative and dedicated staff, grew into the National Centre for Applied Technology (www.ncalt.com). I led this new unit as a collaboration between the MPS and National Police Training, now the National Policing Improvements Agency. It now delivers training to 187,000 police and police staff and recent statistics show 35,000 course completions through NCALT per month. Clearly another dividend, or legacy, from Stephen Lawrence.

Another Stephen Lawrence dividend, or legacy, was that the Minerva methodologies were to be applied to other areas of policing. The complex world of hostage negotiation and crisis management, or crimes in action, such as kidnap and armed sieges, were to be simulated within a Minerva exercise. Here the whole team could experience the interdependences of the incident. Using pods to represent the Forward Command Post, the Firearms Control Post, the Hostage Negotiation Cell, the Stronghold and Borough Headquarters, Minerva enabled complex exercises to be run where the entire incident team were immersed in the operation, *together*. It addressed the problems of silo thinking and accorded with the research evidence, which showed that cross-team training is the key method for enhancing team effectiveness (Marks *et al.* 2002). Now there could not be a reductionist view of the problems. Solutions generated by the hostage negotiators had a direct impact on the Forward Commander; advice to the Forward Commander from the Firearms Advisor had to be considered alongside advice from the Hostage Negotiator Coordinator; negotiations from the stronghold would now become an added complexity to the other officers: real complexity, real problems, real teams.

The second solution was an adaptation of Minerva into a new system that I called Hydra. This would be designed on Minerva principles and allow Senior Investigating Officers the opportunity to immerse themselves into a murder investigation and to live, in full colour, the emotions of the decision-making and feel the weight of their absolute accountability not only to the criminal investigation but also to the victims, their families and the communities. It was essential that these simulations had the highest level of content fidelity possible. I was able to generate an environment which had sufficient process fidelity that the aspiring Senior Investigating Officers found immersion inescapable. These simulations included deep analysis of the evolving investigation, strategic direction, interaction with the victims' family, and engagement of Family Liaison. The officers had to design, deliver and own the communication strategies with the media, and work alongside their communication advisors. The five-day event brought them in contact with role-plays with family, in front of press conferences, and under scrutiny from senior officers. I called the learning environment 'safe', and it was safe in the regard that the students were practising these skills within the safety of a training environment. For some, the environment was dangerous; for the first time they were not able to provide the textbook answers that their legal training had prepared them for. Here, within the Hydra event, they had to deal with the consequences (often unintended) of their decision-making.

Hydra took all the learning from Minerva but recognised that the strategic decisions made by the investigators needed to be examined. Minerva ran at the pace of the football match, whereas Hydra had to operate within the projected timescale of murder investigations, in many cases days, weeks and months.

I recognised the importance of the development of a naturalistic approach to studying and training decision-making. Known as naturalistic decision-making (NDM), this approach had recently emerged in the academic world. A group of loosely affiliated academics advocated that NDM should firmly reject the notion of building an evidence base from what happens in a sterile lab (Klein et al. 1993; Lipshitz et al. 2001). Both research and professional training needed the preservation of context in all its siren-sounding, alarm-flashing complexity if results were to be meaningful. I had to replicate, as far as possible, real life.

Instead of immersing an entire team, as in football, I had to design a system that would immerse the key decision maker and simulate his or her team, including analysts, family liaison officers, independent advisors and the media. This was challenging because the technology was in its infancy, the pressure to deliver was immense, and the potential for failure was enormous. To add to my anxiety, I was designing Minerva exercises in Sydney, Australia in preparation for the 2000 Olympic Games. I was, however, supported by some inspired people. We had incorporated research findings into the system to ensure that the exercises would cover all bases, educational as well as operational. For example, exercises regularly withhold information – not simply because that's how it works in the real world – but also because it helps to make officers' reasoning processes explicit (Hoffman 1987). These reasoning processes are likewise made explicit in plenary sessions which demand officers discuss or even draw the various aspects and different domains of knowledge they have been using (Hoffman et al. 1995). It all helps to embed learning.

At three minutes to midnight (GMT) on 31 December 1998 I was working in Sydney, putting together the early scenarios for the Games. My email sprang into life. It was from Sergeant Mick Crick, a video expert. It read, 'This is the last version of the witness statements I am sending this year'. It was so supportive to know that on New Year's Eve, we were all working together on the same problem half a world apart. I worked on the Olympics during the day and the Hydra system at night and the first exercise took place in London on 21 January 1999, one month before the Stephen Lawrence Inquiry reported, in the Driving School, Peel Centre, Hendon.

I suggested that we create a mobile version of the system so that we could enhance the Strategic Management of Critical Incidents (SMoCIT) exercise that had been developed by John Grieve for the most senior officers. This required a truck full of equipment and two days' construction on site.

The person who partnered with me for the SIO development was Bill Griffiths. He was responsible for all murder investigations in London. I met him in the early-morning Critical Incident Briefings but our paths really crossed at the SIO conference he ran to brief the SIOs of the outcomes of the Inquiry (see Chapter 5, this volume). I walked up to him and said, 'I think I can help'. He listened and from that moment we have been joined almost at the hip in the crusade to professionalise investigation and police leadership. Bill Griffiths has facilitated hundreds of Hydra exercises, from SMoCIT (fully explained in Chapter 5) to critical incident management in firearms and hostage negotiation. Bill insisted that the investigators generated a decision log to record their thinking; a major omission in the investigation of Stephen Lawrence's murder. The operational advantages speak for themselves. However, it also builds on academic findings from the naturalistic decision-making (NDM) experts who were advocating the keeping of such records (Omodei and Wearing 1994, 1995; Woods

1995). As those at the cutting edge of research were developing methods of recording the 'who did what and why' to gain insight into the nature of expertise, Bill was already implementing it.

I have watched him lead over 70 SMoCIT exercises and have walked round the car park with him in moments of utter despair during them, when the participants were having trouble working through the gruelling complexities we had laid down for them. There were so many such walks with John and Bill that started with despair and ended with excitement at how we could change the exercise to meet the delegates' needs, dynamically. I used to watch Bill shudder when either John or I said, 'Let's do it differently'. Bill had to be the front man and pull it off with the delegates.

The most moving SMoCIT exercise was when Neville Lawrence, Stephen's father, attended. He watched the deliberations, the immersion, the use of Hydra and the role-plays of a family playing out their anguish and their search for answers following the loss of their child. He touched my heart with his inner strength and humanity, and I could not stop myself from weeping during his closing remarks about the good that he saw in this approach to police training.

It is not the place to detail here the methodology of Hydra; that is well documented in other papers and books (see, for example, Eyre, Crego and Alison 2008; Alison *et al.* 2008). It is important to recognise, however, that without the tragic murder of Stephen Lawrence, it probably would not have been developed to the level of sophistication at which it now operates. It has continued to be refined since its inception and the more completely developed system offers the chance for relatively inexperienced officers to make decisions in a safe environment without the high-stakes consequences that the job entails outside the classroom. Equally importantly, it provides officers of vast individual and collective experience the opportunity to manage rare or even unique incidents. Many individuals could otherwise complete entire careers without the experiences we can offer and some incidents have not yet occurred on anybody's watch. The multiple attack sites in London on 7 July 2005 (mercifully) have happened only once, yet preparation for such events is nonetheless essential. We cannot afford to 'play catch up' afterwards.

It is worth describing the phenomenal complexity that police leaders operate within, the sophistication and emotional intelligence of their teams, and the relationships that exist with both internal and external communities, and policing partners. Since Stephen's murder, the concept of policing without engaging with communities and the wider policing partnerships of local authorities, housing trusts, social services, education and health trusts, would be madness (for a critique of this see Azah, Chapter 8 this volume). The question 'Why does policing seem so simple to outsiders looking in?' is pertinent here because it is so easy to look at the landscape in a mono-dimensional grey-scale representation of the realities of policing in the twenty-first century. If you look, really look, at what's going on in reality, the complexity is breathtaking. Join content fidelity with environmental fidelity and you are truly looking at the real world during training, including the horrific experiences of families. This is a massive legacy from Stephen Lawrence.

There are over 40 locations running a Hydra suite in the UK, Canada, Australia, USA, Ireland, including the Red Cross, the United Nations and now the Los Angeles Counter Terrorism Centre. The Metropolitan Police unit, now called Hydra Operations, lives in the Leadership Academy and is, in my opinion, filled with creative people who believe that immersion is everything as they create and run exercises dealing with scenarios from counter-terrorism to domestic violence, with a passion and love – a national and international legacy from Stephen Lawrence.

The collaborative research spans fire and rescue, policing, criminal justice, humanitarian organisations, medical and social care, all bound together and compelled by the licensing arrangements to share research and collectively build Hydra and Minerva exercises. Hydra users have a forum, which holds conferences and meets regularly, to make development, updating and refinement an ongoing process. More gratifying to know is that beyond this forum, many also informally share tips and suggestions for building scenarios. It makes for a healthy and genuine cross-fertilisation of ideas.

My original supervisor was from the University of Portsmouth and I have continued to work with the Institute of Criminal Justice Studies there. There is also an academic research centre at the University of Liverpool – the International Centre for Critical Incident Decision-making (www.incscid.org). My co-director at the centre is Professor Laurence Alison and we are surrounded by Research Associates and PhD studentships, and a number of Masters courses are run in Investigative Psychology using the methodology. The Centre's staff has a healthy collaborative relationship with their local Hydra team and are regular visitors to the nearby control room to observe simulation exercises. They reciprocally evaluate one another's contributions, with the University psychologists offering advice on the interaction between syndicates, and the facilitators share their vast expertise – as the academics term it – 'in the field'.

Some students undertake placements in the MPS at Hendon each year and the University has its own Hydra installation where students (many of whom are serving police officers) have the chance to design a mini scenario or engage in research. Having to include and plan for every eventuality necessitates a good deal of reflective learning and is a solid way to make explicit the many features and decision-making considerations entailed in an incident. The Hydra users and collaborators now include police forces, academic centres and span international borders. This clearly represents a significant research legacy from Stephen Lawrence.

A more distal legacy from the murder of Stephen Lawrence was the generation of a new debriefing methodology which would capture the learning from critical incidents from the heart of the team that had felt the 'crackle of the electricity' contained within them. Peter Hampson, then Chief Constable for West Mercia Constabulary, when talking about the Telford investigations,[4] said it was like receiving a 10,000 volt shock. He gave me permission to use this name for the debriefing methodologies I was developing. I used this to design the second generation of SMoCIT exercises. In essence, the approach allows teams to use technology to anonymously record what they perceive as significant, without the fear of career-limiting disclosures. It is an evolving methodology and I have now used it to debrief the Iraqi hostage negotiations team, working with the team attempting to gain the release of a British hostage, the multi agency management of major disaster, and the construction of counter-terrorism command centres around the UK. I carried out nine debriefs after the London bombings in July 2005 including family liaison, mortuaries and inter-agency working. The most imminent at the time of writing is the debrief of British agencies on their return from the Beijing Olympics in preparation for the 2012 Games in London. In all, there have now been over 175 operational debriefs. The data from these are analysed at the Centre at Liverpool University, used as raw data for the MSc programmes and, most importantly, feedback for organisational learning and the evidence for the creation of new Hydra exercises. A more complete explanation of the approach can be found in the book *Policing Critical Incidents: Leadership and Critical Incident Management*.[5]

The past ten years have been the most intellectually stimulating of my life. The work continues to help shape the landscape. I'm still here, and with humility, deeply proud of what we have achieved and privileged to work amongst the brave and caring professionals who keep communities safe.

Notes

1 The Hydra Immersive Learning System is a unique, high-fidelity learning environment that enables the monitoring of real-time leadership and decision-making in critical incidents (for example, terrorist attacks, murders, abductions). The system evolved from an original system called Minerva (Newland, Creed and Crego 1997) which was principally designed to support team-based decision-making in the management of football and other public order incidents (see Taylor 1990).

2 The Taylor Report is a document whose development was overseen by Lord Taylor of Gosforth, concerning the aftermath and causes of the Hillsborough disaster in 1989. An interim report was published in August 1989, and the final report was published in January 1990.

3 Hartley, Leslie Poles (L. P.) (1895–1972), writer, born near Peterborough. His early short stories, such as 'Night Fears' (1924), established his reputation as a master of the macabre. Later he turned to depicting psychological relationships, and made a new success with such novels as *The Shrimp and the Anemone* (1944), *The Boat* (1950), and *The Go-Between* (1953).

4 Harold McGowan and Jason McGowan were both found dead within six months of each other. Both deaths occurred within miles of each other in a town near Telford, in Shropshire. Neither family believed that they took their own lives. The head of Scotland Yard's Racial and Violent Crime Task Force, Deputy Assistant Commissioner John Grieve, was a special advisor to the second investigation as a result of the Home Secretary's approval of the steps being taken by the Met.

5 Alison, L. and Crego, J. (2008) *Policing Critical Incidents: Leadership and Critical Incident Management*. Cullompton: Willan Publishing.

Chapter 8

Independent advice, operational policing and the Stephen Lawrence Inquiry

John Azah

I have been employed as Director of Kingston Racial Equality Council (KREC) since March 1990. The main responsibility of KREC is to help victims of racist incidents and racial harassment by providing advice, counselling and support in dealing with these crimes. We campaign on behalf of victims' families locally, regionally and sometimes nationally together with other organisations if we feel there has been injustice based on the race or ethnicity of the victim. We also act as advocates for people facing racial discrimination either through employment or the delivery of services and especially if they are disadvantaged and cannot represent themselves.

One of the main agencies that we have worked with is the Metropolitan Police Service (MPS). The MPS agreed to refer all racist incidents taking place in Kingston within its jurisdiction to KREC as part of the protocol agreements of the Crime and Disorder Reduction Partnership, itself a requirement of the Crime and Disorder Act 1998. Over the years KREC has also developed an 'arm's length' but good working relationship with Kingston Police, especially the senior management, consisting of the Chief Superintendent and Superintendent. KREC are, however, fundamentally advocates for the victims of race hate crime and always vehemently defend the rights of these victims, most of the time against resistance from statutory agencies, particularly the police service.

As a service seen predominantly as a campaigning organisation and advocate for victims, we have tended to be at loggerheads with most statutory sector organisations. The police, however, have taken the brunt of most of our criticism for their non-appreciation of the issues of racism and lack of attention and care for the concerns of victims of racist incidents. As a local activist I was at the forefront of those who saw the MPS as the problem. I campaigned vigorously for the victims and their families. I also had the privilege of being able to contact and meet with senior police officers who could not refuse to meet with KREC or me. This was not a privilege enjoyed by most families who were victims or whose children had become victims.

In the mid 1990s Kingston experienced one of its worst periods when within two years, two people from black and minority ethnic (BME) backgrounds (one Indian and one Korean) were presumed murdered because of their race. I led the campaign from the KREC point of view and worked with families, organisations and individuals to seek information and urge the police and local authority to investigate and bring the perpetrators of these horrible racist crimes to justice.

I became involved in a number of campaigns involving the murders or deaths of people from BME communities in London and Surrey in the 1990s. These included those relating to Michael Menson, who complained about being set on fire by racists in north London but was initially not believed by the police and later died in hospital; Akofa Hodasi, who was found hanging from the branch of a tree in Surrey after racist abuse in a car incident; and Ricky Reel, an Asian university student who was found drowned in the River Thames seven days after he disappeared during a night out with three other friends in Kingston, and who had been subjected to a racist incident earlier in the evening.

These racist murders formed the backdrop to my involvement in the Stephen Lawrence campaign. As the Director of Kingston Racial Equality Council I was particularly astonished by the lack of urgency in the response from the MPS to the murders of these young black people and appalled by the resistance to investigate these racist crimes.

Within the Racial Equality Council movement we needed to work with families and communities and campaign with other organisations to ensure that the police investigated these murders appropriately. The Stephen Lawrence campaign was becoming the vehicle for mobilising communities wanting to draw attention to these murders that were, we believed, being ignored by the MPS and other police services. The major breakthrough came when the 1997 elections resulted in a new Labour Government who had promised Stephen Lawrence's parents, Doreen and Neville Lawrence, an inquiry into their son's murder if they came to power.

I was amazed at the response, particularly from diverse communities, when the Stephen Lawrence Inquiry arrived soon after the
new government took office. I attended a number of sittings of the
Inquiry and became frustrated and disappointed at the evidence of
so many police officers. Some claimed they did not know the rules
of arrest and I was appalled by the contempt shown by others. It
became abundantly clear that a large number of police officers who
gave evidence did not care much for a black person's life. Right in
front of us we were confirming the worrying views that the police
service was both institutionally racist, and that racism of the worst
kind also persisted within the service. As a community activist my
position hardened and I became increasingly negative towards this
blatant display of racist behaviour from serving police officers.

I was therefore both shocked and surprised when I was invited
by the then Chief Superintendent Jeff Brathwaite to join the Ricky
Reel Sub-Committee and to have oversight of the reinvestigation
into the death of Ricky Reel with a new Senior Investigating Officer,
Chief Inspector Sue Hill. I was subsequently asked to join the first
Independent Advisory Group (IAG), which the MPS was setting up to
pre-empt the recommendations from the Stephen Lawrence Inquiry,
in particular to address the loss of confidence from London's diverse
communities and to re-engage with these communities.

After my initial reluctance to be seen working with, or indeed
helping, the police, first I decided to find out for myself what the
police wanted from me, and secondly, I left myself the option of
leaving if I did not like what I was being asked to do. Professionally,
it was also pretty risky to be seen to be working too closely with
the police in those days. When I later asked why they invited me to
become an IAG member I was told that the MPS saw me as one of
its 'sternest critics'.

I joined the Ricky Reel Sub-Committee and was selected as its Chair
at its second meeting. More crucially I joined the IAG, the first of its
kind in the UK, in January 1999, and nominated Beverley Thompson
as its first Chair. The police had named the group the 'Lay Advisory
Group'. We changed the name from *Lay* to *Independent* because we saw
ourselves as a group of experts brought together to advise the MPS,
rather than lay individuals with no expertise. In those days we were
angry and vibrant. We needed and wanted answers and we asked hard
questions. DAC John Grieve acknowledged this by once requesting
that we 'make his eyes water' by asking difficult questions.

We were witnesses to police incompetence that just was not
acceptable. In the event we demanded the resignation of the then

Commissioner of Police, Sir Paul Condon. Unlike today there was no culture or precedent for Commissioners resigning because of the mistakes made by the service, and certainly not for racism, and not when it was demanded by BME communities.

The early days of the IAG were very difficult. Many police officers did not want to share information with us. Some refused outright to work with us. Others openly questioned, often in our presence, why it was that we were allowed into meetings and especially into investigations that were considered sensitive.

After a number of such uncalled for difficulties, and in particular following an incident when two Advisors who were sent to help give advice at the Paddington train crash were treated with contempt and disrespect, the IAG decided to withdraw its cooperation with the MPS until such time that there was sufficient evidence of respect for what the IAG was trying to do. After much debate both parties (the MPS and the IAG) decided to retreat to Bournemouth and spend a weekend trying to sort out their difficulties. This was the genesis of Critical Incident Training.

A history of Critical Incident Training

There were numerous internal and external critical incidents for the MPS before the IAG 'critical incident' in Bournemouth. The most significant of the *internal* incidents related to Gurpal Virdi, an Asian police sergeant who was accused of sending racist emails to his police colleagues. The most significant of the *external* critical incidents for the MPS was the case of Stephen Lawrence. Other cases mentioned earlier, which involved the murder of a black person, were similarly critical incidents for the MPS.

The Bournemouth event involved role-plays written by the IAG. Roles were reversed with police officers playing the roles of community activists and IAG members taking the roles of police officers. My most significant memory and learning from this event came when playing the role of a Borough Commander during a meeting with the community representatives and family members. I was asked my name by a solicitor for the family. I totally froze and forgot my name, entirely due to the pressure and stress I was feeling. All I could repeat was, 'My name is, my name is, my name is …' Another lasting memory from the role-play concerned one of the Vice-Chairs of the IAG who was acting as a family liaison officer (FLO). In the confusion they ordered that all the family members be taken next door and be sedated *'because they were too disorderly'*. A mutual understanding of the difficulties of each other's role had begun to emerge.

The police response to the Stephen Lawrence Inquiry recommendations

By the time of the Stephen Lawrence Inquiry, the MPS had created a lot of enemies, especially within the BME communities. Most police officers, rightly or wrongly, were seen as racist and the police service seen as institutionally racist, but it faced the 70 recommendations with a very positive attitude. The MPS pre-empted the Inquiry's recommendations by setting up the Racial and Violent Crime Task Force (RVCTF) and appointed as its first Director DAC John Grieve, an officer with vast experience and reputation, and effectively charged him with the responsibility of saving the reputation of the MPS. He commanded huge respect and was, in my experience, adopted by the BME communities as 'one of their own'. The Stephen Lawrence Inquiry Report was published on 24 February 1999. At the time the then Home Secretary Jack Straw described it as a 'watershed in the history of race relations in this country'.

Practical issues

In responding to recommendations 48–54 of the Inquiry, the MPS initiated Community and Race Relations training for all police officers to address both the ignorance and the lack of understanding that clearly existed in relation to race issues. The MPS also set up a process of Critical Incident Training, taking a lead from the IAG's model in Bournemouth, and enhanced its management through the setting up of Gold Groups and by inviting IAG members to give advice on the impact of critical incidents on communities.

The MPS also set up IAGs and trained FLOs to help deal with critical incidents. All police services within the UK, and indeed many internationally, have now adopted both processes. IAGs were deployed during the 7 July 2005 bombings in London and helped design the Community Impact Assessment (CIA) process. As noted elsewhere in this book, FLOs have now become an internationally recognised service, having been deployed to many parts of the world where critical incidents have occurred, including the US (9/11) and South Asia (the 2004 Tsunami).

More strategically, the MPS set up senior management training in critical incidents that uses role-play to simulate situations, enabling senior officers to immerse themselves in a safe training environment (see Crego, Chapter 7 this volume). These processes are designed to help the MPS deal with the charge of institutional racism and to help it understand the endemic issues of racism that the Stephen Lawrence Inquiry had proved existed within the MPS.

What else could have been done?

The immediate responses to the Stephen Lawrence Inquiry Report recommendations were quite strategic and designed to reassure communities and regain lost confidence. Morale amongst the rank and file police officers was very low (see Hall, Grieve and Savage, this volume), especially amongst those who did not take time to understand the definition, who resented the accusation of institutional racism and did not understand the operational impact it makes every day on the MPS as well as the communities it serves.

In addressing the issues of racism, the MPS should have sustained the momentum developed by the Lawrence Inquiry by taking further steps to ensure the MPS grew to look like the communities it served, and ensuring that the leadership included black and minority ethnic officers. It should also have continued the strategy of *mainstreaming* race and equality issues within its processes and operational policies. Instead, at some stage, it is my view that the MPS felt that perhaps it had 'done enough' to address the issue of race and somewhat relegated it to a background activity within a wider agenda of 'Diversity and Citizen Focus'.

Lastly, but more damaging, was the gradual but systematic withdrawal of the use of IAGs on Gold Groups, the continuing attempts to review the IAG process, and the giving of conflicting information to different IAGs, all of which, I would argue, served to undermine one of the most significant legacies of the Stephen Lawrence Inquiry. Indeed, one might even suggest that the distancing of the MPS from the IAGs represents a significant step backwards.

What are we doing wrong now?

The MPS pre-empted a number of the Inquiry recommendations and was therefore able to react quickly and, at least to some extent, adequately manage the fallout from the publication of the Lawrence Inquiry. It sustained that activity until it felt communities, especially

BME communities who had been directly affected by the murder and subsequent mishandling of the investigation of Stephen's murder, had been won over.

The MPS then gradually began changing the framework for dealing with race issues and began concentrating activity on developing 'Citizen Focus and Community Engagement'. Constant reminders from the IAG that they were risking reverting 'to type' and going back to their comfort zones of paying lip service to race, rather than to proper and appropriate engagement with what I will call 'racial minorities', were ignored. Organisations constantly have to evaluate their systems and processes. However, they need to ensure that the changes they implement are positive, and also that such changes will serve to move the strategy positively to the next level.

There have been a number of reviews and evaluations of the Racial and Violent Crime Task Force. It metamorphosed into the Diversity Directorate, and then into the Citizen Focus and Community Engagement Directorate. On the numerous occasions that these changes took place there was very little or no consultation. I personally felt these changes were designed to gradually eradicate the legacy of the achievements of the Racial and Violent Crime Task Force. They were also carried out to accommodate a demanding government in the guise of the Home Office which was becoming obsessed with Community Cohesion and Citizen Focus and wanted to move away from addressing racial equality issues and racism in particular. It felt as if collectively they wanted to exclude race and racism from their vocabulary.

In continuing to deal with Engagement, Cohesion and Citizen Focus and not addressing the real concerns people have the MPS have succeeded in causing confusion. But this lack of clarity means that the 'old' issues of complaints from the rank and file black and minority ethnic police officers are back, worse than before. This time also for the first time in the service's history an Assistant Commissioner and a Commander have made serious allegations of racial discrimination.

Putting aside the rights and wrongs of the cases themselves the MPS can be accused of complacency where an atmosphere continues in which BME officers feel at a disadvantage and compelled to go to employment tribunals and cause major disruptions either to be heard or to address their issues.

This phenomenon will continue to create problems for the service until it learns that it can never say that 'it has done race' and therefore will move on to other Diversity and Equality strands.

Black and minority ethnic people will continue to be murdered in numbers proportionately larger than in any other community. Without creating a hierarchy of equalities it will always be a challenge for all service providers who ignore adequate strategies and policies to manage the scourge of racism and deal with their own issues of institutional racism.

Did IAGs become too close to the police service?

I have been an IAG member for almost 10 years. During this period I have had the privilege of being exposed to some of the most challenging critical incidents within the MPS and other police services. These include the case of Ricky Reel; the Notting Hill Carnival murders; Helios (an internal Metropolitan Police discipline investigation); Damilola Taylor; David Copeland, who bombed Brixton, Soho and Brick Lane; the London bombings in July 2005; the shooting of Jean Charles de Menezes at Stockwell Underground station in 2005; and a variety of internal critical incidents when I sat on Diamond or Gold Groups. Throughout the period, except for a time at the very beginning when no one really knew what we were there for, I have always been treated with respect, dignity and professionalism. I was given information as appropriate and we worked to the popular DAC Grieve adage of 'Initiation not Validation'.

Over the years we made friends within the MPS. And it was sometimes easier to work with friends than people with whom you were at loggerheads all the time. In trying to achieve our objective we needed to understand policing, although perhaps not in the detail some of us wanted to. And there was always going to be a compromise between getting up close to the service to understand its culture and being compromised by its processes and bureaucracy. Some of us were successful in keeping the balance right by getting close enough yet continually reviewing what we did, and always wanting to find out if we continued to retain what I called 'the critical edge'.

With hindsight perhaps we could have retained a greater distance between the MPS and ourselves and remained incisive 'critical friends'. I guess the trade-off is a better understanding and an appreciation by IAG members of the difficulties faced on a daily basis by police officers.

What impact did the arrival of the MPA have?

The Metropolitan Police Authority (MPA) was set up (as I understand it) to reflect what was happening in the rest of the UK. In my view it saw itself as the Authority elected to scrutinise the MPS, and therefore initially saw groups such as the IAG either as competitors or 'unelected busybodies' who wanted to do the jobs that they were appointed to do.

It was difficult to put into context what the real responsibility of the MPA was when it was first set up. The MPS in my view found it difficult to be accountable to a set of individuals and politicians who they felt wanted to teach them their jobs and tell them what to do. The MPS has until this point been terribly independent of much of the political interference endured by other police services around the UK.

The IAG failed to gauge appropriately how important the MPA itself felt. Consequently, both organisations spent some time second-guessing each other's intentions. Ultimately relationships developed and respect grew between the MPA and the IAG. Examples of this included the IAG being invited to give evidence at the Morris Inquiry which was set up by the MPA to look at long-standing grievances by black and minority ethnic officers, and issues of retention and progression. The IAG also joined some of the MPA committees, including those relating to Equality and Diversity and Race Hate Crime. Latterly we have worked together to help resolve disagreements between individuals and the MPS and helped in negotiations involving long-standing employment cases.

Should there have been an IAG and MPA joint working committee?

Having worked successfully together on a number of initiatives the MPA and IAG could have better served the MPS if there had been much closer collaboration on strategy and approach to problem solving. There were times when the MPS would set processes in motion, for example a comprehensive review of IAG work, but imply that the review was advocated by the MPA. At other times there would be rumour that the MPA wanted to take over responsibility for overseeing the IAG. A lot of time would be spent finding out where these stories came from, damaging the trust that existed between agencies and individuals, only for the stories to turn out to be rumours spread by people who had a vested interest in creating mischief between all three organisations – MPA, MPS and IAG.

There is still time for the MPA and the IAG to come together and look at strategically working together either by setting up formal systems or informal arrangements which complement each other's expertise. This will only happen, however, if the IAG survives the present review that has already lasted two and a half years.

What are we doing today and where are we going?

The murder of Stephen Lawrence, and the Inquiry and the recommendations that followed, represent a watershed in race relations in the UK. These events should have served as a beacon for organisations, individuals and communities, and helped us all to address racism and its impact as if our very lives depended on it.

And yet, in my opinion, most organisations continue to pay lip-service to the recommendations for dealing with racist incidents and complaints. Others feel political correctness has gone mad and gone too far. There continue to be levels of dismissiveness and complacency within most sectors. It is as if we have learned very few lessons from Stephen's murder. We should be using the legacy of Stephen Lawrence that helped to amend and strengthen the Race Relations Act to prosecute people who break the law rather than wanting to appease people who do not accept the equity argument.

Positive outcomes

1 After the initial shock of dealing with low morale and the charge of institutional racism, the MPS engaged with the Stephen Lawrence Inquiry Report, accepted all 70 recommendations and set about working to implement all the ones that affected them.

2 The Racial and Violent Crime Task Force, led by DAC John Grieve, was established and community members were invited to become Independent Advisors and help the MPS reconnect with communities of London. The MPS set up 'roadshows' across London, talking to all communities and hearing the difficult messages. This was mature and credible.

3 The IAG process was used successfully to work with communities. This spread nationally with the MPS championing independent advice. All London boroughs were required to have their own IAGs and to a large extent this became part of the way policing was carried out in London, and to a lesser extent around the UK.

Negative outcomes

1 It took the police service a long time to have confidence in the skills of the people they had invited as advisors. There was no initial confidence even though that was what the advisory process was set up to address. Police officers had not been fully briefed about the work of advisors, the setting up of IAGs, and the intrusive nature of the advice.

2 BME people who faced persistent racism shared their experiences. This formed some of the basis for the robust advice given to the police service, although elements of the organisation were not entirely ready to take this advice. There was a feeling that these advisors did not know anything about policing and therefore could not give advice despite the fact that advisors were giving advice on *community issues* rather than on the *practicalities of policing*. Some of this position still persists even though some advisors have, through working with the police, now developed a very good understanding of policing policy, strategy and tactics.

3 The police service ignored all warning not to drop the Race Hate Crime priority, perhaps implying that 'it had done race' and was moving on to wider, and more diluted, 'Diversity Citizen Focus and Community Engagement'.

4 Recent cases, especially from BME police officers, seem to show that the reasons that brought the IAG and community representatives into the Met still persist. Even though the police nationally have changed many things and made a lot of progress, one might argue that racism persists in a more covert form where people have become more sophisticated in the way they use racism to exclude BME people and in the ways that institutions behave to keep members of particular groups from achieving the top jobs. My view is that institutional racism still persists in all organisations, but it is in a more subtle, refined and covert form.

What else should we be doing?

Rather than undoing the successes that have been derived from the Stephen Lawrence Inquiry recommendations we should be building on them. The Morris Inquiry recommended that IAGs should be adequately resourced and the membership reviewed to reflect London's populations, particularly in relation to newly arrived communities from Europe. The MPS on the other hand is reviewing the IAG with a view to setting up one 'pan-London' IAG with a limited membership to address all the complex Equality and Diversity issues in London.

We should also be listening to, and taking seriously, the views of communities whose voices are often *hard* to hear, or who might sometimes have views that we might not *want* to hear. The challenges of the London bombings in 2005, together with the generic threats of terrorism, mean that we need all communities to help the MPS defeat the terrorist. Specialist and Counter-Terrorism Commands, for example, could benefit from fully embracing the Independent Advisory Group process and in so doing take advantage of the intelligence available to them from within communities.

A note on institutional racism

There was a premise before the Inquiry that there were a number of definitions of institutional racism (56 is a number I have) and it was impossible to agree on a single definition that helped to move the debate forward. I was under the impression that Macpherson, having identified it, wrestled with the task of finding a working and acceptable definition of institutional racism.

The black and minority ethnic communities went through a period when their victimisation, including a number of deaths, seemed particularly acute. Suspects always seemed to be white, with death seemingly being caused in suspicious circumstances. The police, it seemed, showed very little concern and a lack of enthusiasm to pursue these suspects. They did not believe the relatives of the victims either. It felt to many as if there was almost a 'policy', possibly unwittingly in some cases, but most of the time the impression was that it was intentional, to deny BME people justice, particularly where the evidence in a case wasn't particularly strong.

Most BME people felt that their negative experiences, no matter how the police hierarchy sought to justify these, were due to the way the organisation's policies operated, and indeed how these policies were written, and also the way the organisations were set up. The charge of institutional racism against the MPS therefore came as little surprise to many.

Legacy issues

The Stephen Lawrence Inquiry was responsible for the amendment and strengthening of the Race Relations Act 1976 through the Race Relations (Amendment) Act 2000. The Commission for Racial Equality had tried on three or four previous occasions to review the Act and asked the government to amend it without success. The amended Act required public authorities to have general and specific duties and to have race equality schemes and to promote Racial Equality. It also made discrimination unlawful (see Hall, Grieve and Savage in the Introduction to this volume).

The Inquiry also obliged the Metropolitan Police Service to set up Independent Advisory Groups (IAG). All police services within the UK and Northern Ireland have since replicated this. The IAG process has also been studied by some overseas countries who have used them in the way they manage critical incidents. The IAG process was to address the recommendations of the Inquiry to deal with community confidence and engaging the BME communities in particular, whose confidence had largely been lost.

The Inquiry recommendations also motivated the MPS to set up training programmes to deal with race and community relations. Training relating to the management of critical incidents introduced community advisors on to training sessions for senior managers (see Crego, Chapter 7 this volume) and to sit on Diamond Groups and critique decisions and solutions proposed by police managers.

Other advisory groups (for example LGBT, Traveller/Gypsy, Young People, Disability, Sapphire (serious sexual offences investigations), Trident (investigation of particular categories of murder, many of them firearms or drugs related in the BME communities), Safeguarding Children, Training) have developed as a direct result of the first IAG dealing with race.

Family Liaison Officers (FLO) are also derived from the Inquiry. By engaging with the families of victims, FLOs have become some of the most important personnel in the police service. The FLO remains an investigator but acts as a conduit between the family and the police, both helping to exchange information (and sometimes intelligence) and retaining the families' confidence in the investigation.

Communities that would not have liaised with the police have developed working relationships and overcome some of the barriers that previously deterred them from working with the police.

What remains to be done?

A lot has been achieved by the MPS but a lot more remains to be done. Communities continue to distrust the police service, many just as much as they did 10 years ago. For example, the shooting of Jean Charles de Menezes, an innocent man who was shot dead on 22 July 2005 by police who erroneously believed that he was a suicide bomber, compounds some of this. There needs therefore to be more transparency and a lot more effort put into the opening up of a number of areas of policing. In turn this can help communities understand the complexities involved in some covert operations.

Since the Lawrence Inquiry, the MPS has also worked hard to recruit black and minority ethnic police officers and has been relatively successful at this. But very few of these BME officers have made noticeable progress compared with their white counterparts. The Management Board of the MPS has tended to consist of mainly white males. When this is challenged the organisation deflects attention from race by drawing attention to progress made by women, which, whilst important, unfortunately does not mean the same thing and has a different impact on communities.

IAGs should become an integral part of managing critical incidents. Over time the MPS has discretionally used independent advice on Gold Groups. This means the community voice is potentially absent once more when major community impact issues are being discussed and decisions are being made. The IAG process should be recommended to other criminal justice agencies and government departments who work with communities and want to consult with them. It harnesses expertise and develops trust and confidence. The latter, of course, reflects the ministerial priority advocated by the Lawrence Inquiry.

Part Three:
Lawrence – Widening the Agenda

Chapter 9

Police training and the impact of Lawrence

Phil Clements and John Jones

The publication of the Scarman Report (1981) proved to be the impetus for a number of changes in police training policy and practice. Nearly 10 years later the publication of the Stephen Lawrence Inquiry Report provided a further wake-up call to police training on a number of fronts. In this chapter we highlight a number of these which seem to have been significant. In some ways it is difficult to isolate changes in policing and practice in police training that may be regarded entirely as a legacy of the Stephen Lawrence Inquiry, for example the introduction of the Initial Police Learning and Development Programme, which devolved initial police training from the Central Police Training and Development Authority to more local authorities, can be seen as having been influenced by Lawrence but did not happen as a result of it. That said, the impact of Lawrence can be detected in a range of issues of policy and practice and it is these that are discussed below.

Evaluation and critique of community and race relations training

The developments in police community and race relations (CRR) training (also in some quarters referred to as diversity training) have been well documented by Rowe and Garland in Rowe (2007) and will not be repeated here. In this section we review some of the training recommendations through the lens of experience of being involved in the development and delivery of CRR training projects within the then National Police Training. The Stephen Lawrence Inquiry (Macpherson 1999) made a number of recommendations (48–54) in relation to police training in respect of racism awareness and valuing cultural diversity, and three recommendations (45–47) in relation to first aid training. Recommendations 48–54 are given below for reference and followed by a discussion of them.

48 That there should be an immediate review and revision of racism awareness training within Police Services to ensure:

   a that there exists a consistent strategy to deliver appropriate training within all Police Services, based upon the value of our cultural diversity;

   b that training courses are designed and delivered in order to develop the full understanding that good community relations are essential to good policing and that a racist officer is an incompetent officer.

49 That all police officers, including CID and civilian staff, should be trained in racism awareness and valuing cultural diversity.

50 That police training and practical experience in the field of racism awareness and valuing cultural diversity should regularly be conducted at local level. And that it should be recognised that local minority ethnic communities should be involved in such training and experience.

51 That consideration be given by Police Services to promoting joint training with members of other organisations or professions otherwise than on police premises.

52 That the Home Office together with Police Services should publish recognised standards of training aims and objectives in the field of racism awareness and valuing cultural diversity.

53 That there should be independent and regular monitoring of training within all Police Services to test both implementation and achievement of such training.

54 That consideration be given to a review of the provision of training in racism awareness and valuing cultural diversity in local Government and other agencies including other sections of the Criminal Justice system.

The recommendations led to a number of projects to deliver them, some of which were the responsibility of National Police Training (latterly the Central Police Training and Development Authority – Centrex), but a review of them reveals both strengths and weaknesses.

In terms of the strengths of the recommendations there was an emphasis on the need for a strategic approach that was balanced with the needs of local areas. A further strength lay in the recognition that the effectiveness of community and race relations training would be enhanced by involvement from local representatives of minority ethnic communities. In this way training would be much more of a partnership and it was hoped that the real lived experiences of black and minority ethnic people would have a powerful impact on the effectiveness of the training. Whilst this idea was not new (it had previously for example been tried at Metropolitan Police Training Centre at Hendon from the 1980s) it did represent a significant departure from the previously insular nature of police training generally. Community involvement in training at the national level was also bolstered from 2000 onwards in National Police Training at Bramshill with a panel of lay advisors representing a diverse range of religion, culture and ethnic background. This panel met on a regular basis and advised on matters ranging from strategy through policy to the delivery of training and training materials themselves. This CRR panel had a significant impact on training from the national perspective.

A further strength that lay in the recommendations overall was the way in which they moved community and race relations training firmly up the agenda and provided a strategic driver to engage with issues that had previously not taken so much prominence. The imperative to provide training in this area was taken up by all forces (although at different speeds) and virtually all police officers in the aftermath of Lawrence received either community and relations training or diversity training in the years that followed. Running in parallel with this was the development of National Occupational Standards, work that was first started by the Police Skills and Standards Organisation which was subsequently subsumed into Skills for Justice. These standards resulted from wide consultation and provided a benchmark against which training could be designed, delivered and subsequently evaluated in terms of its impact on police performance.

It is clear from the above that there was a significant impact on training in terms of legacy from the Lawrence Inquiry, arising from the training recommendations. By way of critique, however, it is important to note that the implementation of the recommendations was not unproblematic. The first problem lay in the self-evidently vague and open-ended way in which they were written. Two phrases, 'racism awareness' and 'valuing cultural diversity', illustrate the point. What is racism awareness? In most understandings of the term 'awareness' is about knowledge of something at a fairly peripheral level. It could be argued that most police officers were already 'aware' of racism, indeed some engaged directly in it so the question needs to be asked what value would be added by such an objective in the training of police officers? The phrase falls some way short of being explicit about what changes police officers were expected to achieve; to be aware of racism does not equate to behaving in a non-racist way. The second phrase, 'valuing cultural diversity', can also be seen to be problematic. In what sense can a person be 'trained' to value *anything*? Values (conceptually) are often conflated with beliefs and attitudes but in fact do have a distinct identity. Values are those things that we regard very highly and in some cases would go to extreme lengths to protect or affirm. But can we be trained to do so? In our view the answer is probably not. In the extreme interpretation, trying to train someone to value something could be seen as a process of brainwashing or at least coercion into taking a view that is not genuinely held. It was found in research by Clements (2000) that CRR trainers differed widely in their view of this. Some felt that they had both the authority and right to address people's values and try to change them. Others were much more reticent about making such claims.

A second problem was that some elements of the content of what would need to be delivered was either too non-specific or too poorly understood. Two examples of this illustrate the point. The first was the new definition of 'racial incident', which in the words of the Inquiry was to be, in terms of recommendation 12:

A racist incident is any incident which is perceived to be racist by the victim or any other person.

Whilst it seems clear that the thinking behind this new definition was essentially to take away the discretion of a police officer to decide what was a racist incident and what was not, the 'any other person' criterion left the definition open to question and in terms of training officers in it made the task considerably more difficult. Central to the Inquiry and its aftermath was, of course, the definition of institutional racism. The concept is not an easy one to understand, and in legacy terms has been the subject of considerable attention in the literature. Clearly any training such as that recommended by the Inquiry would need to include attention to the meaning of the definition but, given the lack of understanding that surrounds it, again the question was raised about how could this be 'trained' when so few people had a good grasp of what it actually meant? This lack of understanding of the definition even in the period after most CRR training had taken place was illustrated in research conducted by Foster, Newburn and Souhami (2005: ix).

> Much of the anger officers felt about the Lawrence Inquiry stemmed from use of the term 'institutional racism'. This was the single most powerful message that police officers received from the Inquiry. However, both survey data and observational fieldwork suggested that the term 'institutional racism' is not widely understood in the police service. Almost all front-line officers and some senior officers in the fieldwork sites thought that institutional racism signified a widespread problem of racist behaviour and attitudes among police staff. This misunderstanding was reflected in media coverage of the Inquiry and in broader public reactions. It is, therefore, not surprising that the term created widespread resentment and anger.

A third difficulty in the recommendations lay in the implicit assumption that training *per se* would be able to achieve the objective. The fundamental purpose of the exercise was to ensure that police officers would be able to identify, challenge and lay aside racist stereotypical assumptions in order to provide a policing service that was fair and equitable for all. The achievement of this would lie not in a superficial addressing of language and knowledge of cultural differences but a fundamental shift on the part of some officers of their world view. Too much was expected of training that was generally delivered in a two-day programme, often by police trainers who were signally unprepared for the task. Evidence of this came in the damning screening by the BBC of the 'undercover' documentary *The Secret Policeman* on 21 October 2003. In this documentary, appalling racist attitudes by some police recruits under training were exposed and the trainer who was filmed seemed to have scant understanding of the real issues, at one point being heard to say and write on the board 'here are some words you cannot say' without any explanation of why that was the case. This also illustrated another finding of the research by Foster *et al.* (2005: xi) that one of the main responses by the police seemed to be attention to the use of 'correct' language and the concomitant excision of what was regarded as racist language. Whilst they found that explicit racist language had been almost 'entirely excised from the police service' this seemed to be linked to the apprehension of 'increased scrutiny and a heightened awareness of potential disciplinary action' (*ibid*: xi).

In the above we have outlined some of the strengths and weaknesses of the training recommendations made by the Stephen Lawrence Inquiry. We turn now to one of the outcomes of recommendation 53, *viz* the scrutiny of the training delivery by Her Majesty's Inspectorate of Constabulary (HMIC). It needs to be noted that attention by HMIC to race and diversity issues is not the sole legacy of the Stephen Lawrence Inquiry. Attention was already being paid to the issues before the publication of the Inquiry Report in 1999, the stimulus for which was in part to do with the continuing legacy of Scarman. For example reports (among others) by HMIC (1997, 1999) *Winning the Race* and *Winning the Race Revisited* were published prior to or in the same year as the Stephen Lawrence Inquiry. *Winning the Race: Embracing Diversity* was published in 2000. A major inspection of police approaches to diversity was published in February 2003 in a report entitled *Diversity Matters* (HMIC 2003). The main focus of this report was on the way in which the police service had responded to the challenge of diversity in terms of training post the Stephen Lawrence Inquiry. The headline findings of HMIC were that the service had achieved a reasonable level of efficiency in delivery of training and meeting targets but was not 'totally effective in delivering organizational change' (p. 27). A number of areas were found to be detrimental, and in themselves contributed to the failure to be effective in delivering organisational change. These were summarised as (p. 28):

- Lack of clarity in the strategy;
- The learning requirement not being clearly articulated;
- Inconsistency in training delivery and evaluation;
- Lack of linkage between training outcomes and staff appraisal;
- Ineffective or inadequate line management had the effect of undermining the messages taken from the training;
- Race and diversity content not being fully integrated into other aspects of police training and development;
- Unsatisfactory selection, assessment, management and support for trainers;

- Training for police trainers was seen to be inadequate;
- Insufficient community involvement in all aspects of the training cycle.

Space does not permit detailed discussion of all these aspects but two of them stand out in terms of our experience of working in National Police Training at the time the report was compiled and published.

Firstly, it was clear at the time the decision was taken predominantly to use police trainers in the delivery of the Lawrence training recommendations that many of them were not or would not be up to the task. HMIC found that although there were 'pockets' of good practice many other trainers were at best not skilled enough and at worst not comfortable with delivering race and diversity training. That said, some of the trainers who were more committed to delivering a good quality of race and diversity training formed their own support network the Police Diversity Trainers Network (PDTN 2008) in 1999. From small beginnings, the network grew and still continues to provide a supportive framework for trainers working in the area of race and diversity.

Secondly, HMIC noted that race and diversity was not fully integrated into other aspects of police training and development. This in our experience was a particularly difficult area to manage in terms of training. A key area for debate was whether, given the specialist nature of race and diversity training, its delivery should be handed over to specialist trainers who had demonstrated the appropriate attitudes, values, beliefs and skills and were therefore much more able to achieve the desired training outcomes. The argument against this was primarily that, given an appropriate orientation towards race and diversity was a requirement on all members of the police, to have specialist trainers would send the wrong message and to an extent let others off the hook. The imperative to integrate race and diversity into all aspects of training was also problematic. Trainers were encouraged to seek every opportunity to make sure that reference was made to the race and diversity aspect of whatever they happened to be training – the so-called 'golden thread'. Whilst it is hard in our view to deny that it is essential to acknowledge that policing in all its dimensions is done in the context of a diverse and plural society, the problem was that some aspects of integration could be perceived as 'tokenism' and its credibility was therefore undermined.

Training and education

The section above has outlined some of the legacy aspects of the
Stephen Lawrence Inquiry in terms of the training recommendations.
In this section we glance briefly at a wider issue, namely whether
training *per se* is the appropriate paradigm for achieving the
outcomes that were called for. Heslop (2006: 331) for example has
argued that police training has in latter years been anchored in
humanistic approaches to training that have been criticised for 'its
latent individualism and lack of attention to diversity'. Cashmore
(2002: 329) in an article which rehearses the possibility that many
responses to centrally driven policy changes could be described as
'window dressing', notes that 'increased recruitment and valuing
cultural diversity training, far from being the near panaceas many
accept them to be may actually have detrimental effects'. The
question for us is whether training itself is capable of delivering
long term sustainable change (particularly in attitudes, values and
beliefs) or whether *education* is a more appropriate paradigm. There
are many reasons for this and we have selected three that seem to
be important:

(a) Although the relationship between the police and higher
education (HE) is not a straightforward one, in recent
years the picture has become a little clearer. There has, for
example over the past decade, been a rapid expansion of
higher education provision for police officers in the form of
Foundation Degree programmes associated with particular
police services and this has led to discussion within HE about
the extent to which universities should become involved
with training or whether they exist to provide 'education'
in its purest sense. The debate about the differences between
education and training is ongoing and tends to focus on
inputs and outputs. In the case of inputs it is about the
methods of learning and in terms of outputs it is about
the precision with which we can specify the outcomes of
learning. Kenny and Read (1986) note that the delineations
can be seen in process, orientation, method, content and the
degree of precision involved. It is the last of these that is of
most interest here in that training is associated with precise
outcomes usually framed as objectives, and more often than
not these are the objectives of the trainer rather than the
learner. With race and diversity, however, and given that

people (for example police learners) should have *freedom* to learn, the precise outcomes of what they learn may actually be very difficult to specify.

(b) There is a growing body of knowledge and literature in the area of race and diversity but to what extent can we have confidence that this is making its way into the training milieu? A clear legacy of the Stephen Lawrence Inquiry has been the volume of literature that has come in its wake – a whole new vista has opened up for the literature in the field. Police training tends to be prescribed fairly narrowly in terms of the literature on which it is based. Very often the access to literature equates to texts that have been written in the police for the police. Whilst at the training level this is not surprising, taking a wider perspective is not all that evident. Without doubt the Stephen Lawrence Inquiry prompted discussion about the complexity of a diverse society and in particular how the police should respond to such complexity. The argument here is that this discussion is far more likely to be fruitful if it is informed by the range of perspectives on offer in the literature. An illustration of this is to be found in the way that National Occupational Standards are framed. The typical formation of a standard is the title which is then further broken down into elements – for example 'Promote people's rights and responsibilities'. These elements are associated with performance criteria which delineate what the person must be able to do and the range of contexts in which they are supposed to be able to do it. The whole standard is then supported by statements relating to the knowledge and understanding that is needed to be able to perform at the appropriate level. Many of these statements seem to go far beyond what is likely to be achieved in a training scenario and present as much more in keeping with the sort of discussion that would be had in a higher education programme, for example 'the tensions which people experience between their own rights and responsibilities'. The point is further made by Hyland (1997) who, in discussing the suitability of competence approaches to teacher training, notes a concern that competence alone may actually inhibit the perceived need for further development and may preclude the need for reflexive and reflective practice.

(c) Collier (2001: 451) in an article on valuing intellectual capacity in the police draws a distinction between 'intellectual capital' (as a stock of knowledge) and 'intellectual *capacity*' as the flow of knowledge. The latter echoes thinking about how to think. One of the clear aims of higher education is to encourage the development of critical thinking and the ability to problem solve. It is about reading widely to enable the taking of a range of perspectives and thus being able to see the world in different ways. This seems to be precisely what police officers need to be able to do to respond effectively to the challenges presented by policing a diverse society. So whereas training has of necessity a narrow focus and is (and should be) predictable, specific and uniform, education by its nature will be organic, general, less predictable and variable (Buckley and Caple 1995: 15). This seems to be a compelling indicator that the desired outcomes of the training recommendations of the Stephen Lawrence Inquiry will only be truly achieved when the training/education balance is found.

Specific issues in police training

This section of the chapter is concerned with analysing the extent to which the Inquiry into Stephen's murder and the subsequent investigation influenced police training. In so doing we have had to be selective in identifying specific issues and the limitations of a single chapter prevent a more detailed analysis. We acknowledge that the legacy of the Inquiry is far reaching and that some equally important issues have had to be omitted.

Process v. people management

As is discussed elsewhere in this volume, the Inquiry led to a number of reviews of internal police policies and processes. The next section of this chapter will be concerned with analysing the extent to which the Inquiry questioned the balance of police policies, procedures and operational practices. In this regard, and taking the totality of the recommendations into account, the Inquiry provided the catalyst for debate which focused on the extent to which an effective police response and police training should be concerned with addressing *people* management issues as well as *process* management issues.

Process management is typically characterised as a top-down analysis of all of the business processes which then translates into operational deployment (Smith and Fingar 2003). An investigation which involves the degree of complexity as that associated with Stephen's murder requires the effective and efficient application of policies and processes which are in themselves fit for purpose. As will be seen later in this chapter and elsewhere in the book many of the recommendations of the Inquiry were concerned with revising existing policies and procedures. Whilst the Inquiry recognised that policies and procedures were in existence it also identified that a number had not been reviewed and updated to meet societal needs or the individual needs of victims. In other words unwitting racism (Macpherson 1999) had allowed the processes to remain unchallenged and not fit for purpose.

A people management approach, on the other hand, is one which puts people at the heart of a performance management regime and in this regard it has been argued that:

> The effectiveness with which organisations manage, develop, motivate, involve and engage the willing contribution of the people who work in them is a key determinant of how well those organisations perform. (Patterson, West Lawthom and Nickell 1997: vii)

The legacy of Stephen in this regard, however, is one which has added a further dimension to the nature of people management. As noted by Jones (2008) policing is a people centric business: it involves the delivery of policing services to people on behalf of people. Effective policing, therefore, should involve a response which takes into account both the needs of individuals involved in a policing event as well as the needs of communities who may in some way be affected by the event. The legacy of developing more effective family liaison and community engagement processes is addressed in more detail in Chapters 3 and 4, the issue in question here is the need for police respondents to focus on the needs of victims and witnesses without recourse to stereotypical assumptions or decisions fuelled by racism (Macpherson 1999).

The importance of developing a people-focused police response was later highlighted by the findings of the 7 July Committee into the 2005 London bombings. The Committee notes that '... plans tend to cater for the needs of the emergency and other responding services, rather than explicitly addressing the needs and priorities

of the people involved' (London Assembly 2006: 9). However, it is
the Inquiry into Stephen's murder some seven years earlier which
questioned the balance of police policies, strategies and operational
procedures and addressed the need to apply a people management
approach to policing. This provides a significant challenge to police
training as very often the emphasis in police training is concerned
with teaching internal processes; for example how to complete forms,
identifying which offence has been committed and what police
powers are available to deal with the offence; in other words the
how of policing. On the other hand a people management approach
requires more of an emphasis on the context of policing (see, for
example, Foster 1999); in other words the *why* of policing. As will
be seen later in the chapter the Home Office and the police service
had recognised that police training needed to take more account of
societal issues (Norris and Kushner 1999). However, as noted by
HMIC (2002), the Inquiry into Stephen's murder remains a significant
factor in reforming police training. It is also this Inquiry which led
to significant improvements in the practice of using members of
the community to inform, question and advise police operational
procedures and it is this area which will now be examined.

Experience of community involvement

The benefits of using members of the community in police training
were recognised in 1983 by the Home Office (Oakley 2000) following
recommendations of the Scarman Report (HMIC 2003). As a result
a specialist community and race relations training centre was
established and a number of police trainers attended an extensive
training programme to implement a national strategy in which they
would be responsible for cascading the training when they returned
to their home force (HMIC 2003). Delivery of this strategy was
patchy and as noted by Oakley, 'with few exceptions, police training
establishments have over the years proved extremely reluctant to
enter into genuine partnerships with community groups for help in
delivering community and race relations training' (2000: 1). Earlier,
and prior to the Brixton Disorders in the 1980s, the Metropolitan
Police Service had recognised the need for police training to take
account of contextual issues and the needs of society in introducing
Human Awareness Training, later renamed policing skills (Bull and
Horncastle 1988). Uniquely in police training this programme was the
subject of an extensive external evaluation. However, as with many
similar innovations, the focus was on the training of new recruits and

the vast majority of police officers did not receive similar training input.

In 2000 the authors of this chapter were employed by the Central Police Training and Development Agency, Centrex (now part of the National Police Improvement Agency) to implement a national training programme designed as a direct consequence of the Inquiry, part of which was to develop a greater degree of community involvement in training (Clements and Jones 2008). Our challenge was to achieve a difficult balance eloquently set out by HMIC (2003):

> ... a fine balance has to be drawn in relation to the number of external contributors used; too many, and training loses the ability to contextualise the learning into the policing environment; too few, and the result will be the Service maintaining an insular view. Careful consideration must therefore be given to creating the right balance of in-Service trainers and external contributors to gain the greatest learning from a training event. (103)

However, Centrex had no mandate in respect of the training delivered by forces (see for example Hermitage 1999) and it was not until 2004 that firmer guidance, in the guise of an Association of Police Authorities document (Association of Police Authorities 2004), was forthcoming. Additional impetus was added by Home Office Circular 4/2005 (Home Office 2005e) and community involvement in training became a requirement of the Police Race and Diversity Learning and Development Programme (PRDLDP). These two documents addressed the need for community involvement in all aspects of police training whilst the training of new recruits was the subject of a new Initial Police Learning and Development Programme (IPLDP) with a specific requirement for community involvement. It is also the case that a number of forces had already commenced a police training community involvement strategy and were evaluating the outcomes of these initiatives (see for example Essex Police 2006).

The legacy of Stephen, therefore, is one which has led to police training moving away from a traditional model which is characterised by police officers being trained by police officers in police establishments to one which is best described by one Head of Police Training as one of 'training in the community with the community for the community' (Boon 2007). Whilst community engagement in police training had been recognised as an issue prior to the Inquiry, the same cannot be said of first aid training and it is this area which will now be explored in more detail.

First aid

The arrangements for police first aid training throughout the country had been in place for a number of years and remained unchallenged until the service responded to the recommendations of the Inquiry. Police recruits received basic first aid training which was delivered using a St John's Ambulance syllabus and they were subsequently awarded a 'First Aid for Police Officers Certificate' once they had passed an examination. In this regard it should be noted that no further refresher training was available (ACPO 2001). It was possible for an officer to complete 30 years' service without any additional training to that provided when they joined the police service. The limitations of this policy are clear and they were specifically addressed by three recommendations in the final report of the Inquiry as follows:

45 That First Aid training for all 'public contact' police officers (including senior officers) should at once be reviewed and revised to ensure that they have basic skills to apply First Aid. Officers must be taught to 'think first aid', and first and foremost 'A (Airways), B (Breathing) and C (Circulation)'.

46 That training in First Aid including refresher training should include testing to recognised and published standards in every Police Service.

47 That Police Services should annually review First Aid training, and ensure that 'public contact' officers are trained and tested to recognised and published standards. (Macpherson 1999).

The ACPO response was to establish a working party which included health care professionals. Its subsequent report went further than proposing changes to the ways in which first responders were trained, for example, extending its recommendations to the delivery of first aid in custody suites and guidance on the use of defibrilators (ACPO 2001).

The lack of attention to police first aid training is of particular significance given the likelihood of police officers arriving first at an incident which involves injured parties and the enactment in July 1998 of the Police (Health and Safety) Act 1997 which placed a legal duty on the police to apply health and safety legislation which had been previously enacted under the Health and Safety At Work Act 1974. Moreover it should be noted that earlier legislation such as the

1974 Act, and the Health and Safety First Aid Regulations 1981, was in existence prior to Stephen's murder and that failure to comply with the 1981 Regulations was a criminal offence (ACPO 2001).

Stephen's legacy is an important one in an area which is often ignored by the police service as the Inquiry served to highlight some significant failings in police training which were likely to reduce police capability. Whilst first aid training might be viewed by some as a 'poor relation' in the police training family the same cannot be said of critical incident training which we will now explore in more detail.

Critical incident workshops

In Chapter 7 the pioneering work to engage senior police staff in critical incident workshops is described in more detail. This initiative was necessary for a number of reasons and using specially designed computer software to manage the workshop it provided participants with a significant insight into the nature and complexities of critical incidents such as Stephen's murder and the impact of a failed investigation. The benefits of this approach to individuals, the police service and to communities are significant and cannot adequately be outlined in full; we would, however, like to highlight four benefits. Firstly, it enabled police staff to engage in a simulated critical incident which required live-time decision-making and by using a challenging, ever-changing scenario it required delegates to organise and deliver speedy responses to a critical event as it unfolded. Secondly, it enabled delegates to explore the differences between rational decision-making processes (see for example Flin 1995), naturalistic decision-making and recognition primed decision-making (Eyre, Crego and Alison 2008). This takes delegates away from the type of decision-making associated with business planning and objective setting and places them in a less orderly and more time-pressurised decision-making environment. Thirdly, it immerses delegates in a safe learning environment in which they can explore individual strengths and weaknesses and develop individual and team strategies to deal with critical incidents (for a more in-depth overview of the development of critical incident workshops see Alison and Crego 2008). Fourthly, it enables delegates to understand how their decisions could impact on communities and how individuals and communities could react to those decisions.

The originality and importance of this innovation cannot be overstated. However, given the development of police specific formal assessment frameworks such as National Occupational Standards (NOS) and an Integrated Competency Framework (ICF) published by the criminal justice Sector Skills Council, Skills for Justice, it might be timely to assess the extent to which critical incident workshops could be further refined and related to other areas of learning and development to build a stronger command capability within the police service. Firstly, we argue that without regular retraining and/or operational practice learning can diminish over time; it is a phenomenon described as skills fade (Deakin *et al.* 2005) and is one of the reasons why the armed services engage in regular exercising when not operational. Secondly is the extent to which there is a requirement for critical incident commanders to more formally demonstrate competence and capability in critical incident command skills (Forbes and Jones 2008). Thirdly, and linked to the previous issue, is the question of professional certification and whether or not critical incident commanders should be required to achieve a licence to practise. We acknowledge that critical incident workshops are linked with the Integrated Competency Framework and that officers can receive command training elsewhere. However, we argue that the complexity and demands of critical incident command are such that it should only be undertaken by qualified personnel who have demonstrated competence in a rigorous assessment environment. That said, critical incident workshops have substantially contributed to the building of this capability and in conversations with participants we have been told of the important part these workshops play in building individual confidence and, in team-based exercises, building team capability. Many of the workshops are built around the types of issues faced by those officers responding, at a number of levels, to Stephen's murder and it is right that officers can learn how to respond to those issues in a safe learning environment, and in this regard this remains a significant legacy. We noted the development of competency-based assessments and NOS above and it is this issue which we now turn to.

Competency assessment

Assessing competency was an integral part of the recruit training programme delivered by us when we first joined the staff of the MPS Recruit Training School in 1987. Skills Development Exercises were designed nationally and became an integral part of a new probationer training programme known as the Stage II programme (Norris and Kushner 1999) whilst a substantial component of national Sergeants and Inspectors promotion examinations was an assessment of competences. However, the competences were not in any way accredited against existing national competency standards nor did they form part of a qualification pathway. The MPS had developed Minimum Effective Training Levels (METLs) in police community and race relations training which were later adopted nationally (Oakley 1999) and our work on the Centrex programme included establishing national police training standards designed to meet the recommendations of the Inquiry and were all designed to provide a competency-based approach to police training. However, it was not until the establishment of the Policing Skills and Standards Organisation, later to become Skills for Justice, the Sector Skills Council for the criminal justice employment sector, that a unified set of National Occupational Standards (NOS) were developed (Skills for Justice, n.d). Together with earlier work undertaken by the MPS to develop an Integrated Competency Framework the NOS provide the underpinning standards around which the IPLDP has been designed.

The IPLDP is an NPIA (National Policing Improvement Agency) centrally designed programme of training delivered by each individual police service to new police officer recruits and provides the framework within which additional training is delivered throughout the two-year probationary period. The NOS have informed the content of the IPLDP which is further defined into topics, subjects, learning descriptors and bodies of knowledge as outlined in Table 9.1 below.

The topic shown in Table 9.1 is supported by six subjects and the depth of coverage in this approach is such that the subject *Origins of Police Values and Ethics* comprises six learning descriptors which

Table 9.1 IPLDP design levels

Topic	Underpinning Ethics and Values of the Police Service
Subject	Origins of Police Values and Ethics
Reference	IND1.1
Learning descriptors	6 Demonstrate knowledge of significant public inquiries
Body of knowledge	a Explain the key findings of the Stephen Lawrence Inquiry

include issues such as policing by consent, partnership policing and the police code of ethics. This provides a total of 25 bodies of knowledge within a single topic. Demonstrating knowledge of significant public inquiries has four bodies of knowledge and in addition to the Stephen Lawrence Inquiry, reports into the murder of Victoria Climbié, murders committed by Harold Shipman and the Scarman Report are also considered.

Whilst the use of the NOS does provide a national framework of standards and they have enabled the IPLDP to be accredited against a Level 3/4 NVQ, we have concerns that an over-reliance on competency frameworks can be limiting. As argued by Foster (1999) and as will be explored in more detail below, police officers need to understand the context within which policing operates. However, the NOS have provided a benchmark in all aspects of police training and from our involvement in the Centrex programme it is clear that recommendations of the Inquiry have substantially influenced how police officers are trained not just in respect of process issues but increasingly in people issues. What is also clear is that whilst the initial focus in reforming police training was directed towards issues of race, as directed by Macpherson (1999) the police service, as with other organisations, has reformed training to take greater account of the wider issues of equality and diversity such as gender, sexuality, disability, religion and faith. This is an important legacy.

Behavioural approaches to training

Police training was the subject of an unprecedented level of scrutiny leading up to and beyond the new millennium. In addition to Macpherson's (1999) criticism of police training, other inquiries included a Home Office review (Home Office 1998), an HMIC training inspection (HMIC 1999), a Home Affairs Committee Inquiry (House of Commons 1999) and a government white paper (Home Office 2000b). Whilst the focus of much of this work was concerned with structural issues, in addition to Macpherson's criticisms of specific areas of police training many of the witnesses presenting written evidence to the Home Affairs Committee noted the limitations of police training and in particular the absence of teaching police officers the context within which policing operates, as noted by Foster:

> The problems which currently face the police service stem in part from the absence of an awareness and understanding of the broader context in which policing takes place. Officers

require such knowledge in order to exercise their discretion appropriately. (1999)

In response to these concerns the Home Affairs Committee recommended that a pilot higher education policing qualification be developed and as a result the Home Office funded 500 police officers to study for a Foundation Degree in Policing developed by the University of Portsmouth. Following introduction of the IPLDP a number of forces engaged with local universities and in some cases the delivery of the IPLDP became the responsibility of those universities. Whilst it is difficult to directly link this development to the Stephen Lawrence Inquiry our involvement in designing the national training response to the recommendations is such that we can identify the Inquiry as a significant influencing factor in the design of the IPLDP and attempts to highlight the importance for police officers to learn about the context of policing within society.

For Foster (1999), context should be taught within a university environment and is not something for which training can be given in a police training environment. Moreover, she argues that the police service needs to develop an approach which encourages reflective professional practice. This type of understanding and approach is more normally associated with an educational approach as opposed to a competency-driven training approach and, as highlighted in the BBC documentary *The Secret Policeman*, described above, is unlikely to result in the attitudinal changes required to refute future allegations of institutional racism. However, we acknowledge that the incident shown in the documentary occurred prior to implementation of the IPLDP and also note the specific requirements of some NOS. For example, the NOS developed in response to policing racist incidents is set out in Table 9.2.

There does appear to be an increasing acceptance that what was known as police training with an emphasis on behavioural approaches may not meet the needs of an increasingly complex police service. In this regard common usage of the term 'police learning and development' as opposed to 'police training' (see for example Association of Police Authorities 2004 and Essex Police 2006) may be more than cosmetic. Moreover, initiatives such as the Recruit Training Modernisation project developed by Surrey Police and the University of Portsmouth involving the delivery of the knowledge elements of the IPLDP prior to joining the police continue to push police training boundaries.

Table 9.2 Content of IPLDP LPG 1.3.10

Subject	Ref.	Learning descriptors	Body of knowledge
Protecting people – racist incidents	LPG 1.3.10	1 State the definition of a racist incident as defined by the Macpherson Report (S. Lawrence)	a Definition from Macpherson Report
		2 State the ACPO definition of Hate Crime	a ACPO Manual
		3 Outline Sec. 18 POA 1986	a Sec. 18 Public Order Act 1986 – legislation
		4 Explain any additional police action when dealing with an incident which is racially motivated	a ACPO Manual
		5 State what additional action should be taken when the victim cannot speak English	a Knowledge of interpreters procedures
		6 State how racist incidents are included in the police planning process	a Police planning process
		7 State how officers can become aware of the problems affecting the community in the area in which they police	a Community scanning processes
		8 From a given scenario identify when a racist incident and hate crime have taken place	a Meaning of racist incident b Meaning of hate crime
		9 Give examples of other agencies that can offer support to victims of racist and hate crime incidents	a List of agencies

Summary and conclusion

We previously noted the difficulty in making tangible links between the Stephen Lawrence Inquiry and some of the issues surrounding police training. However, it should be noted that this inquiry was one of a number of related studies which collectively challenged the thinking around the governance, structure, delivery and content of police training. This chapter has attempted to assess the extent to which police training has changed following the Inquiry. We began by critically reviewing the delivery of community and race relations training and noted some definitional problems which may make training in this area problematic. We sketched out a debate which continues to challenge those involved in deciding how to meet the learning and development needs of police staff – is training more appropriate or should the needs be met by an educational approach? Finally we reviewed some of the related inquiries into and issues facing police training. Whilst it is difficult to comment in the absence of formal evaluative data, our experience of being involved in responding to those inquiries has left us with the view that the Stephen Lawrence Inquiry has had a significant impact in reforming police training. Learning the lessons from this Inquiry remains a central part of police training curricula.

Chapter 10

Talking a different language? Racist incidents and differing perceptions of service provision

Ben Crane and Nathan Hall

The public inquiry into the murder of Stephen Lawrence highlighted a lack of confidence in the police among black and minority ethnic (BME) communities. The Report's first recommendation was that the Home Secretary establish a ministerial priority for all police forces to increase such confidence. The way the service dealt with racist incidents was identified as a key part of improving this confidence (Macpherson 1999) and a code of practice dealing with the reporting and recording of racist incidents quickly followed (Home Office 2000).

It is now 10 years since The Stephen Lawrence Inquiry reported and despite progress being made the overall satisfaction levels of victims of racist incidents remain below the aggregated satisfaction levels (Home Office n.d.). It has been acknowledged that BME people collectively have a different experience of policing from that of the white majority and this is evidenced by disproportionality at all stages of the criminal justice system from victimisation, stop search, arrest, conviction to sentence (Home Office 2006b). Over this 10-year period work has been done to understand these differences and despite the research base expanding, the reasons for these differences remain as much debated today as ever. Where the experience of racist victimisation has been widely researched, the perceptions of police officers in this area has a far more limited research base and has predominantly been in the form of focus groups exploring general issues (Docking and Tuffin 2005), or what could be described as macro case studies, for example the Lawrence Inquiry (Macpherson 1999). Additionally, the perceptions of police officers and victims have not been compared in an empirical manner in order to identify the extent and polarity of any differences in perception.

This chapter reports on a small-scale empirical research study that sought to evaluate the difference between police officer and victim perceptions of the same racist incident, a *perception gap*, and thereby contribute to understanding how to improve the victim's perceptions of the service delivered by the police. The scope of the research does not include an examination of the perception gap in relation to other categories of incidents, nor does it break down racist incidents by crime type. This work can therefore be regarded as an exploratory study that develops understanding of police officers' perceptions of the quality of service they deliver, comparing it with victim perceptions and then signposting for further research.

Context of the study

The recognition that BME communities had a different relationship with the police than the white majority, and perceived a lesser level of service, cannot be attributed to an exact date. Reiner (2000) regards the 1950s as the heyday of British policing; a high level of support was enjoyed and an essentially white working-class police service was policing communities it recognised, identified with and shared values with. Solomos (2003: 119) identifies the period between 1967 and 1970 as when the police gradually began to acknowledge that the approaches they had adopted were not going to work in the developing multi-ethnic society and in 1970 the Metropolitan Police Service publicly acknowledged their failings, stating that BME people posed 'special problems' which they had failed to deal with (Mark 1970; cited by Solomos 2003: 120).

Between 1979 and 1986 a number of official reports were published that identified the theme of the police service not providing an adequate response to minority communities and victims of racist violence, and at worst hostility towards these groups (Bowling 1999: 69–70). Perhaps the most influential report during this period is Lord Scarman's report on the 1981 urban disorder in Brixton, London. He emphasised the need for community policing and concluded that the breakdown in trust and confidence in the police by certain groups had come about because of a lack of communication and securing consent for action. He identified the problem of 'bad apples' within the police service, but concluded that institutional racism was not present (Scarman 1981). This view of institutional racism was of

'... knowingly, and as a matter of policy' (1981: 28). Nevertheless Scarman proposed a raft of institutional reforms, which perhaps suggests that the type of institutional racism identified by Macpherson had indeed been recognised by Scarman. Scarman also noted generally different perspectives between black and Asian groups, the former complaining of police harassment whilst the latter felt unprotected by the police (Scarman 1981: 31). Although the recommendations in Scarman's report were not taken on board in their entirety, they were acknowledged by the police service which did seek to make improvements (Bowling 1999: 99).

In April 1993 Stephen Lawrence was murdered. The investigation was followed by two internal inquiries and finally the public inquiry chaired by Sir William Macpherson (Macpherson 1999). In contrast to the Scarman Inquiry, which focused on process and structural issues, the Lawrence Inquiry went to the heart of police culture and concluded that the investigation was badly conducted and tainted by institutional racism. Macpherson challenged Scarman's 'bad apple theory', pointing to a wider and deeper form of racism. He defined institutional racism as:

> the collective failure of an organisation to provide an appropriate and professional service to people because of their colour, culture or ethnic origin. It can be seen or detected in processes, attitudes and behaviour which amount to discrimination through unwitting prejudice, ignorance, thoughtlessness and racist stereotyping which disadvantage minority ethnic people. (Macpherson 1999: para. 6.34)

The Inquiry extended far beyond the events of Stephen Lawrence's murder, the subsequent investigation and the collapsed trial, and widened to deliver recommendations for improved race relations. For Macpherson it was no longer good enough for the police service to avoid *knowingly* discriminating. Rather, he required the service to challenge *unwitting* discrimination and prejudice. The implementation of the recommendations has been described as 'the most extensive program of reform in the history of relationships between police and ethnic minority communities' (Bowling and Phillips 2002: 16) and the progress of implementation is charted by Foster, Newburn and Souhami (2005) and remains ongoing. Both Macpherson and Scarman essentially agree that the Metropolitan Police Service failed to meet the needs of BME communities, but they differ significantly in the way they constructed their arguments. McGhee (2005) describes

Scarman looking to social problems and attitudes of the African-Caribbean communities, thus shifting the attention away from public institutions, whilst Macpherson moved the debate to a view where racism and racists are the social problem.

Despite acknowledging its significance, Solomos observes that Macpherson's report actually contained very little that was new, but collected together the learning of the previous 20 years (2003: 90–93). Skidelsky offers an alternative perspective on some of the events attributed to institutional racism and describes them as '... the product of an understaffed, under equipped, and above all, a low calibre force'. He uses the lack of first aid training as an example of this and notes that Macpherson did not consider social class of the victim as a possible factor influencing the standard of investigation (2000: 4).

Police, community and race relations are examined by Her Majesty's Inspector of Constabulary (HMIC) in a series of thematic inspections. The first, carried out in 1996/97 (HMIC 1997b), was followed by a second in 1998/99 that noted that many of the recommendations in the first had been sidelined (HMIC 1999c: 7). As a result every police force was put on notice of a further inspection in 2000. This latter inspection found a more positive picture of progress during the two-year interval; however, it may be no coincidence that the Lawrence Inquiry reported during this period (HMIC 2001).

The provision of race and diversity training (Macpherson 1999: rec. 49) was subject to a review in 2003 by HMIC. The report acknowledged that the police are drawn from a society that is inherently discriminatory, but the challenge is to prevent inappropriate behaviour or treatment to minority groups being displayed. The report found that the training was not fully integrated into wider training and as such was not 'totally effective in effecting organisational change' (HMIC 2003: 29). Indeed the provision of training remains subject to criticism. Whitfield found that the MPS used the Brixton riots and subsequent inquiry by Scarman as its starting point for police–community race relations and did not explore adequately the cultural and historical legacy of issues such as slavery and immigration (2006, cited by *Police Review* 2006: September 1).

What is a racist incident?

The concept of a *racist incident* emerged in the late 1970s, gradually evolving from one based on evidence to Macpherson's definition

217

(Bowling 1999: 73). In accordance with recommendation 12 of the Lawrence Inquiry, a *racist incident* is now:

> any incident which is perceived to be racist by the victim or any other person. (Macpherson 1999: para. 45.17)

A racist incident need not necessarily be a crime; it is a classification of *incident* which, when given, triggers a certain response from the police and other services (McGhee 2005; Police Standards Unit 2006). *Incident* is not defined, hence it can be *any* occurrence and the link to racism need only be in the mind of *any* one person (Hall 2005: 13).

An incident can therefore be classed as *racist* without any evidential basis and the absence of even a casual link to a racial motivation. For instance, an opportunity-driven crime may be perceived as racial for a variety of reasons by the victim or other person. It could be due to the offender simply being of a different race, a history of racial victimisation or even racism on the part of the victim. As such, Jacobs and Potter's (1998) description of racist incidents and other hate crimes as an expansive concept is apt and, in the words of Skidelsky (2000: 3), 'the perpetrator of racist activity may not know they are racist at all'. Indeed, even if an offender *is* racist this may not have motivated the offence. Jacobs and Potter's (1998) analysis of the US system views the singling out of racist incidents as a blunt instrument that is ultimately not capable of distinguishing prejudice and causation, and Hall (2005) sees no reason not to apply this to the UK. Ignatieff's (2000) critical analysis of the Lawrence Inquiry argues that the definition may have the effect of 'racialising' more and more encounters between BME people and the police to no one's ultimate benefit – a situation raised in the Introduction to this book.

If one accepts that a perception of racism by any person makes an incident worthy of a greater focus of police resources or an offence worthy of a greater penalty on conviction, there are differing opinions on whether the *direction* of the racism is relevant. Blum challenges the view that 'only whites can be racist' (2002: 89), but describes a difference between racism directed from white to black and vice versa, with this difference being a consequence of the social and historical legacy of the relationships between those groups.

How many racist incidents are there?

Racist incidents have been officially recorded by the police in the UK since 1986. The British Crime Survey (BCS) is conducted annually and provides an alternative to police-recorded racist incident figures. This national representative victimisation survey has followed the political agenda and gradually increased its focus on racial incidents and first included white victimisation in the mid 1990s.

The statistics published under section 95 of the 1991 Criminal Justice Act provide a valuable source of information on BME groups' experiences across the criminal justice system. Over the past 10 years there has been a general increase in the number of racist incidents recorded by the police and a step change is evident in 1999. This has been attributed to the Lawrence Inquiry (Home Office 2005c; Hall 2005: 60). The BCS data indicates that the number of racist incidents has been falling, consistent with overall BCS crime estimates (Home Office 2006a; Home Office 2006b) and, despite significant under reporting, when BCS and police data are looked at together, it appears that the proportion of incidents reported to the police is rising.

The BCS is presented by the government as '... the most authoritative basis on which we can track crime' (Blears 2004, cited by BBC 2004). This confidence is open to question because the BCS misses significant areas of crime, such as crime against businesses and juveniles. Therefore, like police-recorded figures, the BCS can only under-represent the full extent of racist incidents. Over zealous recording by police officers is highlighted by Hall (2005: 200) who suggests that some victims may remain hidden under the weight of numbers that this social construction has created. Maguire (2000: 333) argues that the data may tell us more about the activities of the police than the experience of crime felt by the public. Indeed Hall (2005) explains that the only certainty that can be drawn from statistics in this area is that racist incidents do exist.

In addition, Chahal and Julienne (1999) found that reporting an incident to an agency was rarely a victim's first response. The reasons for not reporting a racist incident have been explored by a number of authors and include a perception that the incident is 'minor', fear of creating further problems and a lack of trust in police and the criminal justice system (Bowling and Phillips 2002).

Racist victimisation

Salisbury and Upson's (2004) analysis of the 2001/02 and 2002/03 BCS found that the risk of racial victimisation was 1 per cent or less for white, 4 per cent for mixed, 2 per cent for Chinese or other ethnic groups, 3 per cent for Asian, and 3 per cent for black people.

They also found that people from BME groups were more likely to be victims of any crime than white people. However, when the younger age profile of BME communities was accounted for this difference disappeared. They were also more likely to be worried about burglary, car crime and violent crime than white people.

Research by Docking, Keilinger and Paterson (2003) also found that more often than not, except in the most serious offences, suspects were known to the victim in some way, and that incidents generally occurred in the victims' own areas of living. In many cases the offender is a neighbour, partner, work colleague, customer, business contact or other acquaintance.

Clancy *et al.* (2001) analysis of the 1999 BCS found that victims of racially motivated incidents report being more emotionally affected than victims of other incidents. The impact of racist incidents can stretch far beyond immediate victim and family or friends (Chahal and Julienne 1999) and when official responses are less than satisfactory it can lead to disengagements and lack of trust in the criminal justice system (Bowling 1999: 159; Office for Criminal Justice Reform 2006). Indeed it has been argued that following the physical and psychological trauma of a hate attack, ineffective or insensitive policing is tantamount to secondary victimisation, potentially leaving the victim and the wider community feeling unprotected, isolated and vulnerable (Hall 2005: 194).

Bowling (1999) identifies the most common emotional reactions to racist incidents as anger, shock and fear with effects commonly continuing long after the incident. Bowling contrasts this ongoing and cumulative process of victimisation with the way the criminal justice system is constructed around *events* and *offences*; it is *incident*-based with outcomes measured in quantitative terms such as offences brought to justice (OBTJ) and response times (1999: 157–168, 286). Within this system an incident of racist victimisation is reduced to an act and a state of mind; *actus reus* and *mens rea*. It is thus removed from its wider context and the dynamics of the victim, offender and community relationships. MacLean (1986, cited by Bowling 1999: 158) likens this view of racial victimisation to trying to understand the context of a film by viewing only one frame. The Protection from Harassment Act 1997 has allowed 'courses of conduct' to be examined by the court and the law that restricted evidence of relevant previous convictions or 'bad character' – in other words the context – being admitted as evidence has recently been relaxed (Criminal Justice Act 2003).

Bowling and Phillips (2002), Bowling (1999) and Maynard and Read (1997) found that the impact of victimisation is worse where BME people are more isolated, and Chakraborti and Garland (2000), for example, explore this phenomenon in some detail. Victims of racist incidents may also be driven to be more antisocial and racist themselves as a consequence of their experience (Kohatsu and Sasao 2003).

Clarke and Moody (2002) identify that the support needed by victims of racist incidents cannot be predicted by their membership of a particular ethnic group. They found that in some cases victims would prefer support from someone from within their own community with appropriate language skills, whilst in other cases victims expressly did not want to be supported by someone from within their own community for reasons of confidentiality.

Experiences and perceptions of policing

Police forces measure victim satisfaction according to national guidelines (Home Office 2005a). Evidence suggests that victims of racist incidents and BME victims are typically less satisfied with the service they receive from the police than victims of other crimes and white victims (Home Office n.d.). In particular, Docking and Tuffin (2005: 37) identify the keys to victim satisfaction as follows:

1 Providing a quick response to the initial contact
2 Keeping them informed of any progress; and
3 Dealing with perpetrators effectively.

The BCS also examines confidence in the police in addition to victim satisfaction. Nationally, BME respondents report a higher level of confidence in their local police and the police in general, but then report a lower level of satisfaction when they do call for service (Allen et al. 2006).

Perceptions of the service provided to victims have also been explored in research by Victim Support (2006). This study examined service provision by a range of agencies to victims of hate crime and found that the police were rated poorly by 80 per cent of those surveyed. Areas of dissatisfaction included perceptions that the police did not provide enough support, did not keep victims informed of case progress, criminalised the victim, did not treat cases seriously, and were not culturally aligned to victims. Such views mirror those aired at the public meetings held as part of the Stephen Lawrence Inquiry a decade ago. However, the Victim Support study also found that, where they existed, many victims held positive views of *specialist* police investigative units (themselves a legacy of the Lawrence Inquiry), leading Victim Support to recommend that the police should examine ways of incorporating the features of specialist units into mainstream policing.

More generally, Kitchen, Michaelson and Wood's (2006) analysis of the 2005 Home Office Citizenship Survey finds that black people and those born in the UK have a lower level of trust in the police than Asian and white people and those born outside the UK, with younger black people having significantly less trust than older groups. Whilst there are dangers in making direct comparisons between the Citizenship Survey and the BCS, this seems to present something of a contradiction. Kitchen, Michaelson, and Wood (2006) also report how people felt they would be treated by their local police compared with other ethnicities and found significant variations according to ethnicity. Only 4 per cent of white respondents felt that they would be treated worse than other ethnic groups, whilst 18 per cent of BME respondents felt that they would be treated less favourably.

Personal experience of the police has been found to be negatively related to people's attitudes. Nicholas and Walker's (2004) analysis of the BCS finds that the police were more likely to be rated as doing a good job by people who had no contact with them or had not been a victim of a crime over the previous year. Additionally the impact of 'vicarious experience' is considered by Rosenbaum *et al.* (2005) who demonstrate that experiences passed on from others do influence perceptions and expectations.

The literature examined here illustrates both the rationale for, and a path to, an improved police response to racist incidents. It is noteworthy that the embedding of changes within the service since Scarman and Macpherson has been a long journey which has required periodic external pushes to keep moving. Despite ultimately being able to recognise that change is necessary and delivering significant improvements, the police service has not been able to deliver an equitable level of satisfaction to the victims of racist incidents. BME people, and victims of racist incidents, who are predominantly BME, have a greater fear of crime, expect to receive a low level of service from the police and are less satisfied with the service they do receive. In an apparent contradiction, BME people collectively have greater confidence in the police than white people but, as with all groups, this confidence decreases with contact. These are complex dynamics for the police service to wrestle with and when considered with the service's cultural resistance to change (Reiner 2000; Neyroud and Beckley 2001) and not least the volume of racist incidents (Hall 2005), the challenge of raising perceptions of service levels may seem significant. With exceptions, most authors argue for the identifying of racist incidents as worthy of special attention and arguably the focus on performance information around racist incidents itself could be regarded as a social barometer of race relations.

Perceptions of victims of racist incidents have been widely researched. However, the perceptions of police officers has a far more limited research base. This has been limited to focus groups exploring general issues (Docking and Tuffin 2005; Wells, Horney and Maguire 2005) or macro case studies such as Scarman (1981) and Macpherson (1999). When we look at those macro case studies we find that a path to improvement has been set out, but progress seems to continually come up against well documented barriers. Hence this research sought to explore the perceptions of police officers at a more micro level by examining the routine rather than the exceptional that make up the vast majority of the recorded racist incidents.

The police force in which the research was conducted is a medium-sized force policing an area including a diverse city, market towns and many rural villages. This work is focused on incidents that took place in the city. The force uses a model where the majority of racist incidents remain within a local policing team supervised by local inspectors. More serious incidents are investigated by more specialist investigators and the force has a recognised policy lead.

Methodology of study

The research compared the data from surveys of victims of 11 racist incidents with data from interviews conducted with the officers who dealt with the same incidents. The intention was not to measure the incidence of any particular factors or make a firm quantitative assessment of differences in perceptions, but rather to establish and analyse areas of deviation between these groups.

The views of victims were available from the Statutory Performance Indicator 3a (SPI3a) survey findings. A mixed methodology interview was developed to obtain the investigating officers' satisfaction with the level of service they delivered. This contained closed questions mirroring the SPI3a survey on a Likert scale, with a range from completely dissatisfied to completely satisfied, and additional open questions. The overall approach therefore allowed victims and investigating officers' perceptions of the same racist incident to be obtained and compared and the investigating officers' perceptions to be probed.

Within the findings issues are reported for 'some officers' or 'some incidents' when two or more officers made reference to them. To aid analysis the Likert scale was translated into numerical values with 7 being completely satisfied and 1 being completely dissatisfied. This allows satisfaction levels and perception gaps to be expressed numerically.

Key findings

The findings are presented across five of the areas of satisfaction used within the Statutory Performance Indicators; those being time to arrive, actions taken, follow up, treatment and satisfaction with the whole service. The difference between the mean satisfaction levels of victims and police officers provides what is described as the perception gap (Figure 10.1, below).

It can be seen that investigating officers regard themselves as giving a higher quality of service than the victim perceives across

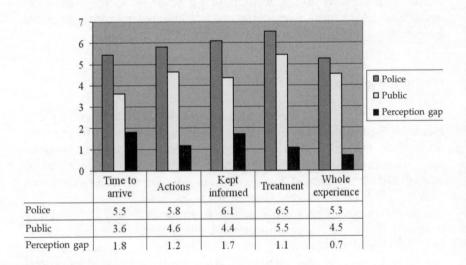

	Time to arrive	Actions	Kept informed	Treatment	Whole experience
Police	5.5	5.8	6.1	6.5	5.3
Public	3.6	4.6	4.4	5.5	4.5
Perception gap	1.8	1.2	1.7	1.1	0.7

Figure 10.1 Mean perceived satisfaction levels and perception gaps across five key areas

each of the five areas. The lowest perception gap was reported with the whole experience and both victims and officers are most satisfied with the treatment given. The qualitative findings in each of the five areas of satisfaction are explored below.

Time to arrive

This area of satisfaction could be regarded as differing from the others because the time at which an officer is dispatched to an incident in relation to the time at which it was reported is normally a function of the control room or a supervisor. In this way the officer usually has less control than in the other areas. Evident from most officers was a sense of blame towards other parts of the organisation for the way the initial response was handled. The following comments characterised the feelings of these officers.

> We were dispatched by control room. It had sat on POLIS (command and control system) for about four hours before we were sent. I don't know why.

> It was allocated to me during leave. It was appalling how the victim was left.

> It was recorded as a suspicious incident so was not allocated for two weeks.

Despite these officers blaming others for the failings of the initial response, it is interesting that the officers then went on typically to grade their level of satisfaction with the initial response as higher than that felt by the victim. Some clues to this apparent contradiction are given by officers who attempt to justify the failings for internal organisational reasons rather than their being at fault themselves, for example:

> It was extremely quick for my section that does not have many officers.

> On response we can't really keep appointments and this is a problem.

Actions taken

The pressure to 'detect' the incident emerged in the majority of

225

officer interviews and arguably not always in a healthy manner, as evidenced by the following comments.

> There is pressure to detect and I definitely felt that I was doing the opposite to what the victim had requested, which I think could have an adverse effect on people reporting incidents to the police, as it makes the victim feel that the decision is taken from their hands.

> A good job for me would have been to get a conviction. Ultimately the best possible thing is detecting the job, that is what we are measured on.

> I told her at the time that the crime would be undetected unless any more evidence came to light ... She felt it was the neighbour but I told her that we need to work on evidence.

> I told him that I would be seeing the suspect because I had to finalise it. She ended up being reprimanded.

> She did not want him prosecuted and was a bit annoyed that I arrested someone.

Evidence of a problem-solving approach was only described by two officers and only in one case did the investigating officer make mention of involving other agencies. Time pressure was identified by some officers as the reason for not giving a greater level of service.

> With all the jobs that we have on response I would like to have been able to speak to the victim more often, but the only time I seem to get is at night.

> The biggest problem is time. Beat managers have to do domestic violence visits as well and they can take ages.

Keeping the victim informed

When different perceptions of discrete incidents are examined the perception gap is sharply exposed in this area. For example, in three incidents the gap is notable with officers describing themselves as completely or very satisfied whilst the victims of these same incidents described themselves as completely dissatisfied. Time pressures, shift patterns and workloads arose as reasons for not meeting victims' expectations, although overall officers just did not seem to perceive the level of dissatisfaction felt by victims.

Treatment

This is the area where officers and victims perceive the greatest satisfaction. Some officers identified listening to the victim as key to their treatment of the victim and identified the length of time they spent with the victim as important.

> I sat down and listened for a good half an hour and gave them the chance to talk to me.

> I spent about one and a half hours there. I listened and explained as much as I could.

> I listened to what she had to say, even about the other things not related.

An apology from the investigating officer is part of the interaction in some cases, examples being:

> I was very apologetic. I was honest about the job being allocated in my absence.

> I am open and honest and I apologise, as in this case.

Whole experience

Some interesting contrasting perspectives on the same incident emerged in this area. For instance, in one incident the officer describes themselves as completely satisfied with the whole service offered, whilst the victim is completely dissatisfied. This victim comments:

> They don't care and don't ever want to hear what we have to say. They do nothing. The police are racist themselves. The police need retraining in how to handle the public.

Although not specifically explored in this study, the views of investigating officers when assigned to a racist incident emerged during the interviews. Evident was an acknowledgement of the importance of racist incidents and this manifested itself in what could be regarded as both healthy and unhealthy attitudes.

When you hear that a racist incident has come in your heart sinks. You think that you are going to get a complaint. If you don't do it right it will be seen as racist.

There are certain jobs you want to do a good job on and racist jobs are one of them.

Discussion of study

Although this was a relatively small study, it has been shown that in the 11 incidents examined, a perception gap emerges in each of the five areas, and in each case the investigating officers have a higher regard for the service they delivered than the victim. Perhaps the first question to ask is does this actually matter? If the police were charged with applying a set of standard operating rules to each incident, in the manner of a production line, perhaps it simply matters that those rules are followed. However, as discussed earlier, racist victimisation is complex and multidimensional and every incident requires a response sympathetic to the cultural and political imperatives. It can therefore be suggested that simply delivering a service by a set of rules or instructions will not suffice and officers need to be able to tailor their response accordingly and self assess the service they are delivering. Indeed this was a key message from the Stephen Lawrence Inquiry, which stated that:

> The provision of policing services to a diverse public must be appropriate and professional in every case. Every individual must be treated with respect. 'Colour-blind' policing must be outlawed. The police must deliver a service which recognises the different experiences, perceptions and needs of a diverse society (Macpherson 1999: para. 45.24)

As such it would appear that the smaller the perception gap the better. Arguably, the police service can't expect to leave all victims completely satisfied. However, recognising when the service does not meet victims' expectations, and acknowledging this as a failure, is an important part of service delivery.

In seeking to find meaning within the findings, the five areas could be viewed in two parts: the *doing* and the *feeling*. The first three areas – time taken to arrive, actions taken, keeping victims informed – could be regarded as the *doing*. They are predominantly about the process aspects of the investigation and have much in synergy with Docking and Tuffin's (2005) key drivers of satisfaction, those being speed of response, keeping the victim informed, and dealing with perpetrators effectively. These areas are additionally defined and prescribed within the force's policies. The assessment of the treatment and whole experience are the final SPI3a categories and could be regarded as the *feeling* areas. The policy requirements of the first three areas are monitored in a transactional manner, whilst the treatment of the victim and an overall assessment are less readily monitored. It is in the three transactional areas that the perception gaps are the largest. This suggests that officers and victims have a more similar understanding of the transformational *feeling* area of the interaction and their perceptions diverge in the *doing* transactional areas.

The 'whole experience' area expresses the investigating officer's overall assessment of their handling of the incident and it can be seen from Figure 10.1 above that investigating officers express a lower satisfaction in this area than in the four preceding areas. It could be suggested that officers are assessing that they are completing their tasks in relation to the incident fairly well, but are aware that the victim is less than fairly satisfied and are reflecting this in their relatively low overall assessment. This could be supported by the victim's assessment of their treatment by the officer as their highest area of satisfaction, above the organisational aspects.

A *blame culture* is evident from the very beginning of some incidents. These organisational frustrations are sometimes shared with the victim and this exposure of the blame culture to the victim cannot engender confidence and satisfaction, nor contribute to creativity or flexibility in dealing with racist incidents.

Investigating officers evidently acknowledged the importance that the organisation places on racist incidents, but it appears that this can then become muddled by the 'blame culture' or a 'performance culture', and most officers perceived a pressure to detect the incident. Some officers were able to identify the tension this pressure created. No officers articulated victim satisfaction as being a successful outcome and only two described problem-solving approaches. This pressure to detect led some officers to take decisions out of the victims' hands and press ahead with arrests against their express wishes.

Most of the officers appeared to be seeking to make the racist incident fit within the police and criminal justice structures; they seek to complete a crime report, an investigation log and finally a detection. The structure is *imposed* on the victim, even if it does not fit with their continuum of victimisation, and is particularly evident in the cases where the officer describes the victim as not wanting a formal outcome against an offender, but rather wanting their problems to cease. The result of taking this route was, however, not predictable. For instance in one such incident the victim described themselves as reassured by the officer's actions and in another they did not. This appears to suggest that going against the wishes of the victim can sometimes actually deliver satisfaction, thus highlighting the complex decision-making that is required of an officer.

A number of these issues were similarly identified a decade ago by Bowling (1999), who argued that as a racist incident is transformed from the world of the victim's experience into an object for policing it is placed in the context of the police organisational and cultural milieu, an environment that is usually antithetical to that of the victim. A consequence of this, Bowling suggests, is that whilst the police may feel that they have responded appropriately and effectively, the victims are frequently left with feelings of dissatisfaction, fear, and a perception of being under-protected. Evidence of problem-solving emerged strongly in only one incident and at the time of the interview this officer regarded the case as still ongoing and a satisfactory conclusion yet to be achieved. This was a number of weeks *after* the victim had completed the SPI3a telephone survey, hence their recorded satisfaction with the police's handling of the incident had been *frozen* at a point in time prior to the conclusion of the police action. Due to the complexity of racist incidents, taking a problem-solving approach to its conclusion can be a long process. Indeed, even attempting to speedily problem solve could further drive the process of racist victimisation to fit neatly within police and criminal justice culture. The SPI3a survey methodology and performance culture would therefore appear not to encourage and recognise longer-term problem-solving work.

As has been discussed, officers and victims can have completely polar perceptions of satisfaction when describing the same aspect of an incident. A victim can be imagined explaining their problem to an officer and saying they would like help to cause it to stop. The officer replies with an explanation of how they are going to arrest and caution the suspect and starts to take details for a crime report. The officer is looking for a single transaction to record and detect and is treating the victim as a commodity whose value is the information that they hold (Ackerley 2007). During the analysis it appeared at times that two actors were actually talking about different incidents. Even some simple closed questions produced evidence of very different perceptions. For example in four incidents the officer and victims disagree about whether there has been any further contact since the initial report and in three incidents they disagree about whether the officer explained that the case has been closed. Somewhere a common understanding or compact is not being reached between the officer and the victim.

Despite the differences in perceptions, victims assessed the treatment they received from investigating officers higher than any other area. It may therefore appear that investigating officers have the appropriate personal style and communication skills, but are not meeting expectations in what they are actually *doing*. In other words, it is the organisational process and cultural aspects that are failing to deliver the desired result.

This may indicate that the barriers to improvement are predominantly organisational rather than emanating from the individual officers and this observation is supported by the observance of a strong culture of *detection* being a measure of success. When this observation of organisational barriers to improvement is reflected on, Macpherson's definition of institutional racism comes to mind. It was also identified that the victims and officers can have very different perceptions of the same aspect of an incident such that the researchers noted that they felt the actors were *talking a different language*. No evidence emerged of officers delivering victims of racist incidents a lower quality of service than victims of other crimes; in fact there was some evidence of the opposite.

Conclusion

The stage has changed for the better in many obvious ways since the murder of Stephen Lawrence in 1993. This has been further evidenced in research by HMIC (2008), which has yielded some encouraging results in this area. In 2006 and 2007 HMIC conducted an inspection, *Duty Calls*, which covered the impact on service delivery and organisational capability of compliance with race equality legislation, notably the Race Relations (Amendment) Act (RR(A)A 2000) and related provisions. Fieldwork was conducted in six police forces with a focus on hate crime, stop and search, black and minority ethnic (BME) staff progression and retention, and procurement as well as comment on community engagement and consultation. HMIC (2008: 1) was encouraged to find, on the whole, 'a palpable commitment to do what is right, many people working hard to good effect, and significant progress since 2001'.

With particular reference to hate crime, HMIC (2008: 1) concluded that:

> In responding to reports of alleged hate crime, the forces had much of the necessary infrastructure in place, were demonstrating effective leadership in many areas, and were using third party reporting processes effectively. Overall performance and satisfaction levels were up to standard. Attention was required to internal hate crime, training and supervision and full compliance with the ACPO manual ... The way ahead involves building on what has been achieved to date.

From the research undertaken, the authors of this chapter now suggest that the service gap is not predominantly about 'indifference on the ground at junior level' (Macpherson 1999: para. 45.12), but rather a vision of success at the front-line that was driven by the translation of the Police Performance Assessment Framework into a small number of easily measurable targets for front line officers with *detections* prominent amongst these. This resulting desire to be businesslike did not always match the victim's vision of success. This study indicates that, despite the emphasis shifting nationally towards more victim-focused approaches, a cultural legacy may remain where police performance, or 'success', is interpreted by most officers as detection.

This interpretation by the people actually delivering the service contradicts the views of some researchers in this area (Bowling 1999; Hall 2005) who have argued that the nature and characteristics of hate crime effectively mean that the clear-up rate is a relatively meaningless measure of police performance, and that it is therefore important to measure 'success' in other ways. For example, 'success' might be better measured against the numbers of hate crimes reported by victims, or by victim satisfaction with the police response as indicated by qualitative and quantitative surveys. Indeed, shortly after the publication of the Stephen Lawrence Inquiry report, the Metropolitan Police Service recognised both the limitations of using detections as a key measure of 'success' and the importance of recognising the needs of the victim. The MPS stated that whilst the investigation, identification and prosecution of perpetrators to the satisfaction of both the victim and the community is a priority, so too is the identification and pursuit of alternative courses of action when prosecutions aren't possible, and the need for officers to 'resolve hate crime imaginatively' (1999d: 12). The continuing challenge is to translate this vision down to busy front-line officers. Furthermore it is important that the police avoid providing a service that is done *to* the public, otherwise, as Macpherson (1999: para. 46.40) suggested in the Stephen Lawrence Inquiry, policing by consent may be the victim.

Chapter 11

Educational policy and the impact of the Lawrence Inquiry: the view from another sector

Nicola Rollock

The public inquiry into the circumstances leading to the murder of Stephen Lawrence was announced on 31 July 1997 and formally began in March 1998. The Inquiry panel, led by Sir William Macpherson with Tom Cook, the Reverend John Sentamu and Dr Richard Stone, held a series of public hearings, collected evidence and received countless submissions from a number of individuals and organisations. This information supported the direction and content of the final report *The Inquiry into matters arising from the death of Stephen Lawrence* which was presented to Parliament and published on 24 February 1999. In his summation of the Inquiry, Macpherson (1999: 46.1) stated:

> The conclusions to be drawn from all the evidence in connection with the investigation of Stephen Lawrence's racist murder are clear. There is no doubt but that there were fundamental errors. The investigation was marred by a combination of professional incompetence, institutional racism and a failure of leadership by senior officers.

The majority of the Lawrence Inquiry's 70 recommendations pertained mainly to specific areas of the criminal justice system. For example, as has been discussed in other chapters in this volume, far-reaching changes were proposed to the ways in which the police service conducted and reviewed murder investigations; in the recording and reporting of racist incidents; and to the ways in which victims and witnesses were treated within the Crown Prosecution Service (CPS). In addition, Macpherson and his team considered organisational change within the police service in relation to race equality and cultural diversity issues fundamental to addressing some of the failings of the investigation and repeatedly, in the Inquiry Report, pointed to the lack of progress that had been made in this area since the seminal report by Lord Scarman into the Brixton riots some 18 years earlier (Scarman 1981). Specifically, a number of the Lawrence Inquiry recommendations also argued for clearer objectives and leadership around cultural diversity training; improvement in the recruitment, retention and progression of black and minority ethnic police officers and staff, and the monitoring by ethnicity and publication of 'voluntary' stops or what are now termed 'stop and account' procedures. The overall aim of the 70 recommendations was the 'elimination of racist prejudice and disadvantage and the demonstration of fairness in all aspects of policing' (Macpherson 1999). An examination of progress and some of the challenges encountered in attempting to address these recommendations has been discussed at length elsewhere (Rollock, forthcoming 2009).

While there was no explicit recommendation pertaining to institutional racism, the Inquiry was perceived as instrumental in fixing the concept, admittedly not without considerable controversy, at the forefront of public and political consciousness (see Murji 2007). Further, while the panel's use of the term and their failure to make the distinction between institutional and other forms of racism has been subject to extensive criticism (e.g. Solomos 1999; Stenson and Waddington 2007), the seriousness with which Macpherson and his colleagues viewed (institutional) racism and its impact on society is clearly conveyed throughout the Report, Chapter 6, in particular. It is analogised as a 'corrosive disease' deeply embedded in the very policies, leadership and structures of organisations, and addressing and eliminating racism is seen as central to establishing long-term change and improvement in British society. The responsibility for such action is seen to extend beyond the sole remit of the police service and the broader criminal justice system:

> If racism is to be eliminated from our society there must be a co-ordinated effort to prevent its growth. This need goes well beyond the Police Services ... Just as important, and perhaps more so, will be similar efforts needed from other agencies, particularly in the field of education. As we have indicated, the issue of education may not at first sight sit clearly within our terms of reference. Yet we cannot but conclude that to seek to address the well-founded concerns of minority communities

simply by addressing the racism current and visible in the Police Services without addressing the educational system would be futile. The evidence we heard and read forces us to the conclusion that our education system must face up to the problems, real and potential, which exist. We therefore make a number of Recommendations aimed at encouraging schools to address the identified problems (Recommendations 67–69).

(Macpherson 1999: 46.34)

This chapter provides an overview of progress in implementing the education recommendations of the Stephen Lawrence Inquiry. Key debates and government responses to each are examined. In closing, consideration is given to whether, by failing to include specific parameters for the successful elimination of racism within education and by failing to include recommendations aimed at teacher trainees, teachers and school governors, Macpherson and his team went far enough to meet their overall aim of seeking to prevent and eliminate racism.

The Stephen Lawrence Inquiry recommendations on education

The Macpherson panel's three education recommendations focus on changes to the National Curriculum; the recording and reporting of racist incidents; the recording and publication of exclusion data by ethnic group; and the role of Ofsted inspections in relation to each of these (Figure 11.1).

These recommendations should be understood alongside a wider context of legislative change to the Race Relations Act 1976.

The Race Relations (Amendment) Act 2000

The new Race Relations (Amendment) Act 2000 (RR(A)A 2000) placed a statutory duty on schools to eliminate unlawful racial discrimination, to promote equality of opportunity and good relations between people of different ethnic groups. It placed specific duties on the governing bodies of schools to have in place by May 2002 a written race equality policy (REP) that would set out how they would assess and monitor the impact of their policies, including the REP on pupils, staff and parents of 'different racial groups' and in particular how they would assess and monitor differences in attainment by ethnic group (CRE

67. That consideration be given to amendment of the National Curriculum aimed at valuing cultural diversity and preventing racism, in order better to reflect the needs of a diverse society.

68. That Local Education Authorities and school Governors have the duty to create and implement strategies in their schools to prevent and address racism. Such strategies to include:

- that schools record all racist incidents;
- that all recorded incidents are reported to the pupils' parents/ guardians, school Governors and LEAs;
- that the numbers of racist incidents are published annually, on a school by school basis; and
- that the numbers and self defined ethnic identity of 'excluded' pupils are published annually on a school by school basis.

69. That OFSTED inspections include examination of the implementation of such strategies.

Figure 11.1 The Stephen Lawrence Inquiry recommendations on education

2002). An initial survey evaluating the response to the public duty received a markedly poor response rate from schools (20 per cent of the total sample) compared with other targeted educational institutions (a remarkable 47 per cent response rate). Gillborn (2008) has argued that amongst the possible reasons for such a low response may have been an apprehension on the part of schools to respond to a survey sponsored by the very body – the Commission for Racial Equality (CRE) – responsible for the enforcement of the public duty. However, this does not explain the comparably better response rate received by other surveyed education institutions. He also suggests that schools may simply have been too busy with their other commitments to respond to the demands of research. It is likely, therefore, that those who did take part in the survey were those who perceived that they had made notable progress in the area. Yet, the findings do not support this. Only 65 per cent of schools believed their race equality work had produced positive benefits compared with an average of 69 per cent across all public bodies surveyed. In addition, schools were least likely to report that they required further guidance and support in this area, despite having made the least overall progress (CRE and Schneider-Ross 2003).

The RR(A)A 2000 was initially seen by many to provide an ideal opportunity, through a formal legal framework, to challenge the persistent inequalities in relation to ethnicity that have remained at the forefront of educational debates over at least the past 50 years. These contentious debates have been particularly concerned with the lower academic attainment of black Caribbean pupils (especially boys) across all stages of the maintained school system (e.g. Coard 1971; Gillborn 1999; Gillborn and Youdell 2000; Rollock 2007a; for detailed overview see Gillborn and Rollock, forthcoming) as well as their continued over-representation in the national figures on exclusions from school (discussed further below). Despite the possibilities for change presented by the legislation the main focus, albeit an important one, has been reduced to a mere concentration on monitoring attainment by ethnicity with little significant long-lasting change to the overall national figures on educational outcome (see DfES 2006a; DCSF 2007).

The National Curriculum

Recommendation 67 That consideration be given to amendment of the National Curriculum aimed at valuing cultural diversity and preventing racism, in order better to reflect the needs of a diverse society.

Citizenship

There have been general revisions to the National Curriculum (NC) which include the incorporation of a single statutory inclusion statement (the inclusion statement was previously mentioned separately to the aims of the NC) which clearly references the need for teachers to be aware of legislative provisions relating to race (as well as gender and disability). However, one of the main ways in which the government has claimed to address recommendation 67 has been through the introduction of the Citizenship subject area (Home Office 1999; Home Office 2005d). Introduced as part of the statutory curriculum for key stages three and four (11- to 16-year-olds) in September 2002 (it is non-statutory for key stages one and two), the Citizenship curriculum aims to equip young people with the 'knowledge, skills and understanding to play an effective role in public life' (Qualifications and Curriculum Authority 2008).

The move towards implementing a Citizenship subject area received wide criticism from academics and practitioners largely because the plans for its introduction were already well under way when the Lawrence Inquiry was published and therefore it was not seen as to genuinely engage with the recommendation proposed by Macpherson and his colleagues. In fact, the plans for a Citizenship subject area were announced on exactly the same day as the publication of the Stephen Lawrence Inquiry Report. In the government press release, the then Education and Employment Secretary David Blunkett offered an uncritical causal link between the murder of Stephen Lawrence and the need for the teaching and learning of Citizenship in schools:

> The tragedy of Stephen Lawrence's death shows how much more needs to be done to promote social justice in our communities. This is about how we treat each other and, importantly, how we learn to respect ourselves and one another as citizens. That learning comes from within the home, at school and the wider community. That is why we are promoting the teaching of citizenship at school, to help children learn to grow up in a society that cares and to have a real equality of opportunity for all. (Blunkett 1999)

No mention was made of how this new subject area would address racism, institutional or otherwise (Osler 1999). Indeed, further criticism was levelled at the fact that its rapid introduction into the curriculum in September 2002 was done without sufficient guidance to schools and resulted in its being taught by existing non-specialist teachers (Robinson and Robinson 2001). Indeed, a key review published many years later, led by former secondary headteacher Keith Ajegbo, examining Diversity and Citizenship across the curriculum supported some of these earlier concerns (Ajegbo, Kiwan and Sharma 2007). The academic research which informed this review found that the teaching and practice of Citizenship varied considerably across the country and that it continued for the most part to be taught by non-specialist teachers who struggled to locate useful, practical resources to support their classroom delivery (Maylor *et al.* 2007).

The Government's interest in Citizenship education should not be isolated from the wider political agenda, including what would come to signify an increasing anxiety about issues of immigration, asylum and citizenship. The tightening of policy in this area can be evidenced, for example, by changes in the new Nationality, Immigration and Asylum Act (2002) which required future British citizens to pass an English language and citizenship test (see Tomlinson 2005; also Rollock, forthcoming 2009). Such policy changes have been accompanied by narrow, anxious discussions, involving, for example, concerns about maintaining 'safe borders' and attempts to define the parameters of Britishness (e.g. Blair 2006; Brown 2006). Some have insisted that these debates have in turn contributed to the racialisation of immigrant groups and those seeking asylum (Bhavnani, Mirza and Meetoo 2005). Therefore, the Lawrence Inquiry came to be seen by many as a conduit to promoting the idea of Citizenship rather than as having generated a genuine critical engagement with recommendation 67 *per se* (also Stanford 2001).

Community cohesion

While initial preoccupation about 'community cohesion' stemmed from the riots in Bradford, Oldham and Burnley in 2001, the recent, statutory introduction of the Community Cohesion duty for schools from September 2007 can be regarded as supporting the part of recommendation 67 aimed at 'valuing cultural diversity'. In the Government's guidance, community cohesion is defined as:

> ... working towards a society in which there is a *common vision* and *sense of belonging* by all communities; a society in which the diversity of people's backgrounds and circumstances is appreciated and valued; a society in which similar *life opportunities* are available to all; and a society in which strong and positive relationships exist and continue to be developed in the workplace, in schools and in the wider community. (DCSF and DCLG 2007: 3, emphasis in original).

The aim for schools is to help children and young people to understand others; to value diversity while also promoting the concept of shared values; and to develop skills of participation and responsible action (Knight 2007). Defined in this way, community cohesion clearly has links to the Citizenship subject area described earlier and is seen to complement the existing duties for race equality with which schools are already expected to abide. Ofsted will, from September 2008, begin to inspect schools on community cohesion. There have been concerns, however, that the Government's implementation of this duty and the time taken to train inspectors have reflected a greater commitment to community cohesion than that shown towards race equality, especially in light of research which has in the past questioned Ofsted's commitment to inspecting for race equality (Osler and Morrison 2000).

History

The new secondary curriculum, implemented from September 2008, has seen an expansion, following much lobbying by specialist groups and practitioners, of topics included for study within the history subject area. Specifically, the inclusion of teaching and learning about the British Empire and slavery and its abolition might also be regarded as a further way of attempting to reflect and value Britain's cultural diversity (see Boston 2007).

Racist incidents

Recommendation 68 has been divided into two parts; the former relating to racist incidents is discussed here. The last part of the recommendation which relates to exclusions from school is examined in the next section.

Recommendation 68 That local education authorities and school governors have the duty to create and implement strategies in their schools to prevent and address racism. Such strategies to include:

- that schools record all racist incidents;
- that all recorded incidents are reported to the pupils' parents/guardians, school governors and LEAs;
- that the numbers of racist incidents are published annually, on a school-by-school basis.

This recommendation was accepted in part. Schools are required to collect information about each racist incident, including the names of the perpetrators and victims and the action taken to deal with the incident. Parents and governors should be informed of the nature and number of these incidents and schools should, in turn, inform their local authority of the statistics relating to these incidents annually. Authorities have an obligation to collate and monitor the pattern and frequency of this information and offer guidance and support to schools where necessary (see DfEE 1999; Home Office 1999). Schools are also expected to report to the police any racist incident that they suspect to have a criminal aspect (Home Office 2000a). In its study of good practice in schools and local authorities in relation to race equality Ofsted found that, of the 50 surveyed schools, those that were most effective in dealing with 'race-related incidents' tended to be supported by headteachers and local authorities who had a clear and authoritative stance for dealing with such matters. Where there was evidence of under-reporting, it was found to be due to a 'perceived lack of confidence' in defining and reporting incidents and lack of clear local authority guidance (Ofsted 2005).

While the Government accepted the first two elements of recommendation 68 the third, relating to the annual publication of racist incidents on a school-by-school basis, was deemed to risk 'discouraging the reporting of racist incidents to the detriment of minority ethnic children' and to 'effectively penalis[e] those schools which sought to address problems by acting in an open and honest manner' (Home Office 1999: 36). While it is impossible to establish whether such apprehension was warranted, a key government review, examining the recording and reporting of racist incidents published some six years later, revealed that while there were some good examples of schools and local authorities monitoring and recording racist incidents, there were also significant problems with under-reporting. Schools involved in the study were generally found to be reluctant to record racist incidents due to worries about their reputation in the climate of competition evoked through performance tables. There was also evidence that such incidents were often categorised as bullying behaviour rather than racism *per se*, and that some schools were anxious about the consequences of labelling children as racist (Docking and Tuffin 2005). While information on the frequency of racist incidents and action taken to address them is collated at a local level, the central monitoring of this information seems important to identifying overall national trends and sharing examples of effective recording and reporting. It may also be helpful to examine the extent to which the pattern of occurrence of racist incidents collected by police forces is similar to that occurring locally within schools.

Exclusions

Permanent exclusion is the most serious sanction a school can take against a student. While the local authority has a legal duty to make sure that excluded students receive education elsewhere, available evidence indicates that being excluded from school tends to be associated with poor educational outcomes, criminal activity and other forms of antisocial behaviour (e.g. Cabinet Office 2006). Such evidence is particularly worrying in light of concerns about the disproportionate number of black pupils who have been, and continue to be, excluded from school (see DfES 2006b; DCSF 2008).

The Government's initial commitment to addressing the issue of exclusion from school was seen in the first report of the newly created Social Exclusion Unit, which focused on exclusions and truancy from school, that was set up shortly after New Labour came to office. Published just a year before the publication of the Stephen Lawrence Inquiry, one of the central recommendations of the report was for the Government to put procedures in place to reduce the number of permanent exclusions by a third from 12,700 in 1996/97 to 8,400 by 2002 (SEU 1998). This target was abandoned in 2001, when the government stated that the reduction had been successfully met (at 8,300 exclusions in 1999/2000) and that no new targets were necessary (DfES 2003). This strategy failed, however, to take account of the disproportionate number of exclusions experienced by black students. In 1996/97, these students were four times more likely to be excluded from school compared with their white counterparts and this rate was still relevant when the target was abandoned two years later. Little attention also seemed to be paid to the fact that, following the relinquishing of the target, the number of students permanently excluded from school dramatically increased (see Table 11.1).

Recommendation 68 (continued) That Local Education Authorities and school governors have the duty to create and implement strategies in their schools to prevent and address racism. Such strategies to include:

• that the numbers and self-defined ethnic identity of 'excluded' pupils are published annually on a school-by-school basis.

By the time of the publication of the Lawrence Inquiry, the Government was already collecting and publishing exclusion data by ethnicity although the practice became much more rigorous following the specific duties imposed on schools with the introduction of the RR(A)A 2000. The ethnic group categories were extended, following their inclusion in the 2001 Census, to include those of mixed heritage.

Table 11.1 shows official data on permanent exclusions from school for key ethnic groups from 1998/1999, the year of the publication of the Stephen Lawrence Inquiry Report, to 2006/07, the most recent year for which data are available. The columns show the number of students in each ethnic group recorded as having been permanently

Table 11.1 Ethnic origin and permanent exclusions from school, England, 1998/99 to 2006/07

Ethnic group	1998/99		1999/00		2000/01		2001/02		2002/03		2003/04		2004/05		2005/06		2006/07	
	N	%	N	%	N	%	N	%	N	%	N	%	N	%	N	%	N	%
White	8,801	0.15	6,890	0.12	7,574	0.13	7,820	0.13	6,800	0.12	7,860	0.14	7,470	0.13	7,230	0.13	6,760	0.12
Black																		
Caribbean	589	0.60	455	0.46	385	0.38	410	0.41	360	0.37	400	0.41	380	0.39	380	0.41	360	0.38
Black African	157	0.21	145	0.17	156	0.17	160	0.15	130	0.12	200	0.16	190	0.14	230	0.16	210	0.13
Black Other	268	0.50	218	0.37	236	0.39	220	0.35	90	0.32	120	0.42	100	0.36	90	0.30	80	0.26
Indian	71	0.04	54	0.03	47	0.03	60	0.03	50	0.03	40	0.02	70	0.04	60	0.04	60	0.04
Pakistani	165	0.10	129	0.07	113	0.06	170	0.09	130	0.08	130	0.07	160	0.08	160	0.08	180	0.09
Bangladeshi	42	0.07	53	0.08	44	0.07	80	0.11	40	0.06	70	0.09	50	0.06	70	0.08	70	0.08
W/Black Caribbean	n/a	n/a	n/a	n/a	n/a	n/a	n/a	n/a	180	0.29	240	0.37	280	0.41	260	0.36	270	0.36
W/Black African	n/a	n/a	n/a	n/a	n/a	n/a	n/a	n/a	40	0.26	40	0.23	50	0.24	40	0.18	50	0.20
W/Asian	n/a	n/a	n/a	n/a	n/a	n/a	n/a	n/a	40	0.11	40	0.12	30	0.09	30	0.06	50	0.11
TOTAL*	10,424		8,314		9,122		9,519		9,270		9,860		9,380		9,130		8,680	

*includes some groups not shown separately above

N = number of pupils permanently excluded
% = number of pupils excluded in that ethnic group expressed as a percentage of that ethnic group in compulsory schooling
n/a = data not available for that period

Sources: DfES (2003); DfES (2004); DfES (2005); DfES (2006b); DfES (2007); DCFS (2008)

It should be noted that while Table 11.1 concentrates on main ethnic groups, the disproportionate exclusion of students of Traveller and Gypsy backgrounds, despite their low numbers in the school population, continues to be evident in the statistics on school exclusion.

excluded. The percentage column shows the number of students excluded as a percentage of their ethnic group in school population. The figure of 0.04 for Indian students in 1998/99, for example, indicates that four Indian students in every 10,000 were excluded for that period.

There are a number of limitations that need to be borne in mind when seeking to interpret this data. For example, as Table 11.1 shows, there have been changes to the ways in which ethnicity has been recorded, with the introduction in 2002/03 of new 'mixed' ethnic group categories, contributing to the disaggregation of some of the data formerly collected within the 'Black' and 'Asian' groups. Nonetheless, it can be seen that distinct differences exist across time and by ethnic group in terms of students' experiences of exclusion (for detailed discussion see Gillborn and Rollock, forthcoming). Irrespective of whether the data are examined from when the Inquiry Report was published (1998/99) or when the RR(A)A 2000 was introduced to schools (2002/03), the pattern of rate of exclusion remains relatively similar across time with only minor fluctuations. For example, it can be seen that students from Indian, Pakistani and Bangladeshi backgrounds are less likely to be excluded from school than their white and black peers. In contrast, black Caribbean, black African and 'black other' have generally been more likely to be excluded than their white counterparts: a pattern that is true in every year since 1998/1999 and for each of the black groups. The one exception to this pattern can be seen in 2002/03 when black African students experienced the same level of exclusion in 2002/03 as their white peers. Black Caribbean students have consistently experienced disproportionate rates of exclusion based on their numbers in the school population. For example, while their overall rate of exclusion has decreased from 60 in every 10,000 in 1998/99 compared with 38 in every 10,000 in 2006/07, they were four times more likely to be excluded from school compared with their white peers in 1998/99 and just over three times more likely in 2006/07. In 2002/03, when the RR(A)A 2000 came into effect, their rate of exclusion stood at three times that of their white counterparts. In other words, while this section of recommendation 68 has been met in relation to the monitoring by ethnicity of school exclusions, black Caribbean students continue to experience similar disproportionate levels of exclusion from school to their levels nine years ago when the Stephen Lawrence Inquiry Report was published. Similar patterns in the rate of exclusion are evident for students in the 'mixed' category to those described for black and Asian ethnic groups.

Additional government data on short-term or 'fixed' exclusions has only been collected since 2003/04 but shows similar patterns to those of the permanent exclusions: i.e. students in the mixed white and black Caribbean, black Caribbean and other black groups tend to experience fixed-term exclusions at around twice the rate of their white peers and the national average (DfES 2005, 2006b).

Academic research has presented varying reasons for the over-representation of black pupils in exclusion statistics but has largely pointed to the inequitable treatment of notably black Caribbean students which has been reinforced by negative stereotypical images of young black men and their families in the media (Blair 2001). Even if the findings of this research were overlooked, government reports have found that black students are subject to harsher reprimand even when engaging in the same behaviour as their white counterparts: 'the lengths of fixed-period exclusions varied considerably in some schools between black and white pupils for what were described as the same or similar incidents' (Ofsted 2001: 23).

Ofsted inspections

Ofsted has traditionally been subject to heavy criticism for failing to engage sufficiently with race equality in its inspections (Osler and Morrison 2000) or failing to comment on the ethnic group disproportionality in school exclusion figures (Parsons *et al.* 2004). Writing in 2002, three years after the Lawrence Inquiry report, Acting Chair for the Commission for Racial Equality Beverley Bernard, while recognising Ofsted's efforts to update inspection materials, remained apprehensive about its commitment to include criteria relating to race equality and educational inclusion, warning that 'failure to incorporate racial equality into the self-evaluation materials w[ould] make it more difficult for schools to meet the requirements of the positive duty' (Bernard 2002: 14).

Ofsted have since revised their inspection framework and as from September 2005, inspections have been shorter, with greater emphasis placed on school self-evaluation. The aim of self-evaluation is to help inspectors with their pre-inspection work, to enable them to form judgements about the school and identify any issues that they believe require prioritising for examination during the inspection. While self-evaluation provides scope for schools to comment on the experiences of learners from different ethnic backgrounds (Home Office 2005d), it is not immediately clear from the statistics on educational attainment or school exclusion data, for example, that the new form of inspection is translating to a difference in practice and outcome for minority ethnic students.

In addition Ofsted's already fragile reputation for engaging with race equality in its inspections has only been further weakened in a final handover report from the CRE to the newly formed Equalities and Human Rights Commission regarding the performance of regulatory and inspection bodies in relation to monitoring race equality in the public bodies for which they are responsible. In a damning statement, the report revealed that:

> [Ofsted] has the poorest record of any inspection or regulatory body. It does not accept that it has a responsibility to monitor RED [race equality duty] performance of public authorities within its arena of responsibility. It is arguably the most uncooperative public authority the Commission has had to deal with over the last two years. (Johnson and McCarvill 2007)

Ofsted's race equality scheme was found to be non-compliant and due to its consistent poor record in meeting its race equality duties, the CRE recommended that legal compliance action be taken against it. Therefore, while the Government accepted, in 1999, the Lawrence Inquiry recommendation that Ofsted inspections include examination of strategies relating to racist incidents, a culturally diverse curriculum and exclusions, there is a lack of confidence by many that the body set up to enforce the RR(A)A 2000 that Ofsted has the capacity or commitment to conduct such inspections satisfactorily.

Discussion

By including recommendations on education, the Macpherson Inquiry team sought to present ways in which racism might be addressed and eliminated from British society. This chapter has discussed progress in meeting these education recommendations during the 10 years since the Inquiry Report's publication in 1999. It has considered Government strategy and policy to address cultural diversity and prevent racism in the National Curriculum; the recording and publication of racist incidents; the monitoring by ethnicity of exclusions from school; and the role of Ofsted inspections in maintaining regulation of these acts.

However, it is suggested that these recommendations while important do not go far enough in uncovering and challenging racism within the education system, let alone wider society. First, they lack a clear and definitive association to outcomes or measurements that might be judged to address or eliminate racism. For example, it is difficult, if not impossible, to determine the extent to which learning about 'valuing cultural diversity' in the curriculum, to take just one example, will necessarily translate to a fair and just approach to other ethnic groups and address racism. Similarly, recording racist incidents and exclusions, while indicative of good practice, does not address the perceptions and actions that contributed to the disproportionality in the first place. This may in part be due to limitations of a Public Inquiry to make overall suggestions for change rather than being able to point to the need for change in specific outcomes.

Second, it is unfortunate that the education recommendations failed to include any mention of the role and responsibilities of teachers, either during training or once they are qualified, in meeting the overarching aim for education to prevent and eliminate racism. This is an important oversight, especially in view of annual survey data from the Training and Development Agency (the body responsible for managing the recruitment and training of potential teachers) which has consistently found newly qualified teachers (NQTs) judge their training as not sufficiently effective in preparing them to teach learners from minority ethnic backgrounds. In 2008, for example, 41 per cent of NQTs rated their training as 'good' or 'very good' in preparing them in this area. This result was higher than in any previous year. However, responses to this question have consistently given lower ratings for this than for any other questions within the survey (along with the question to teach learners with English as an additional language which has also received low ratings) (TDA 2008). While being prepared to teach learners from minority ethnic backgrounds may not automatically imply capacity to prevent racism, the TDA results do indicate a clear gap in provision and in the confidence of NQTs to support and understand the needs and experiences of these pupils. The results point to the need for a detailed examination of trainees' needs and expectations before they start their training and for a better understanding of which training courses have been most effective in supporting teaching in this area. Indeed, such provision should not be limited to teacher trainees. In view of the ongoing poor educational outcomes and high exclusion rates of certain minority ethnic students it would be prudent to extend such course provision, in the form of professional development, to qualified teachers to be repeated on a statutory basis at intervals throughout their professional careers.

Similar concerns are also pertinent to governing bodies who play an important role in supporting headteachers in the management of the school and who have various statutory duties under the Race Relations (Amendment) Act 2000. With governors coming from such a wide range of backgrounds and with varying experiences and committing their time on a voluntary basis it remains difficult to ensure that all are equally committed to and understand wider debates on race equality and education let alone their duties under the Act.

Finally, there are some quite sobering parallels to be drawn between school based research on ethnicity and available government statistics in the area of race and the criminal justice system which suggest that much work needs to be done in both areas to address race equality. For example, similar patterns of disproportionality for black groups also persists in the statistics on stop and search as it does in the figures discussed earlier in relation to school exclusions. Black people (mainly men) are up to seven times more likely to be stopped and searched than their white counterparts (see Jones and Singer 2008). Macpherson viewed this disproportionality as 'the result of discrimination'. As discussed above, black (Caribbean) students are up to three times more likely to be excluded from school than their white counterparts. Despite this inequity there has been resistance to extending the discourse of discrimination to the education system. For example, the priority review *Getting It: Getting It Right*, published at the end of 2006 made an explicit statement, following a detailed examination of the literature, about concerns of institutional racism in relation to black students' over-representation in the exclusion statistics:

> The clear message of the literature is that, to a significant extent, the exclusions gap is caused by largely unwitting, but systematic, racial discrimination in the application of disciplinary and exclusions policies. Many cite this as evidence of Institutional Racism. The Department has a legal duty to eliminate such discrimination under the Race Relations (Amendment) Act 2000. (Wanless 2006: 16)

It went on:

> The exclusion gap is the most obvious manifestation of an effect that seriously threatens to undermine the Department's efforts to extend opportunity to all children and learners. Left to its

own devices, the system will conclude that Every Child Matters, but that Black children's failure and social exclusion is to be expected – that they matter a little bit less. Personalisation could empower Black pupils to fulfil their true potential, but not whilst teachers' view of the person is conditioned by subconscious prejudice. (Wanless 2006: 16)

The review, in effect, lent weight to the large body of research and community concerns that have been voiced for many years about the exclusion of black students. While there were moves within the (then) Department for Education and Skills to carry out a series of projects to address the over-representation, the label of 'institutional racism' was dismissed by former education advisor to the government and subsequent Parliamentary Under Secretary of State for Education, Lord Adonis, as having no particular applicability to the education system as a whole (see Griggs 2006). Today black Caribbean students continue to be up to three times more likely to be excluded from school.

Yet further parallels are evident in the findings of the Morris review into professional conduct and employment matters within the Metropolitan Police and discipline in relation to black (Caribbean) students. The review found that black officers were more likely to be reprimanded for minor incidents compared with their white colleagues and that line managers were more likely to resort to formal grievance procedures when matters involved black compared with white officers (Morris 2004). This echoes findings from Ofsted about the more severe reprimands experienced by black students compared with their white peers even when engaging in similar behaviour.

To conclude, the persistent race inequities in the experiences of black students, the continued under-reporting of racist incidents, and the failure of Ofsted to seriously engage with and monitor how schools meet their race equality duties, unfortunately indicate that much more still needs to be done to meet the Stephen Lawrence Inquiry's ambitious but important education aims, set 10 years ago, of preventing and eliminating racism in society.

References

Ackerley, I. (2007, 23 April) Citizen Focus Briefing. Presented at *The Chief Constables Briefing Day 2007* [Conference]. Papplewick, UK.

ACPO (1985) *Guiding Principles Concerning Racial Attacks*. London: ACPO.

ACPO (2000) *ACPO Guide for Identifying and Combating Hate Crime*. London: ACPO.

ACPO (2001) (2nd edn) *Report and Recommendations on Police First Aid Training*. London: ACPO.

ACPO (2005) *Hate Crime: Delivering a Quality Service (Good Practice and Tactical Guidance)*. London: ACPO.

ACPO (2007) *Practical Advice on Critical Incident Management*. London: National Police Improvement Agency.

Adams, T. (2002) *Performance Report: Homicide. Report to Professional Standards and Performance Monitoring Committee*. London: Metropolitan Police Authority.

Ajegbo, K., Kiwan, D. and Sharma, S. (2007) *Diversity and Citizenship: Curriculum Review*. Nottingham: DfES.

Alison, L. and Crego, J. (2008). *Policing Critical Incidents: Leadership and Critical Incident Management*. Cullompton: Willan Publishing.

Alison, L., Crego, J., Whitfield, K., Caddick, A. and Cataudo, L. (2008) 'Leading, co-operation and context in Hydra syndicates', in L. Alison and J. Crego (eds) *Policing Critical Incidents: Leadership and Critical Incident Management*. Cullompton: Willan Publishing.

Allen, J., Edmonds, S., Patterson, A. and Smith, D. (2006). *Policing and the Criminal*. London: APA.

Association of Police Authorities (2004) *Involving Communities in Police Learning and Development: A Guide*. London: Association of Police Authorities.

Baggini, J. and Stangroom, J. (eds) (2002) *New British Philosophy. The Interviews.* London: Routledge.

Baker, D. (2002) 'Public Order Policing', in T. Prenzler and J. Ransley (eds) *Police Reform: Building Integrity.* Sydney: Hawkins Press.

Baker, R. (1972 reprinted 1999) *The Terror of Tobermory.* Edinburgh: Berlinn Ltd.

Baltes, B.B., Dickson, M.W., Sherman, M.P., Bauer, C.C. and La Ganke, J.J. (2002) 'Computer mediated communication and group decision making: a meta-analysis', *Organisational Behaviour and Human Decision Processes*, 87: 156–179.

Barker, A. (1998) 'Political Responsibility for UK Prison Security – Ministers Escape Again', *Public Administration*, 76(1).

BBC (2004, 11 Oct) *Crime reduction strategy 'flawed'.* Accessed 18 September 2006 from http://news.bbc.co.uk/1/hi/uk/3732244.stm

Beesly, P. (2000) (2nd edn) *Very Special Intelligence. A Story of the Admiralty's Operational Intelligence Centre 1939–1945.* London: Greenhill Books.

Beesly, P. (1990) 'Convoy PQ17: A Study of Intelligence and Decision Making', pp. 292–322, in M. Handel (1990) *Intelligence and Military Operations.* London: Cass.

Bernard, B. (2002) 'The agenda for education in challenging racism and promoting good race relations: implementing the Race Relations Amendment Act', *Multicultural Teaching*, 20 (3): 12–15.

Bhatti, A. (2008) 'The mobiles are out and the hoods are up', in C. Harfield, A. MacVean, J. Grieve and D. Phillips *The Handbook of Intelligent Policing, Consilience, Crime Control, and Community Safety.* Oxford: Oxford University Press.

Bhavnani, R., Mirza, H.S. and Meetoo, V. (2005) *Tackling the Roots of Racism: Lessons for Success.* Bristol: Policy Press.

Blair, I. (1985) *Investigating Rape: A New Approach.* London: Croom Helm.

Blair, M. (2001) *Why Pick on Me?* Stoke-on-Trent: Trentham Books.

Blair, T. (2006) 'The duty to integrate: Shared British values', speech at *Our Nation's Future* series, Downing Street, London, 8 December.

Blakey, D. (2001) *HMIC Revisit re: part II of 'Winning Consent'.* London: HMIC.

Blakey, D. and Crompton, D. (2000) *Policing London – Winning Consent. A review of murder investigations and community and race relations issues in the Metropolitan Police Service.* London: HMIC.

Blakey, D., Nove, P. and Sentamu, J. (2002) *The Damilola Taylor Murder Investigation Review: report of the oversight panel.* London: MPS.

Blum, L. (1999) 'Moral asymmetries in racism', in S. Babbitt and S. Campbell (eds) *Racism and Philosophy.* Ithaca, New York: Cornell University Press.

Blum, L. (2002) *I'm not a racist, but … : The moral quandary of race.* Ithaca, New York: Cornell University Press.

Blunkett, D. (1999) *Ethnic minority pupils must have the opportunity to fulfil their potential.* 24 February, 90/99 www.dfee.gov.uk/news/90.htm, accessed 20 October 1999.

Boin, A. and t' Hart, P. (2000) 'Institutional crises and reforms in the policy sectors', in H. Wagenaar (ed.) *Government Institutions: Effects, Changes and Normative Foundations*. Boston, MA: Kluwer.

Boon, N. (2007) 'Collaborative Working', paper presented to HE Forum, Skills for Justice, 21 March.

Boston, K. (2007) 'Curriculum for the 21 Century', speech at the launch of the new secondary curriculum. (Available at www.qca.org.uk/qca_12423.aspx, accessed 5 November 2008).

Bowers, A. (2008) 'Knowledge management and the National Intelligence Model', in C. Harfield, A. MacVean, J. Grieve and D. Phillips *The Handbook of Intelligent Policing, Consilience, Crime Control, and Community Safety*. Oxford: Oxford University Press.

Bowling, B. (1998a) *Violent Racism. Victimisation, Policing and Social Context*. Oxford: Clarendon Press.

Bowling, B. (1998b) *Violent Racism: Victimisation, Policing and Social Context*. Part II submission to the SLI, July 1998.

Bowling, B. (1999) *Violent Racism*. Oxford: Clarendon Press.

Bowling, B. and Phillips, C. (2002) *Racism, Crime and Justice*. Harlow: Pearson Education.

Brathwaite, J. (2005) *Hard to Hear Voices: A Comparison of Internal and External Ethnic Minority Pressure Groups Within the Policing Sector*. Portsmouth: University of Portsmouth (unpublished doctoral thesis).

Brown, G. (2006) 'The future of Britishness', presentation to The Fabian Society *Who do we want to be? The future of Britishness* conference, Imperial College, London, 14 January.

Buckley, R. and Caple, J. (1995) *The Theory and Practice of Training*. London: Kogan Page.

Bull, R. and Horncastle, P. (1988) 'Evaluating training: the London Metropolitan Police's recruit training in human awareness/policing skills', in P. Southgate (ed.), *New Directions in Police Training*. London: HMSO.

Burden, A., Morris, W. and Weekes, A. (2004) *The Case for Change – People in the Metropolitan Police Service: The Report of the Morris Inquiry*. London: MPA.

Burney, E. and Rose, G. (2002) *Racist Offences: How is the Law Working?* Home Office Research Study 244. London: Home Office.

Butler, Lord (2004) *Espionage and the Iraq War*. London: The Stationery Office, HC 898. Reprinted by Tim Coates, London.

Cabinet Office (2006) *Fairness and Freedom: The final report of the Equalities Review*. London: Cabinet Office.

Carrabine, E. (2005) 'Prison riots, social order and the problem of legitimacy', *British Journal of Criminology*, 45 (6).

Cashmore, E. (2002) 'Behind the window dressing: ethnic minority police perspectives on cultural diversity', *Journal of Ethnic and Migration Studies*, 28 (2): 327–341.

Cathcart, B. (1998) 'An Inspector calls'. London: *New Statesman*, 26 June.

Cathcart, B. (1999) *The Case of Stephen Lawrence*. London: Viking.

Chakraborti, N. and Garland, J. (2000) 'Under-researched and overlooked: an exploration of the attitudes of rural minority ethnic communities towards crime, community safety and the criminal justice system' [electronic version]. *Journal of Ethnic and Migration Studies*, 29 (3): 563–572.

Chahal, K. and Julienne, L. (1999) *'We Can't All Be White!' Racist victimisation in the UK*. York: Joseph Rowntree Foundation.

Clancy, A., Hough, M., Aust, R. and Kershaw, C. (2001) *Crime, Policing and Justice: the Experience of Ethnic Minorities. Findings from the 2000 British Crime Survey* (Home Office Research Study 223) [electronic version]. London: Home Office.

Clarke, I. and Moody, S. (2002) *Racist Crime and Victimization in Scotland.* Edinburgh: Scottish Executive Research Unit.

Clements, P. (2000) 'Fair enough? Improving the teaching and learning of Equal Opportunities in the British Police Service.' Home Office Police Research Award Scheme.

Clements, P. and Jones, J. (2008) (3rd edn) *The Diversity Training Handbook*. London: Kogan-Page.

Coard, B. (1971) *How the West Indian Child is Made Educationally Subnormal in the British School System*. London: New Beacon Books.

Collier, P.M. (2001) 'Valuing intellectual capacity in the police', *Accounting, Auditing and Accountability Journal*, 14 (4): 437–455.

Commission for Racial Equality (2002) *Statutory Code of Practice on the Duty to Promote Race Equality*. London: CRE.

Commission for Racial Equality (CRE) and Schneider-Ross (2003) *Towards Racial Equality: An evaluation of the public duty to promote race equality and good race relations in England and Wales (2002)*.

Crompton, G. and Jupe, R. (2002) 'Delivering better transport? An evaluation of the ten-year plan for the railway industry', *Public Money and Management*, 22 (3).

Cullen, W. (1996) *The Public Inquiry into the Shootings at Dunblane Primary School*. London: HMSO.

Daily Mail, 29 August 2008.

Daily Telegraph, 29 August 2008.

Davis, J. (2008) 'Why Bad Things Happen to Good Analysts.' In R. George and J. Bruce (eds.), *Analyzing Intelligence. Origins, Obstacles and Innovations*. Washington: Georgetown University Press.

Deakin, C.D., Peters, R., Tomlinson, P. and Cassidy, M. (2005) 'Securing the prehospital airway: a comparison of laryngeal mask insertion and endotracheal intubation by UK paramedics', *Emergency Medical Journal*, 22: 64–67.

Department for Children, Schools and Families and Department for Communities and Local Government (2007) *Guidance on the Duty to Promote Community Cohesion*. Nottingham: DCSF.

Department for Children, Schools and Families (2007) *National Curriculum Assessment, GCSE and Equivalent Attainment and Post-16 Attainment by Pupil Characteristics, in England 2006/07*. SFR 38/2007. London: DCSF.

Department for Children, Schools and Families (2008) *Permanent and Fixed Period Exclusions from Schools in England 2006/07*. SFR 13/2008. London: DCSF.

Department for Education and Employment (1999) *Social Inclusion: Pupil Support*. Circular No. 10/99. London: DfEE.

Department for Education and Employment (DfEE) (2001) 'Black and Indian students see big improvement in GCSE results', *press notice 2001/0033*. London: DfEE.

Department for Education and Skills (DfES) (2003) *Permanent Exclusions from Schools and Exclusion Appeals, England 2001/2002 (provisional)*. SFR 16/2003. London: DfES.

Department for Education and Skills (DfES) (2004) *Permanent Exclusions from Maintained Schools in England, 2002/2003*. SFR 42/2004. London: DfES, Table 4.

Department for Education and Skills (DfES) (2005) *Permanent and Fixed Period Exclusions from Schools and Exclusion Appeals in England, 2003/04*. London: DfES.

Department for Education and Skills (2006a) *Ethnicity and Education: The evidence on minority ethnic pupils aged 5—16*. Research Topic Edition 2006. London: DfES.

Department for Education and Skills (DfES) (2006b) *Permanent and Fixed Period Exclusions from Schools and Exclusion Appeals in England, 2004/05*. London: DfES.

Department for Education and Skills (DfES) (2007) *Permanent and Fixed Period Exclusions from Schools and Exclusion Appeals in England, 2005/06*. SFR 21/2007. London: DfES.

Docking, M., Keilinger, V. and Paterson, S. (2003) 'Policing racist incidents in the Metropolitan Police Service'. Paper given to the Research and Development Conference, 3 June 2003.

Docking, M. and Tuffin, R. (2005) *Racist Incidents: progress since the Lawrence Inquiry* (Home Office Online Report 42/05). Accessed 6 March 2006 from Home Office website: http://www.homeoffice.gov.uk/rds/pdfs05/rdsolr4205.pdf.

Dunleavy, P. (1995) 'Policy disasters: Explaining the UK's record', *Public Policy and Administration*, 10 (2).

Essex Police (2006) 'Community Involvement in Police Learning and Development'. Paper presented to Essex Police Performance Committee.

Evans, R.M. (2008) 'Cultural paradigms and change: a model of analysis', in C. Harfield, A. MacVean, J. Grieve and D. Phillips *The Handbook of Intelligent Policing, Consilience, Crime Control, and Community Safety*. Oxford: Oxford University Press.

Eyre, M., Crego, J. and Alison, L. (2008) 'Electronic debriefs and simulations as descriptive methods for defining the critical incident landscape' in L. Alison and J. Crego (eds), *Policing Critical Incidents: Leadership and Critical Incident Management*. Cullompton: Willan Publishing.

FBI (2002) *Hate Crime Statistics 2001*. Washington DC: US Department of Justice.

Fennell, D. (1988) *Investigation into the King's Cross Fire*. London: HMSO.

Fisher, H. (1977) *The Confait Case: Report*. London: HMSO.

Flin, R. (1995) 'Incident command: Decision making and team work', *Journal of the Fire Service College*, 1 (1): 7–15.

Forbes, P. and Jones, J. (2008) 'Vector Command launches Command Assessor-Police system for command training and assessment', *Policing Today*, 14 (4) (September 2008): 20–21.

Foster, J. (1999) *Memorandum by Dr Janet Foster to the Home Affairs Committee Inquiry into Police Training and Recruitment*. London: House of Commons.

Foster, J. (2008) 'It might have been incompetent but it wasn't racist', *Policing and Society*, 18.

Foster, J., Newburn, T. and Souhami, A. (2005) *Assessing the Impact of the Stephen Lawrence Inquiry* (Home Office Research Study 294). London: Home Office Research, Development and Statistics Directorate.

Fricker, M. (2002) 'Power knowledge and injustice', in J. Baggini and J. Stangroom (eds), *New British Philosophy. The Interviews*. London: Routledge.

Gaffney, J. (1987) *Interpretation of Violence: The Handsworth Riots of 1985*. Coventry: Centre for Research in Ethnic Relations.

George, R. and Bruce, J. (2008) (eds) *Analyzing Intelligence. Origins, Obstacles and Innovations*. Washington: Georgetown University Press.

Gillborn, D. (1999) 'Fifty years of failure: "Race" and education policy in Britain', in A. Hayton (ed.), *Tackling Disaffection and Social Exclusion: Education Perspectives and Policies*. London: Kogan Page.

Gillborn, D. (2008) *Racism and Education: Coincidence or Conspiracy?* London: Routledge.

Gillborn, D. and Rollock, N. (forthcoming) 'Education', in A. Block and J. Solomos (eds), *Race and Ethnicity in the 21st Century*. London: Palgrave Macmillan.

Gillborn, D. and Youdell, D. (2000) *Rationing Education: Policy, Practice, Reform and Equity*. Buckingham: Open University Press.

Golding, B. and Savage, S. (2008) 'Leadership and Performance Management', in T. Newburn (ed.) *Handbook of Policing* (2nd edn). Cullompton: Willan Publishing.

Grant, W. (1989) *Pressure Groups and British Politics*. London: Palgrave Macmillan.

Grieve, J. (2002) Public lecture at various sites in London and elsewhere on developments since the SLI.

Grieve, J. (2004) 'Developments in UK criminal intelligence', in J. Ratcliffe (ed.), *Strategic Thinking and Criminal Intelligence*. New South Wales: Federation Press.

Grieve, J. (2008a) 'Lawfully audacious – a reflective journey', in C. Harfield, A. MacVean, J. Grieve and D. Phillips (eds), *The Handbook of Intelligent Policing, Consilience, Crime Control, and Community Safety*. Oxford: Oxford University Press.

Grieve, J. (2008b) 'Understanding critical event learning and leadership: Hydra/10k immersive learning, debriefing and other tools', in L. Alison and J. Crego (eds), *Policing Critical Incidents: Leadership and Critical Incident Management*. Cullompton: Willan Publishing.

Grieve, J., Crego, J. and Griffiths, W. (2007) 'Critical incidents, investigation, management and training', in T. Newburn, T. Williamson and A. Wright (eds), *Handbook of Criminal Investigation*. Cullompton: Willan Publishing.

Grieve, J. and French, J. (2000) 'Does institutional racism exist in the Metropolitan Police?', in D. Green (ed.), *Institutional Racism and the Police*. London: Institute for the Study of Civil Society.

Griffiths, W. (1999) *Special Notice 6/99 Major Crime Review*. Unpublished MPS policy on murder investigation.

Griffiths, W. (2000) *Vision for the Implementation of the Serious Crime Group by DAC Bill Griffiths*. Unpublished.

Griggs, I. (2006) 'Institutionally racist: Report tells how black children are being discriminated against in schools', *The Independent*, 10 December. (Available at www.independent.co.uk/news/education/ education-news/institutionally-racist-report-tells-how-black-children-are-being-discriminated-against-in-schools-427859.html last accessed 6 November 2008).

Guardian (19 September 2008) 'Met Commander ... suspended ...'

Guardian (29 August 2008) 'Top Asian officer sets out race case ...'

Hall, N. (2002, 18 October) 'Crimes of hatred', *Police Review*, 18–19.

Hall, N. (2005) *Hate Crime*. Cullompton: Willan Publishing.

Hall, P. (1993) 'Policy paradigms, social learning, and the State: the case of economic policymaking in Britain', *Comparative Politics*, 25 (3): 275–296.

Handel, M. (1990) *Intelligence and Military Operations*. London: Cass.

Harfield, C. and Harfield, K. (2005) *Covert Investigation*. Oxford: Oxford University Press.

Harfield, C. and Harfield, K. (2008) *Intelligence: Investigation, Community and Partnership*. Oxford: Oxford University Press.

Harfield, C., MacVean, A., Grieve, J. and Phillips, D. (2008) *The Handbook of Intelligent Policing, Consilience, Crime Control, and Community Safety*. Oxford: Oxford University Press.

Hermitage, P. (1999) *Memorandum by Mr Peter Hermitage to the Home Affairs Committee Inquiry into Police Training and Recruitment*. London: House of Commons.

Heslop, R. (2006) '"Doing a Maslow": Humanistic education and diversity in police training', *Police Journal*, 79 (4), 331–342.

HM Government (2008) *The Prevent Strategy. A Guide for Local Partners in England. Stopping people becoming or supporting terrorists or violent extremists.* London: HM Government.

HMIC (Her Majesty's Inspectorate of Constabulary) (1997) *Policing With Intelligence, Criminal Intelligence – A Thematic Inspection of Good Practice.* London: Home Office.

HMIC (1997b) *Winning the Race: Policing Plural Communities.* London: HMSO.

HMIC (1999a) *Winning the Race: Policing Plural Communities – Revisited.* London: HMSO.

HMIC (1999b) *Managing Learning: A Study of Police Training.* London: HMSO.

HMIC (1999c) *Winning the Race Revisited* (1998/99). London: Home Office.

HMIC (2000) *Winning the Race: Embracing Diversity.* London: Home Office.

HMIC (2002) *HMIC Inspection Manual 2002.* London: HMIC.

HMIC (2002) *Training Matters.* London: HMSO.

HMIC (2003) *Diversity Matters.* London: HMSO.

(HMIC) (2008) *Duty Calls – HMIC Inspection of Race Equality Compliance 2006–07.* London: Home Office.

Hoffman, R.R. (1987) 'The problem of extracting the knowledge of experts from the perspective of experimental psychology', *The AI Magazine*, 8: 53–66.

Hoffman, R.R., Shadbolt, N.R., Burton, A.M. and Klein, G. (1995) 'Eliciting knowledge from experts: a methodological analysis', *Organizational Behavior and Human Decision Processes*, 62 (2): 129–158.

Holdaway, S. and O'Neill, M. (2007) 'Black Police Associations and the Lawrence Report', in M. Rowe (ed.), *Policing Since Macpherson.* Cullompton: Willan Publishing.

Home Office (1998) *Review of National Police Training: Draft Report.* London: Home Office.

Home Office (1999) *Stephen Lawrence Inquiry: Home Secretary's Action Plan.* London: Home Office.

Home Office (2000a) *Code of Practice on Reporting and Recording Racist Incidents.* London: Home Office.

Home Office (2000b) *Police Training: The Way Forward.* London: Home Office.

Home Office (2001) *Stephen Lawrence Inquiry. Home Secretary's Action Plan Annual Report on Progress.* February 2001.

Home Office (2001) *Building Cohesive Communities.* London: Home Office.

Home Office (2002) *Stephen Lawrence Inquiry. Home Secretary's Action Plan Annual Report on Progress.* June 2002.

Home Office (2003) *Stephen Lawrence Inquiry. Home Secretary's Action Plan Annual Report on Progress.* March 2003.

Home Office (2005a) *Definitions and Survey Guidance for PPPAF Measures of User Satisfaction 2005/6* [Electronic version]. London: Home Office.

Home Office (2005b) *National Community Safety Plan*. London: Home Office.

Home Office (2005c) *Statistics on Race and the Criminal Justice System – 2004.* [electronic version]. London: Home Office.

Home Office (2005d) *Lawrence Steering Group: 6th Annual Report*. London: Home Office.

Home Office (2005e) Home Office Circular 4/2005: The Police Race and Diversity Learning and Development Programme. London: Home Office.

Home Office (2006) *Statistics on Race and the Criminal Justice System: A Home Office publication under Section 95 of the Criminal Justice Act 1991*. London: Home Office.

Home Office (2006a) *Race and the Criminal Justice System: An overview to the complete statistics 2004–2005* [electronic version]. London: Home Office.

Home Office (2006b) *Statistics on Race and the Criminal Justice System – 2005.* London: Home Office.

Home Office (n.d.) *National Performance Indicator Data 2005/06*. Accessed 19 August 2007 from Home Office website: http://police.homeoffice.gov.uk/performance-and-measurement/performance-assessment/assessments-2005-2006/national-assessments/national-performance-indicators/http://www.skillsforjustice.com/websitefiles/NOS_Common_Standards_Briefing.pdf. Accessed 7 November 2008.

House of Commons (1999) *Home Affairs Committee Inquiry into Police Training and Recruitment*. London: HMSO.

Hyland, T. (1997) 'Teaching, learning and NVQs: Challenging behaviourism and competence in adult education theory and practice'. Paper presented at the SCUTREA.

Iganski, P. (1999) 'Legislating against hate: Outlawing racism and anti-semitism in Britain', *Critical Social Policy*, 19 (1): 129–141.

Ignatieff, M. (2000) 'Less race, please', in D. Green (ed.), *Institutional Racism and the Police: fact or fiction* [electronic version]. London: Institute for the Study of Civil Society. Accessed 25 September 2006 from: http://www.civitas.org.uk/pdf/cs06.pdf

Jackson, R. (2008) 'Conversations in Critical Studies on Terrorism. Counter-terrorism and Communities: an interview with Robert Lambert', *Critical Studies in Terrorism*, 1 (2): 1–16. London: Routledge.

Jacobs, J. and Potter, K. (1998) *Hate Crimes: Criminal Law and Identity Politics*. New York: Oxford University Press.

John, G. (2003) *Race for Justice: A Review of CPS Decision-Making for Possible Racial Bias at Each Stage of the Prosecution Process*. London: CPS.

Johnson, N. and McCarvill, P. (2007) *CRE Monitoring and Enforcement Plan – Final Report*. London: CRE (Available at www.equalityhumanrights.com/Documents/Race/General%20advice%20and%20information/monitoring_and_enforcement_report_2005-7.pdf last accessed 6 November 2008).

Jones, A. and Singer, L. (2008) *Statistics on Race and the Criminal Justice System – 2006/07*. A Ministry of Justice publication under Section 95 of the Criminal Justice Act 1991. London: Ministry of Justice.

Jones, J. (2008) (ed.) *Police Ethics, Values and Human Rights Workbook*. Portsmouth: University of Portsmouth and Surrey Police.

Jones, S. and Mason, T. (2002) 'Quality of treatment following police detention of mentally disordered persons', *Journal of Psychiatric and Mental Health Nursing*, 1 (1).

Juett, L., Smith, R. and Grieve, J. (2008) 'Open Source Intelligence – a case study: GLADA "London – the Highs and Lows", 2003 and 2007', in C. Harfield, A. MacVean, J. Grieve and D. Phillips *The Handbook of Intelligent Policing, Consilience, Crime Control, and Community Safety*. Oxford: Oxford University Press.

Kebbel, M. and Wagstaff, G. (1999) *Face Value? Evaluating the Accuracy of Eyewitness Information* Police Research Series Paper 102 [electronic version]. London: Home Office.

Keeler, J. (1993) 'Opening windows for reform: Mandates, crises and extraordinary policy-making', *Comparative Political Studies*, 25 (4).

Kennedy, H. (2005) *Just Law: The Changing Face of Justice and Why It Matters to Us All*. London: Vintage.

Kenny, J. and Reid, M. (1986) *Training Interventions*. London: Institute of Personnel Management.

Kerr, R.J. (2008a) 'The perfect enemy. Reflections of an Intelligence Officer on the Cold War and today's challenges', in C. Harfield, A. MacVean, J. Grieve and D. Phillips *The Handbook of Intelligent Policing, Consilience, Crime Control, and Community Safety*. Oxford: Oxford University Press.

Kerr, R.J. (2008b) 'The track record. CIA analysis 1950–2000', in R. George and J. Bruce (eds), *Analyzing Intelligence. Origins, Obstacles and Innovations*. Washington: Georgetown University Press.

Kitchen, S., Michaelson, J. and Wood, N. (2006). *2005 Citizenship Survey: Race and faith topic report* [electronic version]. London: Department for Communities and Local Government.

Klein, G.A., Orasanu, J., Calderwood, R. and Zsambok, C.E. (eds) (1993) *Decision Making in Action: Models and Methods*. Norwood, CT: Ablex.

Knight, J. (2007) 'Community cohesion'. Speech presented at 'Promoting Community Cohesion through Schools' conference, *Runnymede Trust Bulletin*, No. 352, December 2007.

Kohatsu, E. and Sasao, T. (2003) 'Perceived racism, racial environments, and hate violence against Asian Americans', in B. Wallace and T. Carter (eds) *Understanding and Dealing with Violence: A Multicultural Approach*. Thousand Oaks, CA: Sage.

Kozlowski, S.W., Gully, S.M., Nason, E.R. and Smith, E.M. (1999) 'Developing adaptive teams: a theory of compilation and performance across levels and time', in P.R. Ilgen and E.D. Pulakos (eds) *The Changing Nature of Performance* (pp. 240–292). San Francisco: Jossey-Bass.

Kuhn, T. (1962) *The Structure of Scientific Revolutions.* Chicago: Chicago University Press.

Laming, Lord (2003) *The Victoria Climbié Inquiry.* Cmnd. 5730. London: The Stationery Office.

Lawrence, D. (2006) *And Still I Rise. Seeking Justice for Stephen.* London: Faber and Faber.

Lea, J. (2000) 'The Macpherson Report and the question of institutional racism', *The Howard Journal*, 39 (3), 219–233.

Lipshitz, R., Klein, G., Orasanu, J. and Salas, E. (2001) 'Taking stock of naturalistic decision making', *Journal of Behavioural Decision Making*, 14, 331–352.

London Assembly (2006) *Report of the 7 July Review Committee.* London: Greater London Authority.

Lowenthal, M. (2008) 'Intelligence in transition: Analysis after September 11 and Iraq', in R. George and J. Bruce (eds) *Analyzing Intelligence. Origins, Obstacles and Innovations.* Washington: Georgetown University Press.

Macdonald, I., Bhavnani, R., Khan, L. and John, G. (1989). *Murder in the Playground.* The Burnage Report. Report of the Macdonald Inquiry into Racism and Racial Violence in Manchester Schools. London: Longsight Press.

Macpherson, W. (1999) *The Stephen Lawrence Inquiry.* London: HMSO.

Maguire, M. (2000) 'Researching street criminals: a neglected art', in R. King and E. Wincup (eds), *Doing Research on Crime and Justice.* Oxford: Oxford University Press.

Marks, M.A., Sabella, M.J., Burke, C.S. and Zaccaro, Z.J. (2002) 'The impact of cross training on team effectiveness', *Journal of Applied Psychology*, 87, 3–13.

Martin, J. and Evans, D. (1984) *Hospitals in Trouble.* Oxford: Blackwell.

Maylor, U., Read, B., Ross, A., Mendick, H. and Rollock, N. (2007) *Diversity and Citizenship in the Curriculum: Research Review.* Research Report RR819. London: DfES.

Maynard, W. and Read, T. (1997) *Policing Racially Motivated Incidents: Police Research Group Crime Detection and Prevention Series, Number 59.* London: Home Office.

McGhee, D. (2005) *Intolerant Britain? Hate Citizenship and Difference.* Maidenhead: Open University Press.

McLaughlin, E. (1999) 'The search for truth and justice', *Criminal Justice Matters*, 35: 13–15.

McLaughlin, E. (2002) 'Rocks and hard places: The politics of hate crime', *Theoretical Criminology*, 6 (4): 493–8.

Metropolitan Police (1993) *Fairness, Community, Justice Conference. Report and the Way Forward.* December 1993. London: Metropolitan Police.

Metropolitan Police (1998a) *Racial and Violent Crime Task Force CO24. Action Plan,* version 6, 18 September 1998. Operation Athena. London: Metropolitan Police.

Metropolitan Police (1998b) *The London Beat.* London: Metropolitan Police.

Metropolitan Police (1998c) *MPS Strategy – Policing Plan 1998/9.* London: Metropolitan Police.

Metropolitan Police Authority (2001) *The Virdi Inquiry Report.* London: MPA.

Metropolitan Police Miscellaneous Documents, 1998–2004.

Metropolitan Police Service (1999a) Independent Advisory Group minutes dated 16 June 1999. London: Metropolitan Police Service.

Metropolitan Police Service (1999b) *Briefing Note: Lay Involvement Analysis of MPS Borough Commanders' Survey.* London: Metropolitan Police Service.

Metropolitan Police Service (1999c) *Minutes of the Independent Advisory Group Conference,* dated 17 December 1999. London: Metropolitan Police Service.

Metropolitan Police Service (1999d) *Minimum Investigative Standards for Community Safety Units: Special Notice 7/99.* London: Metropolitan Police Service.

Metropolitan Police Service (2000f) *Communities: Making the Difference. National Independent Advisory Groups Conference, 13 November 2000.* London: Metropolitan Police Service.

Metropolitan Police Service (2000g) *Outstanding Recommendations and Requests from the Anti-Racist Subgroup,* dated 27 July 2000. London: Metropolitan Police Service.

Metropolitan Police Service (2002b) *A Guide to the Management and Prevention of Critical Incidents.* London: Metropolitan Police Service.

Morris, W., Burden, A. and Weekes, A. (2004) *The Report of the Morris Inquiry: An Independent Inquiry for Professional Standards and Employment Matters in the Metropolitan Police Service.* London: MPA.

Murji, K. (2007) Sociological engagements: Institutional racism and beyond. *Sociology,* 41 (5): 843–855 (available at http://soc.sagepub.com/cgi/content/abstract/41/5/843 last accessed 21 October 2008).

Newburn, T., Williamson, T. and Wright, A. (2007) (eds) *Handbook of Criminal Investigation.* Cullompton: Willan Publishing.

NCIS (2000) *National Intelligence Model.* London: Home Office.

Neyroud, P. and Beckley, A. (2001) *Policing, Ethics and Human Rights.* Cullompton: Willan Publishing.

Nicholas, S. and Walker, A. (2004) *Crime in England and Wales 2002/2003: Supplementary Volume 2: Crime, disorder and the Criminal Justice System – public attitudes and perceptions.* London: Home Office.

Norris, N. and Kushner, S. (1999) *Memorandum by Professor Nigel Norris, University of East Anglia and Professor Saville Kushner, University of the West of England to the Home Affairs Committee Inquiry into Police Training and Recruitment.* London: House of Commons.

O'Hara P. (2005) *Why Law Enforcement Organisations Fail. Mapping the Organizational Fault Lines.* North Carolina, USA: Carolina Academic Press.

Oakley, R. (1999) *Memorandum by Dr Robin Oakley to the Home Affairs Committee Inquiry into Police Training and Recruitment.* London: House of Commons.

Oakley, R. (2000). The NAPAP project: promoting community involvement in police training. *The Runneymede Bulletin.* June 2000.

Observer, 31 January 1999, 'Let's Nick Some Racists'.

Office for Criminal Justice Reform (2006) *Report of the Race for Justice Taskforce.* London: Office for Criminal Justice Reform.

Ofsted (2001) *Improving Attendance and Behaviour in Secondary Schools.* London: Ofsted.

Ofsted (2005) *Race Equality in Schools: Good Practice in Schools and Local Authorities.* London: Ofsted.

Omodei, M. and Wearing, A. (1994) 'Perceived difficulty and motivated cognitive effort in a computer-simulated forest firefighting task', *Perceptual and Motor Skills,* 79: 115–127.

Omodei, M. and Wearing, A. (1995) 'The Fire Chief microworld generating program: an illustration of computer-simulated Microworlds as an experimental paradigm for studying complex decision making behaviour', *Behavior Research Methods, Instruments and Computers,* 27: 303–316.

Open Source (2008) *Prospectus for MPS Crime Academy and Leadership Academy and MPS Values and Behaviours under 'Together'.* Accessed from www. teamMet.com.

OPSI (2005) *The Police Authorities (Best Value) Performance Indicators Order 2005* (retrieved October 2008 at http://www.opsi.gov/uk/si/si2005/20050470. htm).

Osler, A. (1999) 'Citizenship, democracy and political literacy', *Multicultural Teaching,* 18 (1), 12–15 and 29.

Osler, A. and Morrison, M. (2000) *Inspecting Schools for Racial Equality: Ofsted's strengths and weaknesses.* A report for the CRE. Stoke-on-Trent: Trentham Books.

Paddick, B. (2008) *Line of Fire.* London: Simon and Schuster.

Parekh, B. (2000) *The Future of Multi-ethnic Britain.* Report of the Commission on the future of multi-ethnic Britain. London: Profile Books for the Runnymede Trust.

Parsons, C., Godfrey, R., Annan, G., Cornwall, J., Dussart, M., Hepburn, S., Howlett, K. and Wennerstrom, V. (2004) *Minority Ethnic Exclusions and the Race Relations (Amendment) Act 2000.* Research Report 616. London: Department for Education and Skills.

Patterson, M.G., West, M.A., Lawthom, R. and Nickell, S. (1997) *Impact of People Management Practices on Business Performance*. London: Institute of Personnel and Development.

Police Complaints Authority (1997) *Report by the Police Complaints Authority on the Investigation of a Complaint Against the Metropolitan Police Service by Mr. N. and Mrs D. Lawrence: Presented to Parliament by the Secretary of State for the Home Department by Command of Her Majesty, December 1997*. London: Home Office.

Police Review (1998a) 'A long hard slog', 11 September, p. 5.

Police Review (1998b) 'Watching the detectives', 11 September, pp. 16–18.

Police Review (2006) 'Met recruits learn black culture', 1 September, p. 4.

Police Standards Unit (2006) *Guidance of Statutory Performance Indicators for Policing 2006/2007 Version 1.0*. London: Home Office.

Policy Studies Institute (PSI) (1983) 'Police and People in London, IV: The Police in Action', D.J. Smith and J. Gray. PSI Study No. 621. London.

PDTN (2008) Police Diversity Trainers Network, from http://www.pdtn.co.uk/.

Punch, M. (2000) 'Police corruption and its prevention', *European Journal of Criminal Policy and Research*, 8.

Punch, M. (2003) 'Rotten Orchards: "Pestilence", police misconduct and system failure', *Policing and Society*, 13 (2).

Qualifications and Curriculum Authority (2008) *National Curriculum: Citizenship* (Available at http://curriculum.qca.org.uk/key-stages-3-and-4/subjects/citizenship/keystage3/ last accessed 3 November 2008).

Ratcliffe, J. (2004) *Strategic Thinking and Criminal Intelligence*. NSW: Federation Press (2nd edn in press).

Reiner, R. (1991) *Chief Constables*. Oxford: Oxford University Press.

Reiner, R. (1992) *The Politics of the Police* (2nd edn). Hemel Hempstead: Harvester Wheatsheaf.

Reiner, R. (2000) *The Politics of the Police* (3rd edn). Oxford: Oxford University Press.

Richards, L. (2006) 'Homicide prevention: Findings from the multi agency domestic violence homicide reviews', *Journal of Homicide and Major Incident Investigation*, 2 (2): 53–72. London: ACPO.

Robinson, I. and Robinson, J. (2001) 'Sometimes it's hard to get a taxi when you are Black: the implications of the Macpherson Report for teacher education', *Journal of In-service Education*, 27 (2): 303–321.

Rollock, N. (2007a) 'Legitimising Black academic failure: deconstructing staff discourse on academic success, appearance and behaviour', *International Studies in Sociology of Education*, 17 (3): 275–287.

Rollock, N. (2007b) *Failure by any other name? Educational Policy and the continuing struggle for Black academic success*. Runnymede Perspectives. London: Runnymede Trust.

Rollock, N. (forthcoming 2009) *The Stephen Lawrence Inquiry 10 Years On: A Literature Review*. London: The Runnymede Trust.

Rosenbaum, D., Schuck, A., Costello, S., Hawkins, D. and Ring, M. (2005) 'Attitudes toward the police: The effects of direct and vicarious experience', *Police Quarterly*, 8 (3): 343–365.

Rowe, M. (2004) *Policing, Race and Racism*. Cullompton: Willan Publishing.

Rowe, M. (2007) (ed.) *Policing Beyond Macpherson. Issues in Policing, Race and Society*. Cullompton: Willan Publishing.

Roycroft, M., Brown, J. and Innes, M. (2007) 'Reform by crisis: the murder of Stephen Lawrence and a socio-historical analysis of developments in the conduct of major crime investigations', in M. Rowe (ed.), *Policing Beyond Macpherson: Issues in Policing, Race and Society*. Cullompton: Willan Publishing.

Rozenberg, J. (1994) *The Search for Justice*. London: Sceptre.

Salisbury, H. and Upson, A. (2004) *Ethnicity, victimisation and worry about crime: findings from the 2001/02 and 2002/03 British Crime Survey* (Findings 237). London: Home Office.

Savage, S. (2007) *Police Reform. Forces for Change*. Oxford: Oxford University Press.

Savage, S. (2007a) 'Restoring justice: Campaigns against miscarriages of justice and the restorative justice process', *European Journal of Criminology*, 4 (2): 195–216.

Savage, S.P., Charman, S. and Cope, S. (2000) *Policing and The Power of Persuasion*. London: Blackstone Press Ltd.

Savage, S., Poyser, S. and Grieve, J. (2007) 'Putting wrongs to right: Campaigns against miscarriage of justice', *Criminology and Criminal Justice*, 7 (1): 83–105. London: Sage.

Scarman, L. (1981) *The Brixton Disorders, 10–12 April 1981: report of an enquiry*. London: HMSO.

Sentamu, J., Blakey, D. and Nove, P. (2002) *The Damilola Taylor Murder Investigation Review. Report of the Oversight Panel*. London: Metropolitan Police.

Shephard, D. and Weiss, J. (2004) *The London Homicide Manual*. Unpublished.

Sheptycki, J. (2004) 'Organisational pathologies in police intelligence systems. Some contributions to the lexicon of intelligence-led policing', *European Journal of Criminology*, 1 (3). London: Sage.

Sherman, L. (1978) *Scandal and Reform: Controlling Police Corruption*. Berkeley, CA: University of California Press.

Sims, J. (1993) 'What is Intelligence?' Paper 1 in A. Shulsky and J. Sims, *What is Intelligence? Working Group on Intelligence Reform*. Washington. Consortium for the Study of Intelligence.

Sissens, J. (2008) 'An evaluation of the role of the intelligence analyst within the National Intelligence Model', in C. Harfield, A. MacVean, J. Grieve and

D. Phillips *The Handbook of Intelligent Policing, Consilience, Crime Control, and Community Safety*. Oxford: Oxford University Press.

Skidelsky, R. (2000) 'The age of inequality', in D. Green (ed.), *Institutional Racism and the Police: fact or fiction* [electronic version]. London: Institute for the Study of Civil Society.

Skills For Justice (n.d.) *Common Standards for the Justice Sector: Briefing*.

Smith, G. (2004) 'Rethinking police complaints', *British Journal of Criminology*, 44 (1).

Smith, H. and Fingar, P. (2003) *Business Process Management: The Third Wave*. Tampa: Meghan-Kiffer Press.

Smith, T.J. (2008) 'Predictive Warning: Teams, Networks and Scientific Methods', in R. George and J. Bruce (eds), *Analyzing Intelligence. Origins, Obstacles and Innovations*. Washington: Georgetown University Press.

Social Exclusion Unit (SEU) (1998) *Truancy and Social Exclusion*. London: The Stationery Office.

Solomos, J. (1999) 'Social research and the Stephen Lawrence Inquiry', *Sociological Research Online*, 4 (1) (available at www.socresonline.org.uk/4/1/lawrence.html, last accessed 4 November 2008.

Solomos, J. (2003) *Race and Racism in Britain* (3rd edn). Basingstoke: Palgrave Macmillan.

Sonhami, A. (2007) 'Understanding institutional racism: the Stephen Lawrence Inquiry and the police service reaction', in M. Rowe (ed.) *Policing Beyond Macpherson: Issues in Policing, Race and Society*. Cullompton: Willan Publishing.

Stanford, J. (2001) 'Race, labour and the Archbishop, or the currency of race', *Race Ethnicity and Education*, 4 (1): 83–97.

Stanko, B. (2008) 'Strategic intelligence: Methodologies for understanding what police services already "know" to reduce harm', in C. Harfield, A. MacVean, J. Grieve and D. Phillips, *The Handbook of Intelligent Policing, Consilience, Crime Control, and Community Safety*. Oxford: Oxford University Press.

Stenson, K. and Waddington, P.A.J. (2007) 'Macpherson, police stops and institutionalised racism', in M. Rowe (ed.), *Policing Beyond Macpherson: Issues in Policing, Race and Society*. Cullompton: Willan Publishing.

Sunday Times, 7 January 2007, 'Top Muslim Officers turn on "racist" Met'.

Taylor, Lord Justice (1989) *The Hillsborough Stadium Disaster, 15 April 1989. Inquiry by the Right Honourable Lord Justice Taylor: interim report*. London: HMSO.

Taylor, Lord Justice (1990) *The Hillsborough Stadium Disaster, 15 April 1989. Inquiry by the Right Honourable Lord Justice Taylor: final report*. London: HMSO.

The Times, 19 October 1998, '"Institutionalised [sic] racism" in police". Letters.

The Times, 29 August 2008, 'Race row policeman told to shut up and get on with his job'.

The Times, 19 September 2008, 'Police Chief's suspension ...'

Tomlinson, S. (2005) 'Race, ethnicity and education under New Labour', *Journal of Oxford Review of Education*, 31 (1): 153–171.

Training and Development Agency (TDA) (2008) *Results of the Newly Qualified Teachers Survey 2008*. London: TDA.

Travis, A. (2001) 'Partners in crime. Policemen and academics', *The Edge (Journal of the Economic and Social Research Council)*, 8: 12–14.

Victim Support (2006) *Crime and prejudice. The support needs of victims of hate crime: a research report* [electronic version]. London: Victim Support. Retrieved 28 August 2006 from:http://www.victimsupport.org.uk/vs_england_wales/about_us/publications/hate_crime/crime_prejudice.pdf

Vincent, C.E.H. (1881) *Police Code. Manual of the Criminal Law*. London: Cassell, Petter, Galpin and Co.

Walker, C. (1999) 'Miscarriages of justice in principle and practice', in C. Walker and K. Starmer (eds), *Miscarriages of Justice: A Review of Justice in Error*. London: Blackstone.

Walker, C. (2002) 'Miscarriages of justice and the correction of error', in M. McConville and G. Wilson (eds), *The Handbook of the Criminal Justice Process*. Oxford: Oxford University Press.

Wanless, P. (2006) *Priority Review: Exclusions of Black Pupils. Getting It: Getting It Right*. London: DfES.

Wells, W., Horney, J. and Maguire, E. (2005) 'Patrol officer responses to citizen feedback: An experimental analysis [electronic version]. *Police Quarterly*, 8 (2): 171–205.

Wennerstrom, V. (2004) *Minority Ethnic Exclusions and the Race Relations (Amendment) Act 2000*. London: Department for Education and Skills (DfES).

Woods, D.D. (1995) 'Process-tracing methods for the study of cognition outside of the experimental psychology laboratory', in G.A. Klein, J. Orasanu, R. Calderwood and C.E. Zsambok (eds), *Decision Making in Action: Models and Methods* (pp. 228–251). Norwood, NJ: Ablex.

Wright, A. (2002) *Policing: An Introduction to Concepts and Practice*. Cullompton: Willan Publishing.

Zahid Mubarek Inquiry (2005) *Report of the Zahid Mubarek Inquiry*. London: HMSO.

Appendix I

The Stephen Lawrence Inquiry – A Selective Chronology and Context 1974–2008

Date and event	Relevance, notes and reference
13 September 1974 Stephen Lawrence born at Greenwich District Hospital	Lawrence 2006: 39
1976 Race Relations Act	
1976 *R v. Turnbull* judge's directions about identification evidence	SLI 1999: 283 and 291. Importance of identification evidence in Stephen Lawrence's murder
1977 Fisher Public Inquiry	
18 January 1981 – Deptford fire, 13 young people killed	PSI 1983 IV: 155
November 1981: Report of Rt. Hon. Lord Scarman into the Brixton disorders	HMSO Cmnd. 8427
November 1983: Policy Studies Institute Report, *Police and People in London*	PSI 1983
1984 Police and Criminal Evidence Act especially Section 87, judge's discretion	SLI 1999: 283

17 September 1986 Murder of Ahmed Ullah in Burnage school in Manchester.

Burnage Report 1988 into violent racism (MacDonald *et al.* 1989)

1991 Bristol Seminars for MPS BME officers. Creation of MPS Black Police Association.

February 1993 Community Fairness and Justice Conference at MPS Hendon.

Paul Boateng MP speech on police role in leading against racism (MPS 1993)

22 April 1993 Stephen is murdered and Duwayne Brooks attacked. Initial murder investigation

SLI 1999:

Cathcart 1999: 40

26 April 1993 Change of leadership in murder inquiry

SLI 1999:
Cathcart 1999: 71

6 May 1993 Mr and Mrs Lawrence enlist the support of Nelson Mandela

Cathcart 1999: 104

May 1993 5 arrests

SLI 1999:

July 1993 CPS discontinue prosecution

SLI 1999:

June 1994 Det. Supt Mellish: 3rd investigation

SLI 1999:
Cathcart 1999: 208

8 October 1993 first flawed murder review

SLI 1999: 199

17 April 1996 Private prosecution by the Lawrence Inquiry – 3 suspects acquitted.

Failure of identification evidence. *R v. Turnbull* cited.
SLI 1999: 28

1996 Shadow Home Secretary Jack Straw pledges an Inquiry into the murder investigation

February 1997 Inquest

SLI 1999:

13 February 1997 Police Complaints Authority supervises Kent Constabulary review of investigations thus far (2nd review)

SLI 1999:

1997 Labour Government returned to power in General Election; Jack Straw Home Secretary	SLI 1999:
1997 4th investigation pursuing Kent 11 lines of inquiry	SLI 1999:
31 July 1997 appointment of Sir William Macpherson and 3 advisors as Public Inquiry Panel	Cathcart 1999: 311
6 August 1998 Creation of the Race and Violent Crime Task Force	Metropolitan Police Miscellaneous documents 1998–2004
29 June 1998 5 suspects at SLI. Ben Bowling book *Violent Racism* published same day	SLI 1999:41 Bowling 1998
12 November 1998–18 December 1998 MPS workshops and Conference on Anti Racist Policing	Metropolitan Police Miscellaneous documents 1998–2004
1999 First full meeting of IAG	Metropolitan Police Miscellaneous documents 1998–2004
29 January 1999 first Critical Incident training for senior officers	Metropolitan Police Miscellaneous documents 1998–2004
January 1999 5th murder inquiry by RVCTF	
24 February 1999: Stephen Lawrence Inquiry Reports	
24 March 1999 Home Secretary's Action Plan	
1999 MPS Diversity Strategy	Metropolitan Police Miscellaneous documents 1998–2004
30 September 1999 Mr Lawrence speaks at the Labour Party Conference.	BBC TV Great Speeches 18 April 2000
Race Relations (Amendment) Act 2000 9 December 2000 3rd MPS review, 11 recommendations	

2001 4th review by external police
service's murder review team

21 October 2003 BBC television documentary,
Secret Policeman, Mark Daley

April 2004 IPCC goes live

5 May 2004 CPS decision insufficient
evidence to prosecute from 5th murder
inquiry

Lawrence 2006: 209

May 2004 'True Vision' reporting systems
launched

2004 6th murder inquiry initiated

2007 BBC Documentary *Murderers of
Stephen Lawrence*, Mark Daley

Continuing interest in
the murder

8 October 2008 BBC television programme
Panorama update on the *Secret Policeman*
5 years later, Mark Daley

Continuing interest in
the findings of SLI

Appendix 2

Recommendations of the Stephen Lawrence Inquiry

We recommend:

OPENNESS, ACCOUNTABILITY AND THE RESTORATION OF CONFIDENCE

1 That a Ministerial Priority be established for all Police Services:

'To increase trust and confidence in policing amongst minority ethnic communities.'

2 The process of implementing, monitoring and assessing the Ministerial Priority should include Performance Indicators in relation to:

i   the existence and application of strategies for the prevention, recording, investigation and prosecution of racist incidents;
ii   measures to encourage reporting of racist incidents;
iii the number of recorded racist incidents and related detection levels;
iv   the degree of multi-agency co-operation and information exchange;
v   achieving equal satisfaction levels across all ethnic groups in public satisfaction surveys;
vi   the adequacy of provision and training of family and witness/ victim liaison officers;

vii the nature, extent and achievement of racism awareness training;

viii the policy directives governing stop and search procedures and their outcomes;

ix levels of recruitment, retention and progression of minority ethnic recruits; and

x levels of complaint of racist behaviour or attitude and their outcomes.

The overall aim being the elimination of racist prejudice and disadvantage and the demonstration of fairness in all aspects of policing.

3 That Her Majesty's Inspectors of Constabulary (HMIC) be granted full and unfettered powers and duties to inspect all parts of Police Services including the Metropolitan Police Service.

4 That in order to restore public confidence an inspection by HMIC of the Metropolitan Police Service be conducted forthwith. The inspection to include examination of current undetected HOLMES based murders and Reviews into such cases.

5 That principles and standards similar to those of the Office for Standards in Education (OFSTED) be applied to inspections of Police Services, in order to improve standards of achievement and quality of policing through regular inspection, public reporting, and informed independent advice.

6 That proposals as to the formation of the Metropolitan Police Authority be reconsidered, with a view to bringing its functions and powers fully into line with those which apply to other Police Services, including the power to appoint all Chief Officers of the Metropolitan Police Service.

7 That the Home Secretary and Police Authorities should seek to ensure that the membership of police authorities reflects so far as possible the cultural and ethnic mix of the communities which those authorities serve.

8 That HMIC shall be empowered to recruit and to use lay inspectors in order to conduct examination and inspection of Police Services

particularly in connection with performance in the area of investigation of racist crime.

9 That a Freedom of Information Act should apply to all areas of policing, both operational and administrative, subject only to the 'substantial harm' test for withholding disclosure.

10 That Investigating Officers' reports resulting from public complaints should not attract Public Interest Immunity as a class. They should be disclosed to complainants, subject only to the "substantial harm" test for withholding disclosure.

11 That the full force of the Race Relations legislation should apply to all police officers, and that Chief Officers of Police should be made vicariously liable for the acts and omissions of their officers relevant to that legislation.

DEFINITION OF RACIST INCIDENT

12 That the definition should be:

'A racist incident is any incident which is perceived to be racist by the victim or any other person.'

13 That the term 'racist incident' must be understood to include crimes and non-crimes in policing terms. Both must be reported, recorded and investigated with equal commitment.

14 That this definition should be universally adopted by the Police, local Government and other relevant agencies.

REPORTING AND RECORDING OF RACIST INCIDENTS AND CRIMES

15 That Codes of Practice be established by the Home Office, in consultation with Police Services, local Government and relevant agencies, to create a comprehensive system of reporting and recording of all racist incidents and crimes.

16 That all possible steps should be taken by Police Services at local level in consultation with local Government and other agencies and

local communities to encourage the reporting of racist incidents and crimes. This should include:

- the ability to report at locations other than police stations; and
- the ability to report 24 hours a day.

17 That there should be close co-operation between Police Services and local Government and other agencies, including in particular Housing and Education Departments, to ensure that all information as to racist incidents and crimes is shared and is readily available to all agencies.

POLICE PRACTICE AND THE INVESTIGATION OF RACIST CRIME

18 That ACPO, in consultation with local Government and other relevant agencies, should review its *Good Practice Guide for Police Response to Racial Incidents* in the light of this Report and our Recommendations. Consideration should be given to the production by ACPO of a manual or model for such investigation, to complement their current *Manual of Murder Investigation*.

19 That ACPO devise Codes of Practice to govern Reviews of investigations of crime, in order to ensure that such Reviews are open and thorough. Such codes should be consistently used by all Police Services. Consideration should be given to such practice providing for Reviews to be carried out by an external Police Service.

20 That MPS procedures at the scene of incidents be reviewed in order to ensure co-ordination between uniformed and CID officers and to ensure that senior officers are aware of and fulfil the command responsibilities which their role demands.

21 That the MPS review their procedures for the recording and retention of information in relation to incidents and crimes, to ensure that adequate records are made by individual officers and specialist units in relation to their functions, and that strict rules require the retention of all such records as long as an investigation remains open.

22 That MPS review their internal inspection and accountability processes to ensure that policy directives are observed.

FAMILY LIAISON

23 That Police Services should ensure that at local level there are readily available designated and trained Family Liaison Officers.

24 That training of Family Liaison Officers must include training in racism awareness and cultural diversity, so that families are treated appropriately, professionally, with respect and according to their needs.

25 That Family Liaison Officers shall, where appointed, be dedicated primarily if not exclusively to that task.

26 That Senior Investigating Officers and Family Liaison Officers be made aware that good practice and their positive duty shall be the satisfactory management of family liaison, together with the provision to a victim's family of all possible information about the crime and its investigation.

27 That good practice shall provide that any request made by the family of a victim which is not acceded to, and any complaint by any member of the family, shall be formally recorded by the SIO and shall be reported to the immediate superior officer.

28 That Police Services and Victim Support Services ensure that their systems provide for the pro-active use of local contacts within minority ethnic communities to assist with family liaison where appropriate.

VICTIMS AND WITNESSES

29 That Police Services should together with the Home Office develop guidelines as to the handling of victims and witnesses, particularly in the field of racist incidents and crimes. The Victim's Charter to be reviewed in this context.

30 That Police Services and Victim Support Services ensure that their systems provide for the pro-active use of local contacts within minority ethnic communities to assist with victim support and with the handling and interviewing of sensitive witnesses.

31 That Police Services ensure the provision of training and the availability of victim/witness liaison officers, and ensure their use in appropriate areas particularly in the field of racist incidents and crimes, where the need for a sensitive approach to young and vulnerable victims and witnesses is paramount.

PROSECUTION OF RACIST CRIMES

32 That the standard of proof of such crimes should remain unchanged.

33 That the CPS should consider that, in deciding whether a criminal prosecution should proceed, once the CPS evidential test is satisfied there should be a rebuttable presumption that the public interest test should be in favour of prosecution.

34 That Police Services and the CPS should ensure that particular care is taken at all stages of prosecution to recognise and to include reference to any evidence of racist motivation. In particular it should be the duty of the CPS to ensure that such evidence is referred to both at trial and in the sentencing process (including Newton hearings). The CPS and Counsel to ensure that no 'plea bargaining' should ever be allowed to exclude such evidence.

35 That the CPS ensure that a victim or victim's family shall be consulted and kept informed as to any proposal to discontinue proceedings.

36 That the CPS should have the positive duty always to notify a victim and victim's family personally of a decision to discontinue, particularly in cases of racist crime, with speed and sensitivity.

37 That the CPS ensure that all decisions to discontinue any prosecution should be carefully and fully recorded in writing, and that save in exceptional circumstances, such written decisions should be disclosable to a victim or a victim's family.

38 That consideration should be given to the Court of Appeal being given power to permit prosecution after acquittal where fresh and viable evidence is presented.

39 That consideration should be given to amendment of the law to allow prosecution of offences involving racist language or behaviour, and of offences involving the possession of offensive weapons, where such conduct can be proved to have taken place otherwise than in a public place.

40 That the ability to initiate a private prosecution should remain unchanged.

41 That consideration should be given to the proposition that victims or victims' families should be allowed to become 'civil parties' to criminal proceedings, to facilitate and to ensure the provision of all relevant information to victims or their families.

42 That there should be advance disclosure of evidence and documents as of right to parties who have leave from a Coroner to appear at an Inquest.

43 That consideration be given to the provision of Legal Aid to victims or the families of victims to cover representation at an Inquest in appropriate cases.

44 That Police Services and the Courts seek to prevent the intimidation of victims and witnesses by imposing appropriate bail conditions.

TRAINING

FIRST AID

45 That First Aid training for all 'public contact' police officers (including senior officers) should at once be reviewed and revised to ensure that they have basic skills to apply First Aid. Officers must be taught to 'think first aid', and first and foremost 'A (Airways), B (Breathing) and C (Circulation)'.

46 That training in First Aid including refresher training should include testing to recognised and published standards in every Police Service.

47 That Police Services should annually review First Aid training, and ensure that 'public contact' officers are trained and tested to recognised and published standards.

TRAINING

RACISM AWARENESS AND VALUING CULTURAL DIVERSITY

48 That there should be an immediate review and revision of racism awareness training within Police Services to ensure:

a that there exists a consistent strategy to deliver appropriate training within all Police Services, based upon the value of our cultural diversity;
b that training courses are designed and delivered in order to develop the full understanding that good community relations are essential to good policing and that a racist officer is an incompetent officer.

49 That all police officers, including CID and civilian staff, should be trained in racism awareness and valuing cultural diversity.

50 That police training and practical experience in the field of racism awareness and valuing cultural diversity should regularly be conducted at local level. And that it should be recognised that local minority ethnic communities should be involved in such training and experience.

51 That consideration be given by Police Services to promoting joint training with members of other organisations or professions otherwise than on police premises.

52 That the Home Office together with Police Services should publish recognised standards of training aims and objectives in the field of racism awareness and valuing cultural diversity.

53 That there should be independent and regular monitoring of training within all Police Services to test both implementation and achievement of such training.

54 That consideration be given to a review of the provision of training in racism awareness and valuing cultural diversity in local Government and other agencies including other sections of the Criminal Justice system.

EMPLOYMENT, DISCIPLINE AND COMPLAINTS

55 That the changes to Police Disciplinary and Complaints procedures proposed by the Home Secretary should be fully implemented and closely and publicly monitored as to their effectiveness.

56 That in order to eliminate the present provision which prevents disciplinary action after retirement, disciplinary action should be available for at least five years after an officer's retirement.

57 That the Police Services should through the implementation of a Code of Conduct or otherwise ensure that racist words or acts proved to have been spoken or done by police officers should lead to disciplinary proceedings, and that it should be understood that such conduct should usually merit dismissal.

58 That the Home Secretary, taking into account the strong expression of public perception in this regard, consider what steps can and should be taken to ensure that serious complaints against police officers are independently investigated. Investigation of police officers by their own or another Police Service is widely regarded as unjust, and does not inspire public confidence.

59 That the Home Office review and monitor the system and standards of Police Services applied to the selection and promotion of officers of the rank of Inspector and above. Such procedures for selection and promotion to be monitored and assessed regularly.

STOP AND SEARCH

60 That the powers of the police under current legislation are required for the prevention and detection of crime and should remain unchanged.

61 That the Home Secretary, in consultation with Police Services, should ensure that a record is made by police officers of all 'stops' and 'stops and searches' made under any legislative provision (not just the Police and Criminal Evidence Act). Non-statutory or so called 'voluntary' stops must also be recorded. The record to include the reason for the stop, the outcome, and the self-defined ethnic identity of the person stopped. A copy of the record shall be given to the person stopped.

62 That these records should be monitored and analysed by Police Services and Police Authorities, and reviewed by HMIC on inspections. The information and analysis should be published.

63 That Police Authorities be given the duty to undertake publicity campaigns to ensure that the public is aware of 'stop and search' provisions and the right to receive a record in all circumstances.

RECRUITMENT AND RETENTION

64 That the Home Secretary and Police Authorities' policing plans should include targets for recruitment, progression and retention of minority ethnic staff. Police Authorities to report progress to the Home Secretary annually. Such reports to be published.

65 That the Home Office and Police Services should facilitate the development of initiatives to increase the number of qualified minority ethnic recruits.

66 That HMIC include in any regular inspection or in a thematic inspection a report on the progress made by Police Services in recruitment, progression and retention of minority ethnic staff.

PREVENTION AND THE ROLE OF EDUCATION

67 That consideration be given to amendment of the National Curriculum aimed at valuing cultural diversity and preventing racism, in order better to reflect the needs of a diverse society.

68 That Local Education Authorities and school Governors have the duty to create and implement strategies in their schools to prevent and address racism. Such strategies to include:

- that schools record all racist incidents;
- that all recorded incidents are reported to the pupils' parents/ guardians, school Governors and LEAs;
- that the numbers of racist incidents are published annually, on a school by school basis; and
- that the numbers and self-defined ethnic identity of 'excluded' pupils are published annually on a school by school basis.

69 That OFSTED inspections include examination of the implementation of such strategies.

70 That in creating strategies under the provisions of the Crime and Disorder Act or otherwise Police Services, local Government and relevant agencies should specifically consider implementing community and local initiatives aimed at promoting cultural diversity and addressing racism and the need for focused, consistent support for such initiatives.

Index

Added to a page number 'f' denotes a figure, 't' denotes a table and 'n' denotes notes.